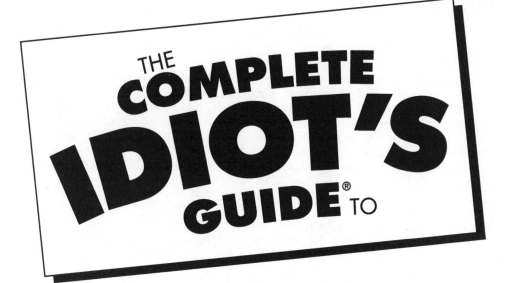

THE COMPLETE IDIOT'S GUIDE® TO

Irish History and Culture

by Sonja Massie

alpha books

A Division of Macmillan General Reference
Pearson Education Macmillan Company
1633 Broadway, New York, NY 10019-6785

This book is lovingly dedicated to Jennifer and David Hald, who know the true meaning of friendship, loyalty, and family ties.

Copyright © 1999 by Sonja Massie

Macmillan Publishing books may be purchased for business or sales promotional use. For information please write: Special Markets Department, Macmillan Publishing USA, 1633 Broadway, New York, NY 10019.

International Standard Book Number: 0-02-862710-5
Library of Congress Catalog Card Number: 98-87600

01 00 99   8 7 6 5 4 3 2 1

Interpretation of the printing code: the rightmost number of the first series of numbers is the year of the book's printing; the rightmost number of the second series of numbers is the number of the book's printing. For example, a printing code of 98-1 shows that the first printing occurred in 1998.

Printed in the United States of America

Alpha Development Team

Publisher
Kathy Nebenhaus

Editorial Director
Gary M. Krebs

Managing Editor
Bob Shuman

Marketing Brand Manager
Felice Primeau

Acquisitions Editor
Jessica Faust

Development Editors
Phil Kitchel
Amy Zavatto

Assistant Editor
Georgette Blan

Production Team

Development Editor
Amy Zavatto

Production Editor
Carol Sheehan

Copy Editor
Heather Stith

Cover Designer
Mike Freeland

Photo Editor
Richard Fox

Illustrator
Patricia Redding

Book Designers
Scott Cook and Amy Adams of DesignLab

Indexers
John Jefferson
Chris Wilcox

Layout/Proofreading
Wil Cruz
Tricia Flodder
Donna Martin
Jeannie McKay
Julie Trippetti

Contents at a Glance

Contents

7 The Seed Doesn't Fall Far from the Tree: The Vikings' Norman Cousins   69

8 Those Blasted Brits   77

Introduction

Have you ever wondered:

> ➤ What's the big deal about St. Patrick? What did he do that was so important?

> ➤ Why do they say there are no snakes in Ireland?

> ➤ Is there really a thing called the Blarney stone and can you actually kiss it?

> ➤ Was the Irish Potato Famine truly all that bad?

> ➤ Why doesn't Great Britain just pull out of Ireland and let it all be one united country?

> ➤ What's with all the "troubles" over there between the Protestants and Catholics? Why can't they just get along?

If you have pondered a couple of these questions, you aren't alone. Some of the answers are simple; others are deadly complex. Greater minds than yours or mine have wrestled with those last few problems and found no solutions. This book is intended to help you understand what it is to be Irish, both the glorious side of the culture and its centuries-old torments. The Irish are so much more than shamrocks and Guinness, St. Patrick Day parades and leprechauns.

Although it would be impossible to tell the complete story of an ancient people whose ancestors built stone passage graves older than Egypt's pyramids in one book, I have included the highlights of Irish history and glimpses into Irish culture. Ireland's story has more titillation than a supermarket tabloid; it's replete with violence, sex, and high-powered political corruption. But it is also deadly serious. Because in Ireland, perhaps more than in many cultures, the past has become the present. Old wounds still ache, and the cruel cuts go deeper every day. Irish culture *is* Irish history; the two are inseparable. In this book, you take a journey through the mystical, magical, and infinitely practical world of the Irish, and you'll feel right at home.

Part 1, "Beyond Leprechauns, St. Patrick, and Shamrocks," introduces you to the Irish people themselves, their customs, their beliefs, their delightful idiosyncrasies, and their celebrations and witticisms. From their colorful Celtic roots to the geography of the Emerald Isle, you'll see the influences that have made the Irish who they are.

In Part 2, "The Story of Eire," you travel back to the days when the only inhabitants of Eire's Land were the four-footed and winged types. Then you'll watch as this Eden is invaded by men and paradise is lost. The Celts arrive and establish a civilization that is strangely pagan, yet amazingly civil. Ireland knows a bit of peace, even converting to Christianity through St. Patrick. But then the Vikings, invaders from the north, descend on the small island, and blood stains the green fields. The terror continues until a champion comes to Ireland's rescue, Brian Boru, the only man who has ever ruled all of this rebellious island.

In Part 3, "Invasions, Repression, and Hunger: You Can't Keep a Good Irishman Down," the British come to Ireland, invited by a disgruntled Irishman named Dermot MacMurrough, who isn't getting along with his neighbors and asks for military assistance. He gets it, along with centuries of British oppression. From the Norman kings to the Tudors, Ireland suffers under the dominion of such notorious rulers as Henry VIII, Elizabeth I, and Oliver Cromwell. Ireland reaches the depths of her miseries during the Great Hunger, the Irish Potato Famine of 1845–1848. The island would never be the same again. Her patriots, enflamed, stage one rebellion after another until the Irish Free State is born. Finally, Ireland rules itself, except for those Northern counties, where the "troubles" still rage.

In Part 4, "Erin's Hall of Fame," you meet Erin's celebrities, whose talents range from great playwrights and authors (William Butler Yeats, Jonathan Swift, Oscar Wilde, George Bernard Shaw, James Joyce, Sean O'Casey, and Frank McCourt to name a few) to skilled politicians, soldiers, and athletic champions. The sons and daughters of auld Erin have given us all a thousand reasons to be fiercely proud!

Part 5, "Ireland and All It Has to Offer: A Story Still Tellin'," shows that the Irish today preserve the customs of their predecessors, while creating traditions of their own. From the glorious handcrafts they produce, to the tourism industry, to the music of today's Irish bands and the flying feet of the *Riverdance* troupe, the Irish people display the beauty and fire of the Celtic spirit. The world is realizing what a marvelous thing it is to be Irish. We always knew!

Extras

To help you along, throughout this book you'll find sidebars with extra information that you won't want to miss:

A Bard's Tale

Because the Irish are famous for their storytellers and bardic traditions, I included tales of yore and modern times for you, too. Here, you'll learn all kinds of fascinating details about the Irish and their culture.

Gift of Gab

Here, you'll find all the blarney you could want, with quotes from and about the Irish.

'Tisn't So!

These little tidbits contain information to surprise (and sometimes shock) you.

Speak Plain Irish

Don't know what a bodhran is? How about the way to say Ireland in Irish? Check these boxes out to get familiar with the lingo.

Acknowledgments

The author would like to thank some very special people who contributed so much to the writing of this book:

Amy Zavatto, a patient, kind, and astute editor, who has enough Irish blood to give her a lovely way with words.

The Irish Tourist Board for a hundred silly questions answered and a bevy of beautiful photographs.

Quirk's Irish Gifts in Massapequa, New York, a delightful store full of charming people and gorgeous things that take your heart back to Ireland.

The best research librarians in the country, Linda Ferraro, Joan Traugott, and Celine Lieffr of the Amityville Public Library. I couldn't have done it without you ladies.

Bruce Hald, who graciously tolerated not seeing his coffee table for most of a year, as it was buried under Irish research materials.

Blanche and George Hald, for asking every day, "How's the book going?" and for cheering miniscule progress.

Gwendolynn Massie, my strength, my rock, who keeps me laughing.

Caitlin Marie O'Leary, whose quiet presence and unconditional love makes a difficult page write faster.

And, most of all, I would like to thank my agent, Laura Tucker, of Richard Curtis Associates, for holding my hand, kicking my arse, patting my back, and being, very simply, wonderful through the whole thing! You sure earned your pittance on this one, darlin'!

Part 1

Beyond Leprechauns, St. Patrick, and Shamrocks

If you've seen the bumper stickers that proclaim, "I'm Proud to Be Irish," you may have thought the driver of that vehicle to be less than humble. You're probably right. We Irish are known for many wonderful qualities, but humility isn't high on the list. If you're the lad or lass sporting that sticker, you may not realize just how proud you can be of your rich, colorful culture.

In Part I, you'll see how the Irish people, bold, articulate, and charming as they are, have excellent reason for being proud. Their heritage, a result of traditions handed down for thousands of years, gives them a strong sense of pride in who they are.

Chapter 1

A Mystical Island of Magical People

In This Chapter

➤ Who are the Irish?

➤ Bards, the great storytellers

➤ Ancient Celtic law

➤ Curses and blessings

➤ Family life

According to the family tree registry, you have a bit of Irish blood flowing in your veins. Forgive me for saying so, but who doesn't? We Irish are a prolific people, and few Americans can study their family tree without finding at least one *O* or *Mc* dangling from a limb.

Ireland, a land of bright-eyed colleens (girls).

The Irish culture has deep roots in Western society (especially in the United States, the United Kingdom, and Australia), where many of us take great pride in our Irish heritage. But few of us know much about it beyond badly painted leprechaun lawn statuettes, gaudy foil shamrocks sold in party stores in March, and the St. Patrick's Day tradition of wearing green. Many assume that being Irish means we have a genetic disposition to drink a bit too much, fight too easily, sing tenor, and wax sentimental over a lad named Danny Boy. Although most stereotypes do contain a seed of truth, there is much more to being Irish.

Speak Plain Irish

Eire, Erin, or Eirrinn are all the Gaelic (or Irish) equivalent of the word Ireland.

The story of Ireland (*Eire*'s Land) is an ancient tale, one that is older than the pyramids of Egypt. Its rich lore runs deeper than the deepest shade of green on the hills of its rolling countryside. Ireland is simultaneously dark and shining, comic and tragic, fiercely violent yet tenderly romantic.

What is it to be Irish? 'Tis a wonder, to be sure. If you have Irish heritage, rest assured, it's that same Irish blood that puts the dance in your step, the twinkle in your eye, the song in your voice, the whimsy in your soul, and the warmth of a *turf fire* in the stories you tell. Those, among many others, are *Erin*'s gifts.

The Magic of Words

An old Irish proverbd says, "If wars were fought with words, Ireland would rule the world." If there is one virtue that sets the Irish apart, it is their deft use of language, written or spoken. On the subject of writing, Nobel Prize-winning Irishman George Bernard Shaw said (with his tongue firmly ensconced in his cheek, no doubt), "My method is to take the utmost trouble to find the right thing to say, and then say it with the utmost levity."

Certainly Shaw could speak for all the inhabitants of the island of poets, saints, and scholars. The Greeks may "have a word for it," but it has always required the agile wit and nimble tongue of an Irish man or woman to string those words together in such a way that can wring both laughter and tears from a listener in the same moment. Ireland has always held a deep affection and respect for those who do this best.

Bardic Tradition

Over the centuries, when even the crudest food and simplest shelter were dear commodities for the Irish peasantry, spoken words and the golden dreams they wove were often the only comfort afforded the bard and his audience. A poor farmer with a leaking sod roof could live in the hero Brian Boru's shining palace at Cashel. A widow with rags for clothes could wear the warrior queen Grania's gold embroidered tunics and have her hair entwined with pearls. The conveyer of those dreams was the *Seanchai,* the *bard.* No higher station could be attained in Irish culture.

Speak Plain Irish

The word **bard** doesn't apply only to that Shakespeare fellow. Traditionally, a bard is anyone from the ancient Celtic order of poets. These folks recited verses, telling the exciting stories of their tribes.

Traveling from village to village, cottage to cottage, the bard provided an evening's entertainment by sharing the mystical tales of Ireland's bravest and best. Given the seat closest to the turf fire, the most tender hock of meat from the soup pot, and the ardent attention of his listeners, the bard used the magic of his words to whisk his listeners away from their humble cottages to the Land of the Ever Young. For a few blissful hours, they could ride along with their mythical hero Ossian on the back of a winged white stallion with silver trappings, led by Princess Niav of the Golden Hair.

The bards of old preserved those stories, the lessons contained therein, and the abilities to relate those tales by handing them down through the generations. Although the old, Celtic, gender- and caste-based laws governing the bequeathing of talent have passed away, the love of good storytelling remains the glory of Ireland. For as long as a drop of Irish blood flows in the veins of Erin's sons and daughters, today's world will be richer for the telling of yesterday's tales.

The Most Just of Men

The Celts, early settlers of Ireland, were known as a fierce, warlike people, who in ancient times swept across Europe, conquering and destroying all that was in their path. Yet for all their barbarism, they had an equally ardent reverence for law and

Speak Plain Irish

The term **brehon** (pronounced *bray*-hon) means judge, attorney, or barrister. But let it be said that the brehons of old behaved themselves far better than their contemporary counterparts.

order. In the first century A.D., the historian Strabo described the Celts as "the most just of men." Adopting laws from each conquered culture, they devised the most elaborate, sophisticated, and, many say, sensible system of government in early times. These laws were administered by *brehons,* judges who traveled from village to village, arbitrating disagreements and enforcing the code.

Loosely modeling certain aspects of the caste system of India, the Celts established a hierarchy of nobles, craftsmen, and artists within their own ranks. Clearly defined laws governed the behavior, responsibilities, and privileges of kings, chieftains, poets, blacksmiths, charioteers, and even public buffoons. From Germanic people, the Celts acquired the custom of charging fines for certain crimes rather than imprisoning the offender.

A Bard's Tale

Under brehon law, if a tribesman wounded a fellow member, he was required to take him or her to his own house, feed the injured party, provide medicine, find a substitute to do his or her work during the healing process, and pay the doctor's fee. Law also required that the victim's house of healing must not be filthy or noisy.

If a male victim were considered "exceedingly lustful" he would be allowed to bring his wife along for the duration of his healing process. A female victim would be accompanied by three female witnesses to protect her from the ardor of her host.

Brehon law was remarkably progressive in its championship of women's rights. Unlike most of the early legal systems, a female was allowed to own property and to obtain a divorce, depending on her status in society. Also, it was a more serious offense to kill a woman than a man. The murderer's sentence was to have a hand and foot cut off and be put to death. The killer's kin was obliged to pay the price of 21 cows to the victim's family.

As an agricultural society, the Celts also respected their animals, endowing them with many of the same legal rights as humans. Brehon law prescribed, "It is illegal to override a horse, force a weakened ox to do excessive work, or threaten an animal with angry vehemence which breaks bones." Although protected by the law, animals were expected to refrain from criminal behavior. An animal that killed someone was hanged as quickly as a human. If a chicken left droppings in the kitchen, its feeding trough might be covered. However, if a cat attacked a member of its family, but 'twas in the work of mousing that it did it, it was exempt from liability.

This system of justice remained in effect until Queen Elizabeth I banned the ancient laws. The manuscripts were buried beneath structures or hidden in secret "keeping holes" in stone hearths. Some have been unearthed and are currently preserved at Trinity College in Dublin and the British Museum of London. The Celts' love of the law has been an integral part of Irish culture over the centuries and remains so today.

To the Devil with You

Although most of us might utter a curse after splashing coffee down the front of our favorite shirt or dropping something heavy on our left foot, to the Irish people cursing is a serious business. Throughout a history of oppression, a deftly articulated curse was often the only recourse available to the poor. A woman whose husband was hanged for looking cross-eyed at a landowner might be heard to mutter at the foot of her mate's gallows, "May the Devil cut the head off all landlords, and may he make a day's work of their necks." Or a lowly peasant, ousted from his humble cottage, might proclaim of his landlord's acting agent, "May the Devil swallow him sideways."

This is not to say that the Irish blithely curse whomever crosses their path. It's one thing to say to someone who's proving themselves a nuisance, "It's a briar on the seat of me britches you are. Wherever I go, it's you behind me." But it's quite another to send someone "to hell, with never a drop o' Guinness to quench your eternal thirst." Every Irishman and Irishwoman knows that an ill-aimed curse directed at an innocent party will "come home to roost," bringing the curser more misery than he had already.

So if a poor widow woman fixes you with a baleful eye, turn tail and run as though the Old Horned One himself had set fire to your backside. If you dally, you might hear this potent condemnation, "May he be afflicted with the rot; may the worms take his eyes and the crows pluck out his entrails, but may he stay alive until we're all sick of the sight of him." That's a grim one, to be sure, but it is reserved for particularly nasty offenders. After all, the Irish are known for painting graphic verbal pictures. As I mentioned before, we're very good with words.

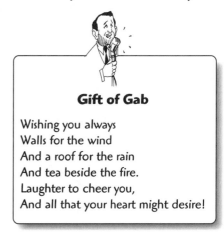

Gift of Gab

Wishing you always
Walls for the wind
And a roof for the rain
And tea beside the fire.
Laughter to cheer you,
And all that your heart might desire!

God Hold You in His Hand

If Irish curses seem morbid or unduly vindictive, understand that, when it comes to verbal expression, the Irish instinctively raise every word and phrase to its superlative degree just to be certain their point is made. Fortunately, the same principle applies when an Irish person is blessing, rather than cursing, you. You haven't received a true and proper benediction until a person of Irish descent bids a ray of sunlight from heaven to shine upon your head.

Accused of being naively superstitious, the spiritual Irish believe that great power lies in words, that something good or bad can literally be "spoken" into being. Therefore, when a blessing is bestowed upon you by one of Erin's children, you can be assured that it is much more than an empty-headed murmuring. Indeed, it's a heartfelt wish for your well-being that the giver fully expects will be manifested.

Some of these traditional blessings might involve the health of your physical body, the destination of your immortal soul, the weight of your wallet, or the fullness of your glass. Some are meant to smooth the rocky road of romance, and some express the poignant desire that you might live your days, every last one of them, on Irish soil. Erin's most valuable resource has always been her people, and in eras of turbulence, that precious commodity has been swept away on the flood tides of emigration. Therefore, no greater blessing could be placed upon a newlywed couple than the following: "May you live together in peace, grow old together in grace, and die in Ireland."

Those who have had to leave that verdant land or whose predecessors were forced aboard emigrant ships bound for another place that was not so green and not so magical can take comfort in knowing that home is only an Irish blessing away. If you feel the need to call a bit of heaven into someone's life, try one of these traditional blessings:

> May the good Lord hold you in the hollow of His hand, and may He not close His fist too tightly on you.

> May I see you with a silver head and combing your grandchildren's hair.

> May we always have a clean shirt, a clean conscience, and a bob in the pocket.

> May you be across Heaven's threshold an hour before the Devil knows you're dead.

> That you might have nicer legs than your own under your table before the new spuds are up.

Life with Ma, Da, and the Wee Ones

Family is everything to an Irish man or woman. Hearth, home, and a dozen children scrambling underfoot—those are heaven's dearest blessings. In times past, when the opportunities to create something lasting and beautiful were few and far between, the Irish delighted in their loveliest creations: their children. Their babies were a couple's hope for the future, as well as a husband's and wife's ultimate gift to each other. Nurturing their wee ones was the life's work that bonded a couple together. Family was, and remains, the center of the Irish universe.

An Irish home of yesteryear.

I've a Wife, Bedamned I Have

No man on God's green earth can woo a woman with more passion and ardor than an Irishman. The gift of gab, highly seasoned with the spice of *blarney*, is never more effective than during the practice of courtship. What lassie could resist the invitation to "come live in my heart and pay no rent?" Delivered in a velvet soft brogue, poetic words of love and undying devotion are impossible to deny.

Irishmen adore their women, and they will tell you as much without apology or fear of appearing overly sentimental. Before the Potato Famine of 1845 to 1848, known in Ireland as The Great Hunger, Irish men and women would tend to marry young and

Speak Plain Irish

Blarney is the ability to use smooth talk to flatter or coax. The Blarney stone is located at Blarney Castle in County Cork. It is said if you kiss the Blarney stone, you will be endowed with the ability to blarney.

Gift of Gab

The Irish can even make the confusion that goes along with love sound beautiful. These Irish proverbs express the quandary of romantic relationships:

Women drive men crazy, 'tis true. Aye, but the asylum would be a lonely place without 'em.

Marriages are all happy; it's having breakfast together that causes all the problems.

Never make a toil of pleasure, as the man said when he dug his wife's grave only three feet deep.

quickly get started on a family. Ireland never truly recovered economically from the famine, and in post-famine Ireland, marriages took place later, because it became far more difficult for couples to provide for their families.

An early, pre-famine custom was that of a groom abducting his bride, literally snatching her from her parents' house, carrying her off, and marrying her. When the newlyweds returned, the parents could do little other than welcome the couple. As barbaric as this custom may sound, usually the abduction was with the enthusiastic endorsement of the young lady. In 1707, the British made such an abduction a capital crime, punishable by hanging, but love-besotted suitors risked their necks to do so anyway.

A more safe, though less colorful, method of obtaining a bride in old Ireland was to hire a matchmaker. Although matchmakers were used in some circumstances, the parents usually conducted the marriage negotiations. These all-important meetings were generally held in a prospective groom's parents' home. The young woman's dowry would be discussed, as well as the gentleman's material worth, to see whether the two were reasonably equivalent. The family doing the entertaining made sure to display generosity in their hospitality. To do less would suggest a miserly attitude and might jeopardize the negotiations.

Marriage dates were carefully chosen, as ill luck would befall those marrying when the moon was waning, rather than waxing. No one in their right mind would schedule their nuptials on a Saturday; to do so would guarantee an unhappy union. Marrying during harvest time assured that the lucky couple would spend their lives gathering. The most fortunate of all omens was the sound of a cuckoo's call on the morning of the wedding or the sighting of three magpies. The couple who was so blessed by their feathered friends was certain to live in harmony for the rest of their days.

Children Growing by the Fire

A couple of old Irish proverbs summarize well the way the Irish feel about children:

"No man wore a warmer scarf than his children's arms around his neck."

"Every mother thinks it's for her child the sun rises."

The birth of a child into an Irish family has always been an occasion for great joy and celebration and for a bit of concern. In long-ago days when superstition ran rampant and "old wives," called *pishogues,* made a living concocting charms and incantations, a young mother worried herself into a dither about the possibility of wicked fairies snatching her newborn from its cradle and replacing it with a fairy child, or a *changeling.* (According to Irish folk tales, fairy spirits have a particular fondness for pretty human babies, especially red-haired ones.) According to the pishogue, the expectant mother should take precautions before the baby's arrival. She should nail a horseshoe to the doorpost, place a prayerbook under her pillow, and make the sign of the cross on a plate of salt.

Once the child was born, even more effort must be employed to protect it from evil. The mother must position a candle so that when the child opens its eyes, the flame is the first thing it sees. This will ensure that the child will choose the acts of light over the deeds of darkness.

In the raising of the child, great emphasis was placed upon the value of industry. Gathering food, whether in the form of grain or game, has always been a task shared by all members of the family. Historically, Ireland was an agricultural society, so strenuous labor, performed with a cooperative spirit, has traditionally been held in high regard. Irish children are taught to work hard, nearly as hard as they play.

Speak Plain Irish

A **changeling** is a child exchanged for another. Commonly, it refers to a fairy child who has been left in place of a human baby. Because the fairy babies are known to be troublesome and mischievous, a human mother might accuse her ill-behaved offspring of being a changeling. **Pishogues,** also more commonly referred to as "old wives," made a living concocting charms and incantations for the superstitious.

The Least You Need to Know

➤ The Irish people's greatest claim to fame is their eloquent use of language, written and spoken.

➤ From ancient times, the Irish have embraced a strict code of justice and maintain a deep reverence for the law.

➤ Despite their love of poetry and justice, the Irish hold hearth, home, and children dearest.

Chapter 2

Celebrating Life, Death, and Everything Between

In This Chapter

➤ Hospitality as only the Irish can serve it up

➤ How to bake a loaf of soda bread

➤ Fine Irish spirits: elixir of the gods or tool of the devil?

➤ Kicking up your heels at a moonlit crossroads dance

➤ An old-fashioned Irish wedding

➤ What's more fun than a wedding? A wake!

Food, drink, a warm hearth, and good company are the ingredients for a fine Irish evening, whether the hours are spent in Dublin, Shannon, Boston, or Queens, New York. The Irish are the finest hosts on the planet, bringing new meaning to the concept, "What's mine is your own." Enter any public place in Ireland, sit down to a table, and you'll straight away have more company than you'll know what to do with. If you want to sip your ale in solitude, feeling sorry for yourself and bemoaning a lost love or fortune, you'll have to do it somewhere outside the company of Irish folks.

Hospitality, Erin's Way

While Ireland may not be renowned for its cuisine (although this reputation is changing), you'll surely not go hungry at an Irish table, especially at breakfast. Your hostess will ply you with delectable sausages and bacon, eggs and fried tomatoes, toast, porridge, and tea until you think you'll never be able to rise from your chair. The Irish seem to live in mortal fear that you might faint dead away in the street from lack of nourishment and with your last feeble breath murmur the fateful words, "'Twas at Mary O'Sullivan's bed and breakfast I ate this morning."

For those who truly enjoy culinary delights, plenty of establishments in Ireland have joined the continental ranks of fine dining. From the coffee shops of Dublin with their freshly baked scones and "sticky buns," to the fresh seafood and produce of the southern counties, and the farm-fresh dairy products of the west, Irish food is a pleasant surprise. Because the lingo may be a bit confusing for some Americans, here are some translations to set the record clear:

➤ Cookies are called *biscuits.* The wonderful, chocolate-dipped varieties go well with the tea the Irish serve that is, as they say, "strong enough to trot a mouse on."

➤ Biscuits are called *scones.* They're fantastic and are often served hot from the oven, with homemade jams and jellies.

➤ French fries are called *chips* and are more commonly served with vinegar than ketchup. What Americans refer to as potato chips are called *crisps.*

➤ Sausages are called *bangers,* and *rashers* are lean strips of bacon.

Pub grub is a term that refers to the meals commonly served in the pubs. Although pub meals are usually just quick, easy, and companionable fare, you can be pleasantly surprised. A simple bowl of potato soup served with fresh brown bread can be lovely on a misty afternoon. Pubs also serve traditional Irish dishes such as bacon and cabbage, lamb stew, shepherd's pie, and *boxty* (a potato cake that inspired the ditty, "Boxty on the griddle, boxty in the pan, if you don't eat boxty, you'll never get a man").

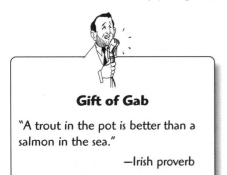

Gift of Gab

"A trout in the pot is better than a salmon in the sea."

—Irish proverb

But, of course, the hospitality extends way beyond the breakfast hours and the dining table. The Irish are truly some of the most welcoming and gracious folks you will ever be lucky enough to encounter.

Irish Soda Bread

Speaking of food, I have a little treat for you. Because it is so easy to make, soda bread is a staple of Irish cuisine, often baked fresh for breakfast and tea in Irish homes. It is a favorite among bed-and-breakfast establishments served as toast, for sandwiches, or with a savory bowl of Irish stew on a cold, misty afternoon. The following is a recipe for this most famous of Irish fare.

Ingredients:

4 cups flour
1 teaspoon salt
1 teaspoon baking soda
1 teaspoon sugar
2 cups sour milk or buttermilk

Preheat the oven to 350 degrees. Sift dry ingredients into a large bowl. Scooping up handfuls of the mixture, allow it to drop into the bowl. This action aerates or "fluffs" the flour. Add enough of the milk to form a soft dough. Working quickly, knead the dough lightly. (Too much kneading will produce bread the Irish call "hard as the hobs o' hell.")

Form a round loaf about the size of your fist. Place it on a baking sheet which has been lightly floured and score a cross on the top of the loaf with a knife that has been dipped in flour. Immediately bake the loaf on the top rack of the preheated oven for 30-45 minutes, until the loaf sounds hollow when you rap it with your knuckles. Hint: If you wrap it in a tea towel as soon as it's baked, the crust will stay softer. Unfortunately, this version will lack that deliciously smoky flavor of a loaf baked on a turf fire, but such is the price of progress.

Whiskey, Y'er the Devil

The Irish have always entertained a love/hate relationship with alcohol. Whether the drink of choice is Guinness, whiskey, or *poteen* (the equivalent of American moonshine), the glow of fine Irish booze has warmed many a heart and lifted many a failing spirit. The consumption of these beverages, examples of some of the finest distilling on earth, is an integral part of Irish culture. The Irish celebrate everything, and whether they are getting born, married, or buried, or celebrating all the other events in between, they use alcohol to intensify the experience.

Yet the excessive use of alcohol has caused countless sorrows for the Irish people. As they say, that which warms the heart also fires the temper and stirs the coals of grievances best left at rest. If, indeed, there is propensity for overdoing it with drink among the Irish, it would appear we should heed a couple of our own proverbs: "Wine drowns more men than water," and "You take your health once too often to the whiskey shop 'til it gets broken."

'Tisn't So!

For those of you who think Ireland is a nation of drunkards, know that Ireland has plenty of teetotalers, as well. Not everyone approves of strong drink, as evidenced by this old Irish saying: "Drink is the curse of the land. It makes you fight with your neighbor, it makes you shoot at your landlord, and it makes you miss."

15

There's nothing like a nice pint of Guinness.

Keeping the virtues of moderation in mind, here are some toasts to share when you heft your next Guinness:

> May your tap be open when it rusts.

> When you look at the world through the bottom of a glass, may you see someone ready to buy.

> Here's to absent friends, and here's twice to absent enemies.

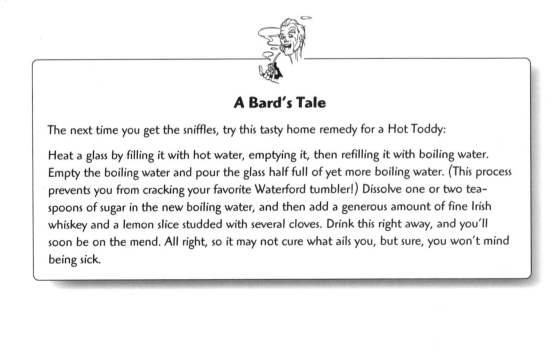

A Bard's Tale

The next time you get the sniffles, try this tasty home remedy for a Hot Toddy:

Heat a glass by filling it with hot water, emptying it, then refilling it with boiling water. Empty the boiling water and pour the glass half full of yet more boiling water. (This process prevents you from cracking your favorite Waterford tumbler!) Dissolve one or two teaspoons of sugar in the new boiling water, and then add a generous amount of fine Irish whiskey and a lemon slice studded with several cloves. Drink this right away, and you'll soon be on the mend. All right, so it may not cure what ails you, but sure, you won't mind being sick.

Where Irish Hearts Gather

The Irish love one another's company; heaven knows, they seek it out often enough. They are constantly getting together for some reason: births and deaths, baptisms and marriages, political meetings, dances and music-making sessions, as well as simple gatherings at the local pub to down a pint and discuss the news.

Formal assemblies have long been a critical element of Celtic society from the early days when such a congregation was required by law. The tribe chieftains called such assemblies for the purpose of reading new laws to their people, sometimes for athletic competition, and sometimes merely for recreation. Strict rules, as well as a few old wives' tales, governed these assemblies. Here's a sampling:

➤ If a king of Leinster neglects preparations for his great assembly, he shall suffer early grayness, baldness, or feebleness.

➤ All arms must be laid aside (during the assembly); all grudges, feuds, and quarreling are illegal.

➤ If you ride your chariot to the great assembly and it is damaged, you may not claim compensation unless it was broken through furious driving.

These regulations assured that all had a nice, peaceful time at the assemblies. Okay, the assemblies probably weren't all that peaceful, but you can be sure that they were hearty good fun!

The Irish Pub, More Than a Tavern

The Irish pub, with its turf fire burning, pub grub simmering on the back burner, and friendly *publican* behind the bar, is a staple of Irish culture, a meeting place for those friendly souls seeking companionship. These colorful establishments are on every corner, it seems, in an Irish town. Even the smallest of towns have more than one.

Speak Plain Irish

A **publican** is a saloon- or inn-keeper.

The large number of pubs isn't so much a result of the Irish propensity for drink as it is an indication of their affection for conversation. Pubs are family-oriented, far removed from the "pickup joint" bars in the United States. It isn't uncommon to see 10 children (possibly from the same family) come charging through a pub, followed by a couple of loping hounds. On Saturday night, the pub might be filled with the town's citizens, from the kiddies to their great-grandparents, and a local band, all making music and dancing the night away.

Pubs are a community staple of Irish culture where friends and family alike gather.

Pubs also provide a forum for political debate, another Irish passion. The intensity of these debates might surprise visitors to Ireland who might not take their politics quite so seriously. Not only do the Irish debate their own politicians' virtues, or lack thereof, but as avid readers, they are well-informed on political situations around the world, and they have strong opinions on those issues, too. The Irish pub has always been a highly entertaining place, even if all a fellow did was sip a Guinness and lend an ear to the gossip and blarney flying through the air around him.

Meet Me at the Crossroads at Midnight

A crossroads marked a well-known, centrally located place for the rural folk to assemble for a bit of music, dancing, singing, drinking, and good-natured carousing. Crossroads dances were a social event eagerly anticipated by all, and the sound of the fiddle tuning, the low, steady boom of the *bodhran,* and the lilting high notes of the pipe summoned lads and lasses from far and wide to come and celebrate each other's company in the silver light of the moon.

Speak Plain Irish

The **bodhran** is a traditional Irish drum.

Some priests were not overly enthused about the practice, probably because it harkened back to the days when the purveyors of pagan charms met at the crossroads beneath the light of a full moon to work their magic. The good fathers might also have been concerned that such activities provided fertile ground for wild oats to be sowed. As the proverb says, "The highway to heaven is well-signposted, but poorly lit at night."

Feelin' Merry When I Marry Mary Mac

Before the Great Famine of 1845, the Irish people were criticized for marrying so young, often in their teens. But the idea of hearth, home, and children, not to mention romance, was a heady incentive for a people who valued those elements of life above all others.

After the Great Famine, so many of the one-room cottages had been razed and so destitute were the masses, that the thought of marrying and bringing more souls into the world, let alone feeding and housing those extra bodies, took the bloom off the rose of matrimony. To this day, Irish men often marry late in life, if at all. Irish women learned long ago they could support themselves, sometimes better than a man could, so many figured, "Why bother?"

For those who chose to set up housekeeping together, the marriage was a wildly gay event, marked with the ubiquitous food and drink, music and dancing, although certain safeguards had to be applied to assure a happy union. The wedding must be held when the moon was waxing, not waning. It was considered a particularly bad omen if the marriage party met a funeral on the road, an event that was sure to put the bride in tears. Also, it must be a man, not a woman, who first wishes the bride joy. More than one disgruntled former girlfriend of the groom has been physically restrained from rushing forward with her Judas kiss and spoiling the marriage entirely.

After the formalities were over, the cake blessed by the priest and cut by the newly-weds, and full glasses passed around to all, the young couple was toasted with the following blessing:

> Health and long life to you,
> Land without rent to you,
> A child every year to you,
> And death in old Ireland.

Paddy, What a Fine Corpse Ye've Made!

Perhaps no aspect of Irish culture has received so much criticism as the behavior of the Irish at a *wake*. You may have heard that Irish folk are sometimes disrespectful of their dead and occasionally engage in excessive drinking, copious smoking, and raucous discourse during this event. Perhaps you've heard rumors of blows being struck, when the hard wood of a *shillelagh* (the traditional Irish club) entertained a passing acquaintance with the only substance on earth more dense than oak, the forehead of an Irishman. It's all true, every word. I can't deny that the revelry at some wakes gets a bit

Speak Plain Irish

A **wake** is a combination of mourning and celebration that takes place between the person's demise and their burial. The family and friends of the dearly departed sit around and discuss the virtues of their loved one. As morbid as it may sound, the corpse is usually present. The idea is to spend as much time as possible with the loved one before that final good-bye.

out of hand. But what good Irishman would send off his fellow Paddy to the next world without the glow of good Irish whiskey to warm his way?

As we discussed earlier, hospitality is as essential to the Irish soul as music and dancing, good food and drink, lively conversation and political debate. So it's only natural that a man's or woman's final extension of hospitality would be to treat their friends and loved ones to a party involving all of these elements.

As important as the quality of the liquor was the volume of the wailing at a wake. Because every Irish person deserved to be mourned with great enthusiasm, professional mourners, called *keeners,* were sometimes hired to take up the slack. These pros were so effective that you might have been tempted to stuff your ears with a plug of tobacco. They hadn't done a proper job of it until residents of neighboring counties were painfully aware that one of their own had gone to meet his Maker.

A Bard's Tale

After a corpse was prepared by the village women, it was laid across a table or bed in the main room of the house. The guest of honor was covered with a linen cloth and surrounded by glowing candles, plates of tobacco, and salt. His big toes were tied together with string to prevent his ghost from roaming about and scaring his poor relatives witless.

Sadly, traditional Irish wakes are few and far between among those who have strayed from Erin's shores. But even generations removed from their Emerald Isle, the Irish people still send their loved ones off with style. An Irish wake remains an excellent place to down a pint, spin a yarn, do a jig, and weep for the dearly departed. And yes, political debate still raises the ire, and the occasional fist will fly. After all, the Irish are a people who celebrate every moment of precious, God-given life; they could be expected to celebrate death just as vigorously.

The Pipe, the Fiddle, and the Bodhran

What would an Irish gathering be without the sounds of the fiddle floating on the air, summoning the folks from far and away to come kick up their heels at a neighborhood dance? Music is as natural to the Irish as conversation. Their ballads express the joys and sorrows of love gained and lost, political struggles, dead heroes, and fair-haired maidens.

In times of British oppression, when it was illegal to sing songs about one's motherland, Irish bards disguised their patriotism with lyrics about the female they loved so dearly that they would die for her honor. These thinly veiled lyrics were about old Erin, not a lass named Deirdre, but the passion was deep, nevertheless. Many of the songs sung at Irish gatherings have the power to bring a tear to the eyes of listeners, but the next tune will probably make them laugh.

Speak Plain Irish

Keening means to mourn loudly, wail even, for the dead. In Gaelic culture, if your loved ones keened vigorously at your wake, this was a sign that you were well-loved and sorely missed. Sometimes professional **keeners** were hired to make sure the dearly departed was properly mourned.

A tune to lift the spirits.

The dancers display amazing agility with fancy footwork that would cause a Flamenco dancer to feel the prick of envy. From the waist up, the dancers hardly move at all, but from there down, there is a fury of action. Pounding feet, flying kicks, and intricate tap patterns make Irish dancing a delight to watch and an extremely vigorous physical workout for the dancers.

The musicians use a variety of instruments to produce a distinctive Celtic sound: the pipe, fiddles, guitars, banjos, and the traditional battle drum of ancient Celtic warriors, the bodhran (pronounced bow-*rawn*). Wherever the Irish have chosen to assemble, this ancient instrument with its deep, stirring boom has defined the heartbeat of a people.

The Least You Need to Know

➤ When it comes to food and drink, Irish hospitality may be simple, but it's the warmest on God's green earth.

➤ The Irish love to get together, enjoy each other's company, and celebrate life to the fullest.

➤ Pubs are the hub of the Irish social wheel. They are family-oriented establishments where the conversation flows as freely as the Guinness.

➤ An Irish wake can be a great place to celebrate a person's life as well as mourn his or her passing.

➤ Music has always been an integral part of any Irish gathering: a wedding, a funeral, or a crossroads dance.

Part 2

The Story of Eire

The first chapter of any book serves as a precursor for the final chapter of that narrative. The story of Ireland is no different. The savage yet civilized Celts, the missionary work of St. Patrick, the Viking invasions, and many other occurrences throughout Ireland's rich past have all left their mark on Ireland and her people. In Part 2, we'll peer through the misty haze of Ireland's early history, where the groundwork was being laid for the Ireland and Irish people of today.

Was the Emerald Isle Always So Emerald?

In This Chapter

➤ Sunny, green Ireland—a land of ice?

➤ Four-foot invaders are the first to discover Paradise, but humans aren't too far behind

➤ Man leaves his mark on the Emerald Isle

➤ The rough and tumble terrain of Ireland

➤ Rainy day people: Ireland's not-so-sunny weather

➤ Water, water everywhere—or at least close by

Why should we study Ireland's past or the rough terrain of this land? If the tales of days gone by are filled with sadness, tragedy, and bitterness, is there any reason to relive such memories and stir up negative emotions? What good can come of coaxing long buried ghosts from their graves and retelling their stories?

The Irish have been accused of being a melancholy people, and we often are. It has been said we hold a grudge, and we sometimes do. We have a reputation for being pensive at times, for having a black sense of humor, and for embracing the dark side of life; that reputation is well-earned. We are a people who appreciate contrast. We know that good shines brightest when surrounded by the darkness of evil. A spring morning is all the sweeter when it follows a harsh winter. We laugh so heartily because we have wept so bitterly.

If you look back over Ireland's long, bloody history, during which wave after wave of invaders—Danes, Normans, and Brits—took turns ravaging the land and its people, you learn a couple of things:

Gift of Gab

"Cast your eyes on other days, that we in days to come may be, still the indomitable Iris   "

—William Butler Yeats

1. The world is a cruel place filled with wicked people. Everyone knows that, because every society has suffered its share of persecution at one time or another.

2. Most importantly, the Irish are an irrepressible people. They have come through hell and back, over and over again, enduring unspeakable horrors with their spirits still intact. When the Irish sing and dance, it isn't a brave front that masks the sorrow buried beneath. It is a joyous celebration of life, because they have seen so much death.

That's the reason to study Irish history. The story of Eire is one of toil, whether the Irish are warring with invaders or amongst themselves. It tells us where we've been so that we can fully celebrate who we are.

A Land Fit for Neither Man nor Beast

If you had decided to take a stroll across a sunlit meadow in County Kerry, Ireland, about 14,000 years ago, you would have needed more than a thick Aran fisherman's sweater to keep you snug. The place was covered with ice. When the glacial sheet withdrew about a thousand years later, it left behind a land that was, for the most part, a lot of soggy bogs and barren tundra.

But over the course of the next 3,000 years, the climate took a turn for the better. Although it still couldn't be called balmy, it was warm enough for a few bushes to spring up here and there. By 10,000 B.C., you could have taken that sunlit stroll through a green meadow, though you still would have needed a sweater.

The First Irish Have Hooves

Not only was the land different back then, but the seas were, too. The North Atlantic had risen by that point in time, covering the land bridge between Ireland and Britain, but the water level between the two was at least 75 feet lower than it is today, and the channel between Scotland and Ireland at one point was only a few miles across.

Some adventurous horses and *megaceros* (giant deer) decided to make the trek across the divide and were rewarded with vast green meadows stretching to the horizon, theirs for the munching. Along with some cattle, pigs, and ordinary-sized deer, who had also made the journey, these animals roamed freely across the island, unhunted by man, who hadn't yet discovered this virgin paradise.

With water everywhere (lakes and rivers were left by the ice), fertile soil, and a climate tempered by the oceans and seas surrounding the island, the vegetation thrived. Meadowlands gave way to trees, which multiplied into dense woods until the island was covered with mighty forests. The enormous herds of horses and giant deer dwindled as their grazing plains matured into woodland. The first wave of Ireland's many invasions, the gentlest of all, had come and gone.

Speak Plain Irish

To say that the deer who initially roamed Ireland were giants is no bit of blarney. Called **megaceros**, they were enormous, standing six feet high, with antlers spanning 10 feet or more.

There Goes the Neighborhood: Humans Arrive

Human history in Ireland started later than in the rest of Europe, which had an Old Stone Age. While primitive folks on the continent were just discovering the advantages of cracking an acorn with a rock, Ireland's inhabitants were still of the four-footed type.

The first people to cross that narrow strip of land and shallow water used by the animals were the *Mesolithic* or Middle Stone Age people of Europe. In the seventh or sixth century B.C., some brave souls (or some people with a reason to get way out of town) decided to climb into their dugout canoe and change addresses. The second invasion was on.

Some of the Mesolithic people came from southern Scotland and the Argyll Islands; others came from southern Britain and Wales. Those more skilled at seafaring came an even larger distance across the waters from southwest Europe. But once these people arrived in Ireland, in the area now known as Antrim, they didn't get much farther than the eastern coast, Ulster, and Donegal.

The Mesolithic people lived close to the beaches or shores of the lakes because of the density of the forests. Mostly, they were nomadic. They wandered along the coastlines, fished, hunted small animals, and caught birds. They domesticated a few animals such as oxen, goats, and sheep. Although they must have found the climate a bit wet to their liking, the temperatures were mild, which was a reasonable trade-off.

These inhabitants, also known as the Late Hunting People, left little of themselves behind, although they lived peacefully in Ireland, in what must have been an almost idyllic setting, for 3,000 years. Some primitive stone tools and bits of crude pottery dropped at a bog's edge, a few garbage dumps, and some charred remains of campfires beside lakes are all the evidence we have of their lives. They made no great impact upon the land and left no burial sites or dwelling ruins. All in all (with the exception of some salmon, rabbits, and crows, who might beg to differ), most would say the second invasion of Ireland was fairly gentle, too.

New Stone Age People Discover Paradise

The next surge of invaders were far more aggressive with their treatment of the land. The *Neolithic* people or New Stone Age People came from nearby Britain and by sea from even farther away, arriving sometime in the fifth century B.C. They conquered the original inhabitants and set to work subduing the land itself. For the first time, Ireland would feel the effects of human hands on its soil. The forests would be felled, the soil churned, and the earth burrowed. Paradise had been invaded.

Poulnabron Dolmen— ancient grave marker.

Farming, Arts, and Crafts

The dense forests presented no great obstacle to the Neolithic people. They cleared the trees and brush and planted their cereal crops wherever they pleased. These ambitious folks were handy at crafting pottery, tools, and weaponry. They manufactured so many axes at their factory in what is now County Antrim that they even exported the surplus to Britain.

Archeological evidence shows that the New Stone Age People were far advanced over the Late Hunting People. They used some form of language and had highly structured local societies. They played flutes, danced, and expressed themselves in stone carvings, the most outstanding being those that decorated the entrances to their amazing stone tombs.

The Great Stone Tombs

The clearest evidence of the Neolithic people of Ireland, and certainly the most spectacular, is the collection of several hundred stone tombs left by them and spread across the island that date back to 4000 to 2000 B.C. The ingenuity demonstrated in the construction of some of these monuments should give us cause to reconsider our attitudes toward "primitive" man.

Newgrange, older than the pyramids.

The Neolithic people preferred to be interred together in large communal graves; the idea of burying people individually wouldn't come into vogue for another 2,000 years or so. The basic design of these graves was a long hallway containing alcoves where the dead were laid to rest. As a result of this design, some of these gravesites were called *passage graves*. In the countryside of County Meath is one of the most glorious and mysterious of these passage graves, Newgrange.

Older than the oldest of the pyramids, Newgrange is dated at 3200 B.C., which makes it 1,000 years older than Stonehenge. The outside of the stone structure is itself impressive: It's 36 feet high, 330 feet across, and made of 250,000 tons of rocks. But the interior is the most astonishing facet of Newgrange.

As you enter the subterranean passageway, you pass the massive Entrance Stone, which is decorated with carved swirls and stylized squares. Beyond the portal, you enter a 62-foot long corridor and travel through the burial chamber with its corbeled roof. For 5,000 years, that roof has keep the interior dry, not an easy feat in a climate as wet as Ireland's. The interior of the chamber is shaped like a cross and lined with recesses that hold large basins, chiseled from stone, which once contained the bones of the deceased.

The most amazing aspect of this chamber is the wonder that occurs for a few minutes once a year. For 364 days, the tomb lies in darkness, its sepulchral gloom undisturbed. But on December 21, the shortest day of the year and the winter solstice, something astonishing happens. Beginning at 9:45 a.m., sunbeams steal across the passage toward the grave chamber. Within minutes, the chamber, from the decorated side chambers to the glorious vaulted ceiling, is set aglow with the sun's light. The wonder is short-lived,

'Tisn't So!

Many folks think that the Egyptian pyramids are the world's oldest man-made constructions. Also, it is widely believed that Stonehenge is the oldest of the mysterious rock formations built by ancient peoples. But Newgrange, a magnificent passage grave in Ireland, is dated at 3200 B.C., which precedes the earliest of Egypt's pyramids and places it 1,000 years before Stonehenge.

only 17 minutes long, and then the chamber is once again dark. But the miracle will happen again, and again, and again, as it has for 5,000 years on every winter solstice.

Stone Gives Way to Bronze

Between 2200 and 2100 B.C., three other groups of Europeans decided to explore Ireland and liked it so much that they stayed. Whether they conquered the established inhabitants by force or assimilation, we aren't sure. But they were so far advanced over the Neolithic people that they wouldn't have had a problem either way. These groups are known by the following names:

➤ The Beaker Folk

➤ The Food Vessel People

➤ The Cinerary Urn People

Speak Plain Irish

In ancient times, after a deceased person was buried, stones were heaped over the grave, which kept animals from digging up those who were trying to rest in peace. This pile of stones, called a *cairn*, also provided a monument for the dead. Sometimes cairns were used to show the spot were someone lost his or her life, especially if that death was violent or untimely.

These newcomers were sophisticated in their farming and stockbreeding techniques and, more importantly, had a wealth of knowledge when it came to metalworking. These latest invaders had metal weapons, which were far more versatile, lighter, and stronger than the stone ones used by the Neolithic people. They congregated in areas where they found copper ore, specifically in the west, in Munster, where they thrived. Ireland's Bronze Age had arrived.

The Beaker Folk

For some reason, archaeologists decided to name these groups of people after the ways they chose to bury their dead. The Beaker Folk buried their dead individually, rather than communally like their predecessors, and in a crouched position in small chambers 2 to 10 meters in diameter. They covered these sites with *cairns,* which are as much a part of the Irish countryside as patches of clover.

Like the Egyptians, who filled their pyramids with goods necessary for housekeeping in the afterlife, the Beaker Folk left articles behind in the chambers of their dead, though none contained anything so glorious as the Tutankhamen stash. The Beaker Folk interred weapons and mundane possessions with their deceased, as well as beautifully decorated drinking vessels, called *beakers* (and you thought it had something to do with concoctions bubbling in a laboratory).

The Food Vessel People

The second group of people, who also arrived from Europe by way of Britain, were the Food Vessel People. They settled in the east, where they, too, buried their dead in a crouched position or in a state of cremation. They also provided utensils for the afterlife in the burial chamber, which was often a stone cist. But the Food Vessel People must have valued food over drink, because they provided bowls for their deceased kin rather than drinking beakers. Bowls were placed with the bodies that were buried in a crouched position, and vases contained the ashes of those who had been cremated.

Some of the Food Vessel People were buried individually, and others were interred in communal graves like the Neolithic folk. In some instances, the Food Vessel People used the same graves created by their predecessors. One of the most well-known examples of a gravesite created by the Neolithic society and later used by the Food Vessel People is the Mound of the Hostages on the Hill of Tara. This site has yielded myriad archeological riches from the many societies who used it millennium after millennium.

The Cinerary Urn People

The Cinerary Urn People can be differentiated from the other two types by the unique way they had of turning their urns filled with cremated remains upside down upon burial. Their interments were always singular, rather than communal. They avoided the stone cists of Food Vessel folk and used simple chambers like the Beaker Folk. They, too, buried some of their deceased at the Mound of the Hostages at Tara in this strange, topsy-turvy manner.

Eire's Land Today: Fierce and Gentle, Like Her People

The ancient High King of Ireland, Cormac MacArt, told his son that the secret to being a great ruler and the most important thing about being a man, was this: To be fierce on the battlefield, gentle in friendship. That wonderful paradox, fierce yet gentle, is an apt description of the character of Ireland today, both the land and the people.

The great "Emperor of Ireland" Brian Boru, who ruled Ireland around the turn of the century (you'll learn more about him later), was renowned for his ferocity in battle. Having learned how to use the weapons of his Viking enemies against them, he could sever a Norseman in half at the waist with one of their terrible battle axes or rip away an opponent's jaw with his bare hands. But that same man who gained a reputation for being a terror on the battlefield would go home to his castle, play the harp, and compose a tender love song for his queen.

In reviewing a Hall of Fame of Irish patriots, you'll find that those who fought the hardest were the gentlest lovers. The rebels were also the poets, and the soldiers were the bards. Those who were willing to spill their own blood and that of others for the prize of freedom were those who loved their nation with a tender, romantic affection that is usually reserved for women.

They say that a people is created by the land it lives upon, and perhaps, therein lies the answer to the dichotomy of the Irish. Ireland is a small country, about the size of the state of Indiana. Yet within her borders, circumscribed by sea and ocean, exist myriad contrasts. In some places, the land meets the sea in a velvety green plain, sloping gently to a sandy beach caressed by gently lapping waves. In others, the land falls away to sheer rocky cliffs hundreds of feet high, and at their base, waves crash with a savagery that has ground many a ship to splinters on the boulders there.

Burren landscape, County Clare.

Fields of Grass, Fields of Limestone

More than one poor Irish peasant has been subjected to this type of sarcasm, muttered by an insensitive neighbor: "That's a fine crop of rocks y'er growin' there, Patrick. And how do ye eat them?" To which he might reply, "Roasted and served hot straightaway with a cup o' buttermilk. The doctor informed me I'm in need o' more roughage in me diet."

Sadly, not all land in Ireland has always been as gentle as the garden lands of County Wicklow. In most areas of the island, you won't find a bare spot of ground anywhere. All types of vegetation fight with one another over the honor of filling any square inch of soil that isn't covered by rock with something green and growing. It makes for some hard soil to hoe.

Hard land and hard labor often spawn hard people, but over the years, the Irish managed to keep their hearts from becoming as calloused as their hands. Family and friends remained dear; and the same peasants who labored all day in the field found the time and energy at the end of the day to nurture the 10 children around their table and have friends over for some conversation and drink besides. Ireland's men and women are hard but gentle.

Soft Rain or Noah's Deluge?

Whatever lad or lass first called Ireland the "Emerald Isle" wasn't just making light of words. To say that Ireland is green is a sad understatement; there are no words to describe the verdant luxuriance of a Kerry field beneath the midday sun or the thousand shades of green you see in the patchworked landscape when you stand at the top of the Rock of Cashel and look across the Tipperary plain.

All that green has to come from somewhere. Contrary to what an Irishman will tell you, it *does* rain in Ireland. It rains cats and dogs, pigs and sheep, chickens and ducks, and you will get wet if you spend any measurable amount of time there. But that Irishman isn't lying to you when he denies that it rains. He just doesn't consider that light, soft mist that falls from the sky many days of every year to be rain. Contrasted with what the sky does on a day when it really rains, you can see why he makes the distinction.

'Tisn't So!

Any Irishman who tells you it doesn't rain much in Ireland is in danger of choking on the Blarney stone. The rainfall in the east can average as much as 30 inches and even more in the west. Which is why in Ireland when something is simple to do it's "As easy got as a wet foot."

While in Ireland, I had the pleasure of visiting Morgan Llywelyn, the author of such magnificent Irish historical novels as *The Lion of Ireland, Bard,* and *Grania.* She took me to see the Cliffs of Moher, one of the wonders of the island. On the way there, she cautioned me that, unless the weather cooperated, we might not be able to properly view this glorious sight. I watched the gathering clouds with apprehension, and by the time we arrived at what seemed to be the edge of the world itself, those breathtaking cliffs that drop straight down as much as 700 feet to the Atlantic, the wind was howling, and the rain coming down in sheets.

She stopped the car, and I said mournfully, "Oh well, I guess it wasn't a good day to try this." She replied, "Nonsense, it's a fine day for it." I looked doubtfully at the windshield, completely obscured by the downpour. I felt the car rocking side to side, buffeted by the near hurricane-force winds. "Oh, yeah?" I said. "How do you figure the weather is cooperating?" She gave me a playful smile, swung her door open, and stepped out into the gale. "Simple," she said. "You can get the car doors open."

A Bard's Tale

For those of you who don't want the blarney, here are a few facts o' the Fair Isle for you:

➤ Ireland is off the northwesterly part of the continent of Europe, situated between 51.5 degrees and 55.5 degrees latitude north and 5.5 and 10.5 degrees longitude west.

➤ The land of Ireland comprises 32,595 square miles and is approximately 302 miles long and 175 miles wide.

➤ The entire Irish coastline is about 3,500 miles long.

➤ The months of July and August are the warmest, averaging about 59 degrees Fahrenheit. Except in the high mountains, snow or ice are rare.

Waters of Life, Watery Graves

Water, water everywhere—that's Ireland. It is surrounded by the Atlantic Ocean to the west, the Irish Sea to the east, and in the middle, it has more lakes than you could shake a bishop's staff at (more than 800 at last count). The Shannon is one of the longest rivers in Europe and is *the* longest in Ireland and Great Britain. All 230 miles of it flow north to south, and it drains one-fifth of the whole island. All this water, combined with that gentle rain mentioned before, guarantees that an Irishman may have many worries, but dying of thirst isn't one of them. From any point on the island, it is only 70 miles at most to the sea and usually a stone's throw to a river or lake.

Lakes of Killarney.

The ocean, rivers, and lakes have always provided life for the inhabitants of Eire, from the earliest settlers thousands of years ago to the present. If you want a fine lunch, drop a line; you'll likely come up with salmon, trout, or some other delectable.

But the waters that have given life have also taken it away. For centuries, the fishermen of Ireland have set out in the morning, met with an unexpected gale at noon, and washed ashore, drowned, at eventide. Then there were those whose bodies were found weeks later or, sadly, not at all.

A Bard's Tale

No doubt you've seen those lovely sweaters that the Irish knit (and for which they are famous), the ones with the gorgeous, intricate patterns. They are enormously popular with the tourists because of their beauty, but those patterns have a dark history. At one time, each family had its own unique design knitted into the men's sweaters. The reason for this was that although a human body might deteriorate when floating in the sea too long, the sturdy, well-made sweaters remained intact. When the corpse of a beloved father, brother, or husband finally washed ashore, he could be identified by the patterns in his sweater.

The Counties and Provinces of Ireland

The island of Ireland is divided into four large provinces: Leinster, Munster, Connacht, and Ulster. These provinces are further sectioned into counties. Twenty-six of those counties make up the Republic of Ireland, and six of the nine counties of Ulster (Antrim, Armagh, Down, Tyrone, Derry, and Fermanagh) constitute Northern Ireland.

Each province and county of Ireland has its own distinct character. Some are lush, green, and meadowlike; others are barren, though enchanting in their own way. Most of the mountains and hills are around the edges of the island; the center is flatter, much like a plate. The rockier areas are in the northwest; the southeast is known for its gentle sloping hills. The southwest, specifically in the County Kerry region, has dramatic scenery: ragged cliffs, lush forests, and rocky coastlines.

Ireland's geography is as diverse as her people and every bit as charming. From the stone-covered plains of Connemara to the gardens of Wexford, gentle and hard, lush and barren—those are the dichotomies of Ireland.

The Least You Need to Know

➤ Ireland was a land of ice until about 10,000 B.C. when the first vegetation began to take root and thrive.

➤ The earliest mammals to inhabit Ireland were horses and giant deer that crossed from the continent via a shallow land/sea divide between Scotland and Ireland.

➤ Between the sixth and seventh millennium, the Mesolithic or Middle Stone Age folks, also called the Late Hunting People, arrived by the same route as the deer and horses. By then, the island was covered with thick, impenetrable forests, so they stayed close to the sea coasts and lake shores.

➤ The Neolithic or New Stone Age people made their way to Ireland and cleared the forests, tilled the soil, and built magnificent stone tombs that exist to this day, including a wonder of "primitive" technology called Newgrange.

➤ Between 2200 and 2100 B.C., three groups of people arrived in Ireland: the Beaker Folk, the Food Vessel People, and the Cinerary Urn People. With their advanced technology and knowledge of metal working, they ushered Ireland into the Bronze Age.

➤ The fertility of the land, or the lack thereof in some areas of Ireland, has had a deep impact on the people trying to scratch out a living from its soil.

➤ They say it never rains in Ireland, just softly mists. This is true much of the time, but when it rains, don't look up, or you'll surely drown!

➤ Ireland is a land surrounded by seas, dotted with lakes and ribboned with rivers. The waters have given life in the form of an abundance of food for the Irish people over the ages, but many Irish have lost their lives to the terrible storms and pounding surfs.

Chapter 4

Those Glorious Celts (Not the Basketball Team)

In This Chapter

➤ Celtic is a state of mind

➤ Barbaric, berserk warriors

➤ Celtics lads and their lack of clothing

➤ Highly civilized savages

➤ The Celts did it their way, but not necessarily the best way

---

Of all the peoples who invaded, conquered, and inhabited ancient Eire, the one group whose influence had the most lasting effect on the Irish of today was the Celts. They were a colorful people, both figuratively and literally. They proudly sported elaborate tattoos, and sometimes painted their nude bodies bright blue before going to war, a sight that must have scared their enemies witless. Gregarious, rambunctious, fiercely proud, and boastful, the Celts loved a good story, a rousing song, plenty of food, and flowing drink, but fighting was their favorite pastime by far. (Sound like anyone we know?)

The Celtic mindset is very different from that of the Anglo-Saxon, and one makes little sense to the other. The Anglo-Saxon relies more on his intellect and his logic for guidance, but the Celt acknowledges the value of that which cannot be viewed, heard, or felt, but is perceived on a spiritual level. A less than charitable Anglo-Saxon might describe his Celtic neighbor as an ignorant, superstitious oaf; a cranky Celt might declare the Anglo-Saxon a soulless fellow with no awareness of the unseen wonders around him. The Anglo-Saxon would be more likely to place great importance on a breakthrough in the field of science. A Celt would be more inclined to celebrate the creation of a great work of literature or a moving piece of music.

Anglos and Celts don't always understand and appreciate each other. This difference doesn't make it easy for those of us with Celtic heritage who find ourselves living in an Anglo-dominated society. Sometimes we feel a bit out of step, not quite in the main flow, and we think something is amiss with us. Perhaps a tear springs to our eye a bit quicker than others when we are touched by an inspiring story or a sentimental song. Maybe our temper flares a tad quicker than our neighbors' does when we believe we have been mistreated. But our compassion and sympathy are just as readily offered to those who have been unjustly wounded. We are accused of being frivolous because of our constant joking by those who don't comprehend the pithy truths contained in our witticisms.

Hopefully, we have evolved a bit from our wildly barbaric Celtic ancestors. No matter how badly you annoy an Irishman today, he isn't likely to slice your head off your shoulders and hang it from his doorpost. But in studying our Celtic forefathers, we can see that the fruit doesn't tumble far from the family tree. The average Irishman and Irishwoman has quite a lot in common with those glorious barbarians. We aren't so very weird after all; we're just Celts living in an Anglo world.

A Bard's Tale

As well as being known for the ferocity of their warriors, the Celts were also renowned for the power of their druids to invoke peace. According to the Greek historian, Diodorus Siculus, when "two armies are in the presence of one another, and swords drawn and spears couched, the [druids] throw themselves into the midst of the combatants and appease them as though they were charming wild beasts. Thus even amongst the most savage barbarians anger submits to the rule of wisdom, and the god of war pays homage to the muses."

Naked Warriors Painted Blue

If you go far enough back into the mists of distant history, you find the Celtic people on the plains of western Russia, in the area of the Volga steppes. As hunters who later became stock-keepers, the Celts were among the first people to domesticate the horse, around 3000 B.C. This skill, along with their deft use of iron for weaponry, gave them a tremendous advantage over their fellow humans. They were a people filled with wanderlust and a love of war, so they decided to invade Europe around 500 B.C. and did so as hordes of fierce, shrieking, naked warriors, thundering over their victims on horseback. It is easy to imagine why some believe that this horrible vision of the nude warriors on their horses inspired the myth of the centaur.

Stiffening their hair with lime, sometimes painting their bodies blue, the Celts would work themselves into a frenzy before riding into battle, where they presented the image of fighters gone berserk. They screamed insults at their enemies on the battle-field, brandishing their own arms and boasting of their great prowess. To this deafening din, they added the clatter and clanging of swords upon shields and cacophonous horn blowing and bellowing. Many of their victims probably died on the spot due to heart failure, sparing them a more violent end.

According to the Greek historian Diodorus Siculus, the Celts beheaded their adversaries and hung the severed heads from their horses' necks. If they considered the victim a particularly prestigious enemy, they preserved his head in cedar oil and stored it in a chest, where the gory trophy could be taken out and displayed to guests.

Finding little resistance to this sort of barbarism, they easily conquered one land after another. Occasional raiding graduated into a full-scale campaign to subdue the continent of Europe, until their domain extended from Bohemia to Austria and southern Germany, Switzerland, and the eastern borders of France. By 300 B.C. they controlled everything from Finisterre to the Black Sea and from the North Sea to the Mediterranean.

The Celts were never a pure race; they were more of a conglomeration of tribes who shared a common language, a love of war, and the joy of conquest. They intermarried with the peoples they defeated and adopted many of the customs and philosophies of those lands. By the time they arrived in Ireland, around the middle of the first century, they were a highly developed, richly complex people who would change the character of Eire's children forever.

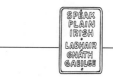

Speak Plain Irish

The **Celts** were an ancient people from western Russia who conquered much of Europe from 500 to 300 B.C. A **Gael** is a Celt of Ireland, Scotland, or the Isle of Man. **Barbarian** is a term coined by the Greeks for anyone who couldn't master the Greek language. To the Greek ear, the language of the Celts sounded like, "ba, ba, ba," hence the word barbarian.

The Delightfully Civilized Savages

When the Celts conquered Ireland, they obliterated nearly every trace of the previous cultures. All aspects of the Neolithic and Mesolithic societies died, and Eire was reborn Celtic. The Celts who took over Ireland were called the *Gaels*, and their language was Gaelic. Although there were various dialects in Gaelic, speakers of those different dialects could easily communicate with one another.

The Gaels were a rowdy bunch. When they weren't waging war with an enemy or with one another, the chieftains spent much of their time in tents, lounging on furs, eating and drinking themselves pleasantly into oblivion, and listening to tales and songs spun by their bards. Hedonistic and earthy, they enjoyed life to the fullest and had no fear of death. Believing in reincarnation, they considered death nothing more than a doorway to the next stage of existence.

By the Gods of My Tribe!

The Celts had gods aplenty in their religion, at least 400 that we know of. Most of them were unique to individual tribes; a common proclamation was, "I swear it by the gods of my tribe!" About 100 of the deities were shared by all, including these favorites:

Gift of Gab

The early Celts considered a person's word of honor to be sacred. According to a collection of civil laws called the *Seanchus Mor,* recorded in the fifth century A.D., "There are three periods of evil for the world: the period of plague, of a general war, and the dissolution of verbal contracts." It adds, "The world would be evilly situated if express contracts were not binding."

➤ Dis was god of the underworld and believed to be the father of mankind.

➤ Esus was the god of arts and crafts and the patron deity of travelers and tradesmen; he was equivalent to the Greek god Hermes.

➤ Taranis was the Celtic equivalent of Zeus. From his name comes the Irish word *torann,* which means thunder.

➤ Lug was a well-loved fellow because he was the god of fertility and the harvest.

Aspects of nature, such as trees and rivers, also played important parts in the Celtic religion. Some rivers, such as the Boyne and the Shannon, were considered divine, as was the earth itself, personified as the female protector of and provider for mankind.

Every Celt Knows His Place

Celtic tribes were divided into groups called *tuaths,* sects belonging to a particular family branch. Specifically, a tuath consisted of the five generations of descendants from one patriarch. The leader of the tuath was elected by the majority. Often this leadership would continue within one immediate family for generations. Sometimes, when a family was voted out of office, that family didn't take the news so well. As a result, homicide among relatives wasn't an uncommon occurrence. In other words, during election time, if you were a likely candidate, you would do well to watch your back. Your cousin twice removed by marriage might be following you with a dagger in his fist.

The individual tribes had virtually no political ties to each other, unified only in a common language and a religion with cultural similarities. But within those tribes, the Celts had highly structured societies, divided into three distinct categories of persons: aristocrats, freemen, and slaves.

Those High-Falutin' Aristocrats

The elite aristocratic class contained the kings and chieftains, warriors, judges, druids, poets, historians, and advisers to the kings. These members of Celtic society received honor and wealth above that of others because their services to the community were considered more valuable:

➤ The kings and chieftains were responsible for the military protection of the tribe under their domain. When they weren't fighting, eating, drinking, and lolling about on fur rugs, they were farmers.

➤ The warriors served their chieftains, fighting their battles when necessary.

'Tisn't So!

Many believe that the Christian priests condemned the druids and their rites, as well as the old Celtic laws. In many cases, this was true, but St. Patrick himself ordered that the laws and customs of ancient Gaelic Ireland be written down and preserved in A.D. 438. Without his action and the efforts of Irish monks, we might have lost much of our knowledge of Irish heritage.

➤ The judges, or brehons, as they were called, tried cases presented to them, adjudicating disputes. For this service, they were paid a fee by the opposing parties. They were fined for unfair judgments, so in spite of their power, they were subject to checks and balances.

➤ The druids were priests, counselors, and teachers all in one and were highly valued members of the Celtic society. The Celts believed their druids possessed supernatural powers; one had to demonstrate evidence of such abilities as soothsaying and fortune telling in order to achieve druid status. Upon their shoulders rested the responsibility of educating the future generations.

➤ The bards, who were musical poets, were also greatly esteemed, because the Celts have always loved a good story and a fine song. As well as writing glorified accounts of their kings' and chieftains' accomplishments, the bards ridiculed his enemies. The bards' disfavor was to be avoided at all costs, because their satires or curses were believed to be so powerful that they could cause not only public disgrace, but also illness, disfigurement, or even death.

Free and Breezy

Among the second category of Celtic citizens were the freemen. The freemen were the basis of the society, because they produced most of what the people consumed. This category, called *cele* in Irish, was the common folk, and it was subdivided into at least 27 other classes according to occupation, such as farmers, tradesmen, and merchants.

The highest level of freeman was a cattle man. Because cattle were the monetary exchange of the Celtic society, the fellow entrusted with the husbandry of the livestock held an enormous amount of responsibility. For this he was richly rewarded in the terms of those days. According to Gaelic law, he was given a cauldron with its spit and handles, a vat in which a measure of ale might be brewed, and small vessels, such as iron pots and wooden kneading boards and mugs, so that he wouldn't be required to borrow them. His larder should be capable of receiving a king, a scholar, or a brehon who might stop by and require a bit of hospitality. He would own seven buildings, a kiln, a barn, a house 27 feet long, an outhouse of 17 feet, 20 cows, 2 bulls, 20 sheep, 20 pigs, 4 boars, and a riding horse. He and his wife could have four suits of clothing.

Slaves: Working Their Way to Freedom

The lowest-ranking position in Celtic society was that of slave. Usually, slaves were enemy soldiers, captured during battle. Prisoners of war were put to death only if they were committing atrocities or other acts of cowardice at the time of their capture. Others were enslaved, but could possibly attain their freedom by learning and faithfully practicing a trade, such as blacksmithing. Although the slave had the fewest rights and privileges and the least wealth in the Celtic society, they were considered extremely valuable by the standards of the day. For instance, a hearty female slave was worth six heifers, a vast amount in an agriculturally based culture.

A Bard's Tale

In his *History of the Gallic Wars,* Julius Caesar wrote of the Celtic druids: "It is said that they commit to memory immense amounts of poetry, and so some of them continue their studies for 20 years. They consider it improper to commit their studies to writing... They also have much knowledge of the stars and their motion, of the size of the world and of the earth, of natural philosophy, and of the powers and spheres of action of the immortal gods, which they discuss and hand down to their young students.

A Celt Is Worthy of His Hire

Once in Ireland, the Celts settled down to a fairly pleasant, rural existence and raised cattle, the primary currency of the society. A ruler's wealth was gauged by the size of his herd, and each member of the tuath was paid annually in cattle or other livestock. The amount he was awarded differed according to his position, whether it be lofty, like that of a bard or brehon, or that of a lowly gravedigger.

Although it might seem incongruent with such a barbaric people, the Celts championed the rights of women and even of their animals. They also considered education extremely important. Although they had no form of written language, they revered the art of oral tradition, and the druidic and bardic scholars memorized enormous genealogies and facts of historical significance, as well as rousing tales of heroes, real and mythical, and a vast knowledge of astronomy, geography, and mathematics.

The gift of eloquence was considered divine, as revered as bravery on the battlefield. To this day, the art of recitation is greatly valued in Ireland. Tiny, copper-haired lads and lasses can prattle off a poem from Yeats or sing you a long, woeful song about a fellow named Willie McBride, a soldier who is buried beneath the poppies on the green fields of France. What's more, they fully comprehend the meaning and significance of the words they are uttering.

The Ultimate Hunger Strike

Celtic law afforded many peaceful methods of settling disputes. If a brehon (judge) awarded you a settlement from your adversary, and he refused to pay up, you could nab some of his property, but only after giving him official notice that you were about to take it. If he paid the rightful debt, you had to return the hostage property.

If all the proper steps had been taken to collect a righteous debt, and the debtor still refused to make it right, you had one final trump card: You could

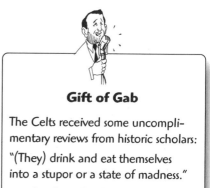

Gift of Gab

The Celts received some uncomplimentary reviews from historic scholars:

"(They) drink and eat themselves into a stupor or a state of madness."

—Diodorus Siculus, Greek historian

"The whole race is madly fond of war."

—Strabo, Greek geographer

"For the great Gaels of Ireland
Are the men that God made mad,
For all their wars are merry,
And all their songs are sad."

—Gilbert Keith Chesterton

camp out on his front porch and starve yourself to death. This action was taken very seriously in Celtic culture. Having a neighbor or relative hold a protest fast in front of your door was a terrible dishonor, one that simply couldn't be borne. Horrified, the debtor would pay to get the famished fellow off his step and the mark of dishonor off his public record.

Contemporary political prisoners sometimes go on hunger strikes, some of which end tragically, in death. It seems the legacy of the Celts continues to the troubled present.

I Gotta Be Me!—Ancient Celtic Philosophy

Much of the fiercely individualistic aspect of the Irish psyche comes from the ancient Celts. They took great pride in themselves as solitary entities within their society. Self-expression was evident in the way they decorated their bodies, sometimes painting, sometimes tattooing their skin and wearing jewelry and brightly colored garments. Especially among the nobles, the quality of their *torques* (heavy collars or necklaces) was extraordinary. Made of gold, these torques were elaborately inscribed with some of the finest, most intricate metalworking the world has ever seen.

The Celts' passion for individuality eventually led to their downfall. They were so full of themselves, so busy fighting each other to prove their own superiority, that when enemies invaded their land, they couldn't mount a unified defense. The Vikings' plundering and pillaging was yet to come. In their serpent ships, the Vikings would steal along Eire's waterways, devouring the Celts in bloody battles with the voracious appetite of a mighty dragon.

43

But first there was to be another invasion of Ireland, a conquering of a spiritual nature. St. Patrick was on his way. And guess what? The most famous Irishman of all time wasn't even Irish.

A Bard's Tale

Fenian warriors (followers of the ancient Gaelic hero Finn MacCool) were held to a strict code of conduct, not unlike the chivalry of King Arthur and his Knights of the Round Table. This code included the following rules:

➤ Choose a wife according to her refined manners and virtue rather than her money.

➤ Never commit an act of violence against a woman.

➤ Always comply with requests for assistance.

➤ Never flee when challenged by less than 10 champion enemy warriors.

The Least You Need to Know

➤ The mindset and personality of Celtic people is quite different from that of Anglo-Saxons. Those differences have caused conflicts over the centuries and even today.

➤ Originally from the plains of western Russia, the Celts were a conglomeration of peoples who were far advanced over the Europeans in the practice of warfare. Riding horses and carrying strong, iron weapons, they rode naked in wild, shrieking hordes through Europe, conquering and assimilating the vanquished societies.

➤ The Celts were barbaric, hedonistic, arrogant, and violent, but they were also highly civilized in many respects. They placed great value upon education, oral tradition, individual rights, and the arts. Their great love of storytelling, poetry, song, recitation, and justice prevails today among their Irish descendants.

➤ Although the strength of the Celts was their appreciation of the individual, it was also their weakness. So self-absorbed were they that they could not present a united defense against the next invaders, the Vikings.

Chapter 5

St. Patrick, Conqueror of Souls

> ### In This Chapter
>
> ➤ Irish raiders bring home more than they bargained for
>
> ➤ A slave boy becomes a priest and then a bishop
>
> ➤ Patrick returns to the land of his enslavement as a missionary
>
> ➤ The fire of Christianity challenges the pagan flames
>
> ➤ The saint leaves his mark on Irish history and the human race

One of the first people one thinks of when Ireland comes to mind is St. Patrick, the Emerald Isle's patron saint. Ireland is predominantly Catholic, and St. Patrick himself is largely responsible for that. His missionary work in Ireland in the 400s A.D. laid the groundwork for not only Ireland's conversion to Christianity, but also, through his spiritual descendants, for the Catholicism of much of Europe.

The monasteries founded by St. Patrick and his followers were repositories for history, astronomy, mathematics, philosophy, and higher learning in general, educating the elite of Europe for generations. Some have made the bold statement that the Irish saved civilization itself. Thanks to the work begun by St. Patrick and his disciples, that is no idle boast.

Not Your Average Day of Pillage and Plunder

The invaders of Irish history weren't always the ones coming from the continent to the Emerald Isle. The Celtic Irish themselves weren't above a bit of piracy and adventure on foreign soil. They set out for unfamiliar shores with pillage and plunder on their minds and the ever-profitable occupation of slave raiding.

In the second, third, and fourth centuries, as the mighty Roman government began to crumble and its armies ceased to guard its previously conquered territories, the unprotected lands presented a special temptation to the Irish. One king in northern Ireland, a fellow by the name of Niall Noigiallach (also called Niall of the Nine Hostages), saw these unprotected areas as the land of opportunity and conducted routine raids on these fallen Roman areas.

There was one invasion, however, that was in no way ordinary. On this particular assault, Niall of the Nine Hostages would bring back one very special young man, a lad named Maewyn of the family Succat. This boy would later refer to himself in writing as *patricius,* which means "well-born" in Latin. Maewyn would change the course of Irish history forever, not to mention that of Christianity and the world itself. Niall of the Nine Hostages could not have foreseen that this boy he brought back to Ireland as an ordinary slave would one day become a most extraordinary man: Niall had stolen his most important captive, the future St. Patrick.

'Tisn't So!

You might be wondering how St. Patrick's grandfather could be a priest, as priests generally don't go around creating offspring to carry on the family name (or at least that's what is in the job description). In the days of St. Patrick, celibacy was not a requirement for the priesthood.

Speak Plain Irish

A **druid** (pronounced *droo*-id) was a member of a Celtic religious order of priests, judges, fortune tellers, poets, and so forth.

Kidnapped and Sold into Bondage

The boy Maewyn is believed to have been born in western Britain, in the district of Severn in the year A.D. 390. He was the son of a British administrator known as Calpurnius, who was a tax collector for the Romans. His grandfather was a Christian monk. The lad was raised as a Christian in Cumbria, though not much is known of his childhood until he was kidnapped in a raid by the Irish king Niall of the Nine Hostages.

At the age of 16, Maewyn was nabbed by Niall of the Nine Hostages. He was whisked away from his family's small farm and taken from his homeland to a strange place, a land the Britons called Hibernia and the Romans knew as Juverna. Hibernia was an island of great natural beauty, but it was ruled by pagan kings and their mysterious *druid* priests. The young Maewyn was sold to a farmer named Milcho from Dalaradia, County Antrim and was put to work herding cattle on Slemish Mountain.

Enslavement on the Isle of the Druids

Slemish Mountain was a lonely place. On this, one of the highest, most dramatic spots in Ireland, the young boy, who at some point began to call himself "patricius" or Patrick, performed his duties for Milcho diligently, with skill, determination, and honor. But the natural beauty of the place inspired him to spend many solitary hours communing with the Almighty.

Patrick existed on a diet of herbs, roots, and the spiritual nourishment of constant prayer. Through the rain and cold of winter and the warmth of summer, he would prostrate himself there on the mountainside and pray to the Christian God whose presence he could feel, even in a land of pagan religions. Later, he would write of that period of his life, saying: "Every day was spent in frequent prayer. I felt no evil, nor was there any laziness in me because, as I now see, the spirit was burning within me." He also wrote that he recited 100 prayers a day.

Six Years in Hell for a Future Saint

Patrick learned the Gaelic language, the Celtic customs, the pagan religion, and all of its colorful tales of ancient heroes. As time passed, he found he loved his new country almost as much as his homeland, which he still missed sorely. He longed for the day when he would escape and return home, even as his affection for the green island grew, bonding him to the place.

Croagh Patrick, where St. Patrick fasted and prayed for 40 days.

The years spent in slavery were difficult for the young boy, but the hardships he suffered toughened and strengthened him, physically and spiritually. He grew to an extraordinary height and developed a religious awareness and maturity far beyond his young years. But considering the difficulty of his life's mission that lay before him, this trial period was merely preparation for what was to come.

Finally, Patrick's sentence on Slemish Mountain came to an end. Six years after he had been sold into bondage, he escaped and boarded a ship, which took him back to the continent. Patrick got away at last, but not forever. Eire still tugged at his heart.

A Bard's Tale

King Laoghaire, son of the Irish king Niall who had kidnapped the young boy Patrick, was afraid of the man whom his father had enslaved and the new religion he represented. Laoghaire's fear mounted when he received this disturbing prophecy from his chief druid: "One shall arrive here, having his head shaven in a circle, bearing a crooked staff, and his table shall be in the eastern part of his house, and his people shall stand behind him, and he shall sing forth from his table wickedness, and all his household shall answer—So be it!— and this man, when he cometh, shall destroy our gods, and overturn their altars... He will seduce the people and bring them after him... He will free the slaves... He will magnify kindreds of low degree...and he shall subdue unto himself the kings that resist him...and his doctrines shall reign forever and ever."

Son of the Church

Little is known of the years Patrick spent in Europe after his escape from Hibernia, but we do know that he learned Latin and became an ordained priest. Someone, probably St. Germanus, bishop of Auxerre, appointed Patrick bishop of the Irish. Of his divine calling to minister to the Irish, Patrick wrote: "I saw, in the bosom of the night, a man coming as it were from Ireland...with letters...and he gave one of them to me. And I read the beginning of the letter containing 'the voice of the Irish'...and they cried out then as if with one voice, 'We entreat thee, holy youth, that thou come, and henceafter walk among us.'"

Return to Eire

In A.D. 432, Patrick and 24 followers landed on Irish soil, on the coast of County Wicklow. Legend says that when he was treated badly by the reigning king of that region, Nathy, Patrick placed a curse upon King Nathy's land and turned his fertile ground into a salt marsh. Although placing a curse on someone might seem like a pagan, not Christian, practice, it was perfectly acceptable in those days. Even today, placing a well-worded curse on the head of a deserving person is not considered ill-mannered or unholy in the least. The more colorful the curse, the better.

Patrick and his party continued up the coast, ending their journey at Strangford Lough in County Down. Their reception there wasn't any warmer than in Wicklow. The chieftain Dichu set his dogs loose on Patrick. Once again, a curse was uttered and legend has it that the offending pooch turned to stone. The disgruntled owner lifted a sword to exact revenge on Bishop Patrick and his arm was instantly paralyzed. Apparently, this was enough for Dichu, who decided to embrace the Christian faith right away. His arm returned to normal.

'Tisn't So!

According to popular legend, St. Patrick rid Ireland of its snakes by driving them into the sea with his magic staff. This story is nothing more than a colorful bit of blarney. The truth is that there never were any snakes in Ireland. The tiny land bridge that connected Scotland and Ireland after the Ice Age was covered with water before they could slither across.

Converting an Old Enemy

Patrick and his followers continued on to the Hill of Tara, arriving on the eve of Beltine, May 1st, an important day in druidic tradition. As the legend goes, according to the pagan priests' commands, fires were extinguished all over the island on that day: campfires, domestic fires, forges, and so on. Then a new flame was kindled by the sun's rays in a ritual by the high priest. That fresh blaze, the sun's own fire, was distributed by runners with torches to all points on the island. From the moment all fires were extinguished, until the new flame was given, no one was allowed to kindle a flame, upon sentence of death.

Well-acquainted with the druids' beliefs and rituals from his six-year stint on Slemish Mountain, Patrick concocted a plan to spread the word of Christianity. He built an enormous fire on a nearby hill, which could be seen for miles around, in direct defiance of the druids. It is said that one of the chief druids gave a prophecy that day in the court of King Oengus, High King of Munster. He warned the king, "If you don't extinguish that fire today [the illegal, literal fire lit by Patrick and metaphorically of the fire of Christianity], it will never again go out in Ireland."

But the king didn't have the fire extinguished. Instead, he hauled Patrick before his court. Having an audience with the king himself, Bishop Patrick gave his famous sermon in which he explained the mystery of the trinity and how three can be one, using the example of the humble, three-leafed shamrock. The story also goes that Patrick was so caught up in the fervor of his own message that he drove his bishop's staff into the ground while emphasizing a point in his sermon, and didn't realize that he had speared the king's foot. Like the noble chieftain he was, Oengus made no complaint but stoically endured the pain, believing it to be part of the ritual of the sermon.

The Saint's Everlasting Footprints on Irish Soil

Although the preceding stories would be difficult to classify as fact or fiction, truth or legend, we do have concrete evidence of St. Patrick's life in his own writings: his *Confession* and his "Letter to the Soldiers of Coroticus." The latter was a passionate missive denouncing a raid on some of Patrick's followers by a British chieftain, who massacred them on the very day the bishop had converted them to Christianity.

Patrick described his mission to the Irish in this way: He "baptized thousands, ordained clerics everywhere, gave presents to kings, was put in irons, lived in daily expectation of murder, treachery and captivity, journeyed everywhere in many dangers, and rejoiced to see the flock of the Lord in Ireland growing splendidly with the greatest care and the sons and daughters of kings becoming monks and virgins of Christ."

St. Patrick captured the essence of his beliefs in "The Deer's Cry":

> "Christ be with me, Christ before me, Christ behind me,
> Christ within me, Christ below me, Christ above me,
> Christ on my right hand, Christ on my left hand,
> Christ when I lie down, Christ when I sit down,
> Christ when I arise,
> Christ in the heart of every man who thinks of me,
> Christ in the mouth of every man who speaks to me,
> Christ in the eye of every man who sees me,
> Christ in the ear of every man who hears me."

St. Patrick established monasteries from one end of Ireland to the other. In many areas, these monasteries were the first settlements and became the center of the communities that grew around them. In later years, the monasteries of Ireland fulfilled the role of the scholastic centers of the culture, where all areas of learning were explored and taught to eager students, some of whom were the sons of European nobility who were sent to Ireland to receive a high-level education.

Monks from Irish monasteries bore the torch of the Christian faith back to Europe and across the continent, bringing even more souls into the fold. They founded yet more monasteries, which upheld the high scholastic and religious standards begun in those humble, lonely sites established by Patrick and his followers, thus ushering in the Golden Age of the Irish Church.

A Bard's Tale

One of Ireland's greatest national treasures, the beautiful Book of Kells, was product of those early monasteries. The 335-page illuminated manuscript contains portions of the gospels and is believed to have been created sometime between A.D. 760 and A.D. 830 and worked on by at least four monks. Its vivid lettering scrolls, winds, and evolves into breathtaking figures: angels, devils, animals, and humans. The book was never completed, probably because of the Viking invasions. It was stolen during a Viking raid, and its golden cover was ripped away. The book was buried, and then recovered and returned home to the Church at Kells in County Meath, Ireland. Its survival almost as miraculous as its artistry, the Book of Kells is now displayed in the Long Room in the library of Trinity College in Dublin.

The great Apostle of Ireland died in A.D. 461 and is reputed to be buried in Downpatrick, County Down, though another tradition holds that his resting place was in Clonmacnois beside the river Shannon in County Offaly. Whatever his burial site, the druidic prophecy has been fulfilled: The saint's spiritual flame still burns brightly in the hearts of Ireland's faithful Catholics. On March 17, the anniversary of his death, the world celebrates the beloved saint and remembers this most famous of all Irishmen, who wasn't Irish by birthright, but in heart and spirit.

The Least You Need to Know

➤ At the age of 16, Maewyn, who was later known as St. Patrick, was kidnapped by Irish pirates who were raiding Britain. He was taken to Ireland and held as a slave.

➤ During young Patrick's years of captivity, he grew in stature, faith, and self-discipline; these attributes would serve him well in his life's mission.

➤ After six years in slavery, he escaped and returned to the continent, where he studied Latin and became a bishop. He returned to the land of his captivity, determined to convert his old enemies.

➤ The fervent missionary traveled the length and breadth of Ireland, risking imprisonment and death to spread the light of Christianity. In less than 200 years after his death, Ireland was a devoutly Christian land. This movement ushered in the era that historians call Ireland's "Golden Age."

Part 3

Invasions, Repression, and Hunger: You Can't Keep a Good Irishman Down

Invasions came to Ireland one right after another. As if the Vikings weren't bad enough, their cousins the Normans arrived, weapons in hand and plunder on their minds. As you saw in Chapter 6, the Vikings wanted the portable treasures of Ireland: gold, jewels, and pretty lasses. The Normans, however, wanted Ireland as their new home. After they had assumed the throne of England, they turned their attentions to Ireland, and so began its long and arduous conflict with England. Hold onto your seats, because in Part 3 we're going to take a look at the not-so-pretty struggle between Ireland and the Crown.

Green Fields Run Red: The Viking Invasion and Brian Boru

In This Chapter

➤ The arrival of the Vikings and the havoc they wreaked

➤ How the Irish fought back

➤ Invasion, Part II: Bloodier than before

➤ Brian Boru's role in fighting the Viking invasion

➤ The end of Viking terror and the loss of the mighty Boru

The years between the coming of Christianity to Ireland and the Viking invasion were fairly peaceful. Most of the Irish lived in family-based groups called *tuaths* (see "Every Celt Knows His Place" in Chapter 4) and existed in relative harmony, except when those relatives went to war with one another, which happened fairly frequently.

But that peace was about to be shattered. The Irish monks had heard rumors of devil barbarians roaming coastline after coastline in dragon ships, wearing horned helmets, and bearing giant axes that could cleave an enemy in half with one blow. The monks heard chilling tales of vicious raids and unspeakable atrocities committed on their brothers in northwest England, on the islands of Shetland and Orkney, and at the monastery of Iona.

They must have suspected they might be next. Forewarned, however, would not have meant forearmed when it came to the Vikings. It was a mercy the Irish didn't know what was coming, because a centuries-long nightmare was about to begin, and nothing could have saved them from the terrible fury of the Norsemen.

Dragon Ships and Battle-Axes

During the eighth century, many European countries experienced a population explosion that the historians are still scratching their heads over. The countries of Denmark, Norway, Sweden, and parts of Finland were getting a bit crowded. That part of the world had limited farmland; most of the countryside was composed of forests, mountains, rivers, and lakes. The Scandinavians needed more room, and being the adventurous sort, these folks, called Vikings, set out in ships to see the world and grab a bit more of it for themselves.

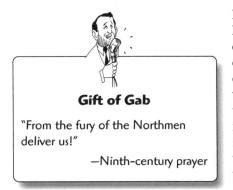

Gift of Gab

"From the fury of the Northmen deliver us!"

—Ninth-century prayer

Being from a land of water (yes, even more than Ireland), the Vikings were magnificent seamen, having developed the keel and mastered the arts of sailing and oarsmanship. To the great chagrin of the Irish, they were experts in another field, as well: warfare. Their weapons were far advanced over most other European societies, their styles of fighting were more bloody, and their methods of torture were more refined. When it came to striking terror in the hearts of the enemy, the Viking warriors were some of the best—or worst, depending on your point of view—the world had ever seen.

The Furious Sons of Thor

The Norsemen were passionately religious people, but their gods weren't benevolent deities who encouraged love, mercy, and goodwill among men. Quite the contrary, Odin, Thor, and the other Norse gods were gods of war. These legendary figures exhorted their sons to take whatever they wished by the power of their might, proving their virility and superiority over those who were considered inferior. Pillage and plunder was not only the right of a proper Viking, but his responsibility. No self-respecting Norseman would sit around on his backside, idling the night away by sipping ale from a mug by the fire, when there was a village nearby to raid and sack. After a good night's work, he could sit by the fire and drink his ale from a golden, bejeweled goblet, pried from the hands of some ill-fated monk who was defending his church's altar.

Of the Vikings who found their way to the Irish coasts, some merely wanted to relocate; others were more inclined to piracy and murder. Whatever they were searching for, the Norsemen found it in abundance on the Emerald Isle: verdant pastures, a climate much milder than their own, beautiful lasses, sturdy lads to serve as slaves, and wealthy monasteries brimming with treasures. What more could a marauding Viking want?

A.D. 795: Year of Blood

The Viking invasion of Ireland began in the year 795 on Recheainn Island off the northeast coast. The monastery there was sacked and burned. For the next 40 years, raids on coastland and island-based monasteries became commonplace.

Why monasteries? Because before the coming of the Vikings, there were no real cities or even large towns to speak of on the island. The monasteries were the community centers, and more importantly to the Vikings, they were repositories for portable booty. The monk artisans of that day were highly skilled in gold and silversmithing, and they created marvelous altar vessels, shrines, relics, and book covers, all made of precious metals. Not only did the Viking pirates steal enough of these treasures to overflow their own personal stockpiles, but there was a surplus to export to the continent. In that day, European trade was flooded with stolen Irish treasure.

'Tisn't So!

Norsemen weren't the only ones robbing churches and setting them afire. The Irish themselves were attacking the monasteries long before the first dragon ship landed. From 800 to 825, the Norse raided 26 settlements. During the same period, the Irish plundered their monastic neighbors 87 times. Those Vikings lads were dirty scoundrels to be sure, but we Irish weren't exactly the image of St. Patrick!

Serpents on the River

Around A.D. 830, the Viking raids became less of the hit-and-run tactics of a single ship and more organized and deadly. Most of the early attacks had been on settlements near the coasts. As the Vikings' thirst for plunder grew, however, large fleets of ships began to glide up the rivers in terrible armadas with the intention of conquering and settling entire areas.

In 837, as many as 60 dragon ships gathered at the mouth of the river Boyne, and another 60 gathered on the river Liffey. The two groups traveled those rivers, ravaging as they went and beginning the deep penetration of Ireland. Great monasteries, known throughout Europe for their scholastic excellence, fell to the Vikings' axes and torches: the mighty Clonmacnois, Lorrha, Terryglass, and Clonfert.

Not all monks turned the proverbial other cheek to the invaders. Quite the contrary, many of the clergy were descended from warring chieftains. They were converted to Christianity, but their fiery temperaments were left intact. As strange as it may seem to the contemporary mind, the concept of warrior monks was common in that day. For example, in 845, the abbot of Terryglass and Clonenagh and the deputy abbot of Kildare were killed while defending their churches in battle against the Norsemen.

A Bard's Tale

"The whole of Munster...was plundered by them. ...neither veneration, nor honor, nor mercy...was felt by this furious, ferocious, pagan, ruthless, wrathful people. They killed the kings and the chieftains, the heirs to the crown. They killed the brave and the valiant...and the greater part of the heroes and warriors of the entire Gaedhil...and they reduced them to bondage and slavery. Many were the blooming, lively women...and the gentle, well brought up youths, and the intelligent, valiant champions, whom they carried off into oppression and bondage over the broad green sea!"

From The War of the Gaedhil with the Gaill, *translated by James Henthorn Todd*

The Irish Strike Back!

As the Vikings swept inland, the local citizenry suffered as attacks were mounted on the family settlements. Children and old people were slaughtered during the raids, and the young, healthy men and women were led away as prisoners and sold into slavery. As with the gold and silver, the Vikings had more than they needed of this human commodity and exported their excess captives to foreign slave markets.

More firmly ensconced in the Irish countryside, the Vikings began to settle in, building military bases and establishing Norse cities, such as Dublin (Dubhlinn, which means Dark Pool) and Annagassan on the south coast. To protect their ships, they constructed harbors, called *longphorts,* that were fortified by earthen walls, wooden palisades, and watchtowers.

Although the longphorts and cities were well-protected, they also provided the Irish with a focal point for a counterattack. Before, the Norsemen had been an incorporeal terror, striking suddenly in the night, seemingly out of thin air, and disappearing just as effectively.

Dragon Ships Afire!

Once the Irish knew where to find the Vikings and their hated dragon ships, they mounted attacks on the longphorts, sometimes setting entire fleets ablaze. Thrilled to finally have a target, local chieftains led their sons and brothers in raids against the Norse settlements, striking some long overdue blows for the Celts.

Unfortunately, the small Irish kingdoms did not have one, unified army. Cooperation between the petty kings was unheard of; they considered each other mortal enemies, not allies. Their manpower, weapons, and energies were too consumed fighting each other to mount a joint defense, let alone offense, against the Norse. But individually, the Irish did what they could, and a few Vikings felt the bite of Irish steel.

A Bard's Tale

The Vikings are credited with teaching the Irish the benefit of stone buildings over wood and wattle, but this is rather like saying the Big Bad Wolf improved the Three Little Pigs' lot by educating them in the advantages of brick versus straw and wood. When enough of the natives' wooden dwellings had gone up in flames from Norse torches, the Irish got smart and began to construct their buildings from stone.

Head for the Tower!

Another "contribution" of the Norse to the island was the Irish's construction of the beautiful and highly practical round towers. In the mid-800s, a hundred or more of these graceful stone spires were built in Ireland. Some remain intact today, including the exquisitely lovely tower at Glendalough in County Wicklow and other fine examples at Nendrum, County Down, and Devenish in County Fermanagh.

The round tower at Ardmore.

The round towers provided a belfry for the monastery, as well as a watchtower from which to spot approaching marauders. But their most important function was that of a refuge during a raid. Standing from 70 to 125 feet tall and as wide as 14 to 17 feet at the base, the towers contained as many as four stories inside. The floors were built of wood and connected by ladders. Their exterior doors were placed at least twice the height of a man and were accessible only by ladder.

When, from one of the four windows at the top, the watchtower guard saw enemies approaching, he would sound the alarm by ringing a handbell. Thus alerted, the monks would grab up the valuables and roar off to the tower. After scrambling inside, they would lift the ladder. With the food and water stashed inside, the monks could hold out a long time, while their frustrated raiders cooled their heels at the base of the tower. As the Vikings were known more for their restless energy than their patience, they weren't inclined to dally about for very long before moving on to a less challenging community.

Look Out! Here Come Some More!

During the last half of the ninth century, the Vikings intermingled with the Irish so much that they became a deeply ingrained part of the countryside. Even their military skirmishes and basic political objectives became synonymous with those of the other warring Irish factions. In other words, they were just one more group living on Irish soil, squabbling with their neighbors.

But in 914, another wave of Viking invaders swept down from the north and landed in Waterford. A year later, another group arrived in Wexford and began to plunder the provinces of Leinster and Munster with a vengeance never before imagined. The first invasion had been bloody, but by the year 950, the second invasion was making the first one seem like a benign dream. This time, the Vikings were already firmly implanted in Irish soil. From their Norse cities on Irish soil, they could raid at will and did, laying waste to vast areas of the countryside and killing everyone in their path.

The Vikings' battle tactics were unbelievably violent. Their philosophy simple: If an attack were vicious enough and its aftermath adequately gory, any remaining survivors would be stunned in its wake. They would be so horrified by the violence and desecration inflicted upon their loved ones, they would be temporarily rendered incapable of seeking revenge. And stunned they were. The Irish had been so busy fighting each other and quarreling over local, petty kingdom issues that, once again, they couldn't mount a unified defense against this ruthless enemy.

By the year 950, Ireland desperately needed a leader, someone of exceptional courage and leadership ability, with the diplomatic skills to unite a factious people. It would be another year, however, before he would be

Speak Plain Irish

Most of the Vikings who settled in Ireland adopted the Gaelic language. Only about 50 of the old Norse words found their way into common Irish usage. Here are a few that made the cut:

bad means boat

stiuir means rudder

dorgha means fishing line

margad means market

schilling means shilling

born, and it would be 20 years after that before the child would be a man, capable of saving his nation from the threat of the Norsemen. Ireland's great emperor, Brian Boru, was on his way.

A Hero Is Born: Brian Boru, Emperor of Eire's Land

Most nations and peoples have heroes whose deeds of valor, feats of courage, and/or acts of kindness have set them above their peers. Ireland has more than her share of such men and women, some of whom have risen to legendary status. Of all the heroes and heroines of Erin, however, one figure towers above all others: Brian Boru, or as he is called in Gaelic, Brian Boruma. He is known as the great emperor of Ireland and the only man in history to rule the entire island under one banner, his own. A scholar, a diplomat, a leader, and a warrior beyond compare, Brian Boru embodied all the qualities of a king—a king that the Irish desperately needed if they were to end the Vikings' siege.

Portrait of an Emperor as a Young Man

Brian Boru was born in the year 951 to King Cennedi, leader of the powerful tribe the Dal Cais of north Munster. The Dal Cais were rich by the standards of the day, though Cennedi didn't spend his days sitting on a throne in a fine palace. Like the other Irish kings and chieftains of tribes, he and his sons were principally farmers and herdsmen, who, when necessary, provided military protection for their kinsmen.

'Tisn't So!

Does the name Cennedi sound familiar? If you think it sounds like Kennedy, you'd be right. Indeed, they are the ancestors of that very bloodline.

Cennedi's Dal Cais achieved a rise in power in the mid-900s as a result of the strategic position of their territory, which straddled the river Shannon, giving them control of the river and its adjoining lakes. In addition to favorable geography, Cennedi had another invaluable asset at his disposal: his sons Mathgamain and Brian Boru.

The oldest, Mathgamain, succeeded to the throne of Munster in 963. An adroit politician and brilliant military strategist, Mathgamain negotiated truces and led attacks against his enemies. In 968, Mathgamain and Brian Boru led a raid on the Vikings of Limerick and carried away loads of treasure that had been taken from the Irish. They also burned the city, giving the Vikings a taste of their own bitter draught and showing their fellow Irishmen that the Norsemen could bleed as freely as the Irish.

This increase in power and reputation for the Dal Cais proved worrisome to the Ui Neill clan in the north, who had decided that the head of their tribe, a fellow named Mael Sechnaill II, was Ireland's *Ard Ri* or "high king." Mael Sechnaill's title was more honorary than practical, because at that time, no one ruler was running the show in Ireland. Regardless of whether he was an effective Ard Ri, though, Mael Sechnaill and his clansmen didn't appreciate the Dal Cais grabbing so much power for themselves.

A Bard's Tale

There are several theories as to why Brian Boru was called Brian Boruma. The word *Boruma* means "taker of tributes" (as in money paid by one king or noble to another as a sign of submission). Some historians say that Brian was a greedy ruler who exacted heavy tributes from his subdued enemies and got the name for his greediness. Others say his name came from the area in which he was born, Boruma, named for the many cattle raised there. The real story is that the name was given to Brian by the poet MacLiag, who recorded the deeds of the great king.

My Brother's Keeper

In 976, Mathgamain was betrayed by some supposedly friendly allies and murdered. Brian didn't take the news of his brother's betrayal and death very well at all. Having idolized Mathgamain, he was devastated by the assassination and was determined to punish the guilty. Among those traitors were some Vikings and Imar, the king of Limerick, and his sons. Brian chased them all the way to a monastery on Scattery Island, where they sought refuge on church land.

Despite the fact that they claimed to be Christians and under the protection of the church, Brian followed them into the church where they had taken refuge, killed them, and desecrated the church where they had been hiding. Not a pretty picture, but Brian's actions demonstrated that he wasn't someone you wanted to cross.

King of Half of Ireland, But It Isn't Enough

In three years, Brian Boru had conquered all of Munster, upsetting Mael Sechnaill and his Ui Neill clansmen even more. Boru was no longer making a secret of his ambitions; he didn't intend to stop until he was Ard Ri and a *real* high king, not just in name. Mael Sechnaill attempted to defeat Boru's purposes, without success. Battles raged between the two of them for nearly 20 years. Then, in 997, they met at Clonfert and negotiated a truce that was bitter for Mael Sechnaill and only half-satisfactory to Brian: Mael Sechnaill would rule the north of Ireland, and Brian would rule the south.

The uneasy peace lasted only a couple of years, until new troubles began to brew. The Leinstermen revolted, and the Dublin Vikings started to kick up their heels, as well—moves that would prove disastrous for them both. Brian met the Leinstermen in battle at Glen Mama and took their king prisoner. Then he turned his attention to Dublin, plundering and burning that fortified city and forcing its Viking king, Sitric Silkbeard, to surrender. Brian would only allow Sitric to return home after he had paid a handsome tribute and vowed allegiance to Boru.

At Last, Ireland Has Her True King

As the year 1000 rolled around, Brian was no longer content to rule half of the island. For two years, he warred against Mael Sechnaill until Mael relinquished the title of Ard Ri. Brian Boru had done the impossible; he had risen from the meager status of prince of a tuath to High King of Ireland through his strength and cunning. He was coronated at Tara, Hill of the Kings, upon the ceremonial Stone of Fal.

A Bard's Tale

According to legend, the Stone of Fal (an ancient gray stone set atop a grassy mound in the heart of Tara) was used as the coronation stone of the high kings of Ireland. It was said that when the one, true king of Ireland was crowned, the stone would "cry" for him. King after king, coronation after coronation, the Stone of Fal remained silent, until the day Brian Boru ascended the stone. According to legend, a rumbling roar issued from the stone that shook the earth, causing those present to fall to the ground, awestruck. In Brian of Boruma, the ancient prophesy was finally fulfilled.

The years passed, and Brian's reign was a peaceful one by Irish standards. He kept both the Vikings and his chieftains in check, and Ireland flourished. Monasteries were rebuilt and stocked with books. In a land with less bloodshed and constant threat to life, art, music and poetry could be indulged. It was a Golden Age for the Emerald Isle. In Boru, Ireland had found her first, and only, true king. Unfortunately, one of Erin's daughters was going to cause a lot of trouble for everyone. She was a beautiful but wicked lass named Gormlaith, and she was Brian Boru's future bride.

Gormlaith, a Wicked Lass, Indeed

Sitric Silkbeard had a secret weapon of his own, his mother, Gormlaith. Although she was old enough to have a son who was king of Dublin, Gormlaith was considered by

Gift of Gab

Even among the Vikings, Gormlaith had a reputation for beauty and treachery. In their historical accounts, she was called the fairest of all women, the best gifted. Though they also added that she "did all things ill over which she had power."

many to be the most beautiful woman of her day. She had been a child-bride to Norse King Olaf of Dublin, by whom she had borne Sitric. Power-hungry, but thwarted because of her gender, Gormlaith tried to rule vicariously through her aged husband. Through her lies and manipulations, she was constantly starting wars among her allies and opponents, bloody conflicts that served her own political purposes. Finally, poor old Olaf was so tired of the constant battles with his enemies and his contentious wife that he deserted Gormlaith and entered a monastery. He died shortly thereafter.

Insulted by Olaf's abandonment, the beautiful and ruthlessly ambitious Gormlaith had her son Sitric arrange a marriage between herself and the Ard Ri of that time, Mael Sechnaill. (This was before Brian took the throne.) But Mael Sechnaill wasn't a feeble old man like Olaf, and Gormlaith found him far more difficult to manipulate. The marriage quickly went sour as Mael Sechnaill tired of her attempts to maneuver politically around him and stir up problems between Mael Sechnaill and his neighbors, friend and foe. When he divorced her, Gormlaith's bitterness against him knew no bounds.

She and Sitric arranged yet another powerful marriage for her with Mael Sechnaill's greatest enemy, the man who was usurping his position as Ard Ri, Brian Boru. Gormlaith expected that the union with Brian would give her the two things she wanted most: power and the opportunity to get revenge on Mael Sechnaill.

Brian was now middle-aged and a widower. (Little is known of his first wife other than that she was beautiful, frail, and sickly, and died young.) When Brian met the captivating Gormlaith, he was smitten and quickly accepted her son's offer of marriage. But it didn't take long for him to see why Gormlaith's other two husbands had shown her the road.

Brian continued to oppose Mael Sechnaill, as he had before, even gaining the coveted title of Ard Ri, high king of Ireland. But Gormlaith was furious that he didn't kill Mael Sechnaill, as she had intended he should. By choosing to make peace with his old enemy, Brian alienated his wife. As she had in her previous marriages, Gormlaith began to make political alliances behind her husband's back, stirring strife among those who needed little coaxing to go to war.

Finally, Brian realized his beautiful wife was more trouble than she was worth, and he divorced her. Being cast aside yet a third time was too much for Gormlaith's vanity to bear. She prodded her son Sitric Silkbeard and her brother King Maelmorda of Leinster into marshalling support among their Viking allies and revolting against Brian.

To gain the support of some of the Viking nobles, Sitric offered them his mother's hand in marriage. He did this secretly, without one knowing of his offer to the other.

Of course, he had no intention of keeping his part of the bargain, having only one mother as a bartering chip. He also promised them kingship of Ireland, a crown that wasn't his to give.

As shallow as these promises were, he had several takers, enough to go to battle against Brian. Sitric Silkbeard would never have to account for his duplicities. A war began, and it was a struggle that would culminate on the bloody fields of Clontarf. When the battle was finished, most of the major players in the game of kings, queens, and pawns would be dead.

Alas, the Mighty Have Fallen

In opposition to his enemies' revolt against him, Brian assembled great armies and prepared to attack Dublin. This time, taking the city proved more difficult for the aging Boru and his troops. Three months later, with Christmas coming, his allies began to drift away. But Brian Boru was determined and began to prepare for an even greater assault.

On April 23, 1014, Good Friday, Boru and his troops were gathered at Clontarf, outside Dublin on the river Liffey. They were engaged by Viking and Leinster forces in one of the deadliest battles in Ireland's history. Some even say that the trees in the area dripped with blood.

At this point, Brian was too old to fight in combat. The aged king watched the action from the sidelines inside a guarded enclosure. The fighting was fierce, and in the course of the battle, Brian's warrior son, Murchad, born of his first queen, was killed, as was the enemy Leinster king (Gormlaith's brother Maelmorda), and the Viking king Jarl Sigurd of Orkney. But the greatest casualty of the battle was Brian Boru himself. A fleeing Viking named Brodar spotted the old king unguarded and attacked. Brian died not the death of a feeble old man, but a warrior's death, struck down by the Viking's axe.

'Tisn't So!

Brian Boru's age at his death is a point of contention among historians. Some say he was over 70, and others claim he was more than 85.

According to the Norse account of the battle of Clontarf, contained in the book *Njal's Saga,* Brodar met a gruesome, horrible death. They say Brodar was captured by Brian's men soon after he assassinated the king. Apparently, Boru's men sliced open his abdomen, fastened his intestines to a tree, and then forced him to circle the tree until he was completely disemboweled.

Gross, huh? Also, not too believable. The Irish weren't saints, but torture wasn't a part of their culture. Undue cruelty committed during warfare was frowned upon; it was one of the few crimes punishable by death in Celtic society, but it was a popular pastime of the Norse. It's more likely that Brodar met with the following, less gruesome end: He was captured almost immediately and killed by Munstermen.

Meanwhile, Brian's other son, Donnchad, led the charge against the Vikings and their allies and chased them into Dublin Bay, where many of them drowned. The Irish armies won a celebrated victory against their enemies, breaking the power of the Vikings in Ireland forever, but the price was terrible. Brian Boru's body was borne with great ceremony to Armagh and buried. The bards composed songs of praise for him and his victory over the hated enemy. Even the Norse poets proclaimed, "Brian fell, but won at last."

The Mark of the Norsemen

Although the mighty Boru was able to defeat the Vikings at Clontarf, the Norsemen left lasting impressions on the Emerald Isle. Some of those marks were deep, painful scars; others were the more positive stamps of civilization.

After Clontarf, the Vikings abandoned their ambitions of conquering the entire island. They adopted a more peaceful approach, concentrating on their Norse cities and building their shipping and fishing enterprises, which greatly benefited Ireland as a whole. In the end, the Vikings became productive, valuable citizens of Ireland, and their contributions to Irish society were incalculable. Here are just some of their contributions:

➤ They established Ireland's first cities: Dublin, Wexford, Waterford, Cork, Wicklow, Limerick, and Stangford.

➤ They introduced coinage to the island, a much more convenient measure of exchange than cattle.

➤ They advanced the industries of fishing and shipping with their superior navigational skills.

The Viking Irish were healthy, hearty souls, who, along with the Celtic Irish, produced sons and daughters with fiery spirits, sturdy, muscular frames, sapphire- and emerald-colored eyes, and burnished gold and copper hair. To this day, you will spy more stunning redheads in the old Norse towns of Dublin, Limerick, and so on than in the rest of the island. Sadly, another heritage they left behind was a spirit of conflict and the quick tendency to war, which came all too natural to the Celtic society and was soon even more deeply ingrained in the Irish culture.

After the Viking invasion, politics in Ireland became far more ambitious. Overlords who had seized control in order to stand against the Vikings, refused to relinquish that power, even after the threat of the Norsemen had subsided. They fought with one another, making life difficult for the common man, who had to decide which of them to align himself with and hope he and his family would live to see the fruits of that decision. So intent were they on securing their own positions, these overlords would never come to a meeting of the minds. Without this necessary unity, they were helpless to mount a defense for the next wave of invaders: the Normans.

The Least You Need to Know

➤ The Vikings were Scandinavians, extremely advanced in seafaring and the art of war. They raided, pillaged, and plundered Ireland, taking whatever they wished.

➤ Enraged by his brother's assassination and the atrocities of the Vikings upon his people, Brian Boru fought his way to the top and became Ireland's Ard Ri, the high king.

➤ Brian Boru was the first and only man to ever truly rule all of Ireland at one time.

➤ On April 23, 1014, Good Friday, the aged King Brian led his armies against the Vikings in the Battle of Clontarf, where he died in battle. Brian had won the final victory against his old enemies, however. The Viking invasion was over.

➤ Although the Vikings terrorized Ireland, they also contributed a great deal to Irish culture with their fine Norse cities and their shipping and fishing industries.

Chapter 7

The Seed Doesn't Fall Far from the Tree: The Vikings' Norman Cousins

In This Chapter

➤ Who the Normans were

➤ How Dermot MacMurrough murdered and maimed his way to the throne of Leinster and became the most unpopular lad in Ireland

➤ What events led to the full-scale Norman invasion of the Emerald Isle

➤ How the Normans eventually adapted to the Irish way of life

Many of Ireland's woes throughout history, even to today, are the result of the British exerting its power over their westerly neighbor. But how did it all start? When did Englishmen first come to Ireland to stake their claim on the Emerald Isle?

You may be surprised to read in this chapter that Ireland was originally given to the British by a Catholic pope! And the first invasion of the British was by invitation from a disgruntled Irish chief. The British arrived in what was called the Norman invasion. No, it wasn't a lad named Norman who came ashore and stirred up all the trouble. It was King Henry II of England, who was himself a Norman. Confused? Read on for a short history lesson about the next wave of conquerors who decided to take an extended vacation on Ireland's fair shores.

Who Were Those Norman Fellows?

Normans, Norsemen, and Northmen are all terms used to describe the raiders who swept down from Scandinavia and robbed, pillaged, and plundered Europe in the 9th and 10th centuries. In general, the earlier raiders were called Vikings and the later ones Normans, but the terms are somewhat interchangeable.

In 843, the Norsemen entered France through her rivers, especially the Seine. After burning, looting, and ruining Paris and Rouen, they began to establish settlements along the mouths of the rivers. From these communities, they continued to raid ever farther inland.

So great was their threat to French commerce and travel that the French king Charles III granted the Norman leader Rollo a duchy, which was named Normandy. This only whetted the voracious appetite of the Norse, who set about expanding their domain. They became Christians, adopted French law and the French language, and were known as Normans from that time forth.

Over time, the Normans lost all connections with their Scandinavian homeland, becoming assimilated into the European culture. In 1066, William the Conqueror, duke of Normandy, became William I, king of England. The Normans had replaced the Anglo-Saxons on the throne of England. They would invade Ireland, as well, but not until they were officially invited by a scoundrel named Dermot MacMurrough, whom you'll hear more about soon.

Beware of Popes Bearing Gifts

Supposedly, in 325 a document called the "Donation of Constantine" awarded the papacy dominion over all islands converted to Christianity. (The "supposedly" is because the "Donation" was later proven to be an eighth century forgery.) Legitimate or not, the "Donation" was the legal grounds by which Pope Adrian IV laid claim to Ireland. Adrian was the only English pope in history, and he entertained some pretty ambitious notions about being a higher authority than the simple kings and secular rulers of the earth.

In 1155, Adrian IV decided to make a present of Ireland to King Henry II of England, a powerful ruler of Norman descent. The Pope's gift was made with the understanding that Henry would "reveal the truth of the Christian faith to peoples still untaught and barbarous." Of course, by then Ireland was devoutly Christian and anything but "untaught," but the Pope was either ignorant of those facts or, more likely, chose to ignore them.

Along with the island, he gave Henry an emerald ring and the following blessing:

> "We regard it as pleasing and acceptable to us that you should enter that island for the purpose of enlarging the boundaries of the Church, checking the descent into wickedness, correcting morals and implanting virtues, and encouraging the growth of the faith of Christ; that you pursue policies directed towards the honor of God and the well-being of that land and that the people of that land receive you honorably and respect you as their lord."

In exchange for his gift and his blessing, Pope Adrian asked that Henry, "pay to St. Peter the annual tax of one penny from each household, and to preserve the rights of the churches of that land intact and unimpaired." It was official; without her consent or the knowledge of her citizens, Ireland had been given to England. Ironically, the deed had been done by the leader of the Catholic Church, which her holy men had served so well for centuries.

Although Henry had been given Ireland as a gift, he was too harried with the business of invading the rest of Europe to mess with the Emerald Isle. He pretty much ignored the little island to the west, until a Leinster knave named Dermot MacMurrough paid him a visit.

Brian Boru's Throne Becomes a Hot Seat

After Brian Boru, a parade of ineffective kings ascended his throne, only to lose it to a usurper who would prove no better at controlling the unruly Irish. The strongest king to climb the ranks and exercise some degree of power over the island of rebels was Rory O'Connor. Considering the political chaos of the times, O'Connor did a fairly good job of holding his kingdom together. Unfortunately, those pesky Leinstermen gave O'Connor a bale full of trouble.

If the lads of Leinster had been a briar on the seat of Brian Boru's britches, they were a royal pain in the backside for O'Connor. Forever rising against him and recruiting others to do the same, the Leinstermen gave O'Connor no end of grief, especially one of their young kings, Dermot MacMurrough.

Rock of Cashel, a coronation site of Irish kings.

Dermot MacMurrough: Bloody Troublemaker

In a time when savagery, cruelty, and vicious ambition were the norm, Dermot MacMurrough made a name for himself as a brute among brutes and one of the most hated individuals by his fellow Irishmen. Dermot had gained his Leinster kingship by killing two Leinster princes and blinding another.

MacMurrough darkened his reputation in 1151 even further by kidnapping the wife of Tighearnan O'Rourke, a principal ally of O'Connor, the high king. Some believe the

'Tisn't So!

The gruesome practice of blinding an adversary had been popular with the Vikings and was thereafter adopted by the Irish, who wanted to disable opposing chieftains, but didn't want to violate their sensitive consciences by killing their enemies outright.

lady Devorgilla might have played a part in her own abduction; the young Dermot MacMurrough was, undoubtedly, a more dashing fellow than the older, one-eyed O'Rourke.

She must have come to her senses, or Dermot tired of her, because a year later she was back at home with her husband. But the damage had been done. O'Rourke would never forget the insult of having his beautiful, young wife snatched away from him, and he vowed revenge on MacMurrough. (Actually, we don't know for sure that she was all that beautiful, but considering the hoopla about her being nabbed, we can assume she was at least mildly attractive.)

Choosing Sides with the Devil

In 1156, MacMurrough found another way to decrease his popularity, this time among his allies, the Leinstermen and Dubliners. He supported a chap with a cumbersome name, Muirchertach Mac Lochlainn, for the high kingship of Ireland. Mac Lochlainn gained his throne through vicious and violent acquisition rather than the loyal support of his subjects. In the eyes of the people, Mac Lochlainn's greatest sin had been that of blinding the king of Ulidia, an act that was particularly vicious because it was unwarranted; the Ulidia king had already submitted fully to Mac Lochlainn. The Irish loathed their new king Mac Lochlainn, along with his most infamous supporter, Dermot MacMurrough.

Dermot, the Most Unpopular Kid on the Block

So disenchanted were the Dubliners with Dermot MacMurrough that they killed MacMurrough's father. Just in case Dermot hadn't gotten the message, they added insult to assassination by burying the corpse, along with that of a dead dog, beneath the floor of their assembly hall.

Astute lad that he was, Dermot MacMurrough began to realize how little his fellow countrymen thought of him. He was even more convinced when his old enemy, O'Rourke, banded together with the Dubliners and a few other Leinster chieftains who had previously been Dermot's allies and attacked him.

Finding himself in highly hostile surroundings, Dermot MacMurrough fled. Although he was certainly no great prayer in any of his fellow Irishmen's rosaries, MacMurrough was about to do something that would cause his name to live forever on Ireland's roster of dastardly scoundrels.

Dermot Runs to the Enemy for Help

On August 1, 1166, Dermot boarded a ship bound for Bristol, taking along his lovely and marriageable daughter, Aoiffe (or Eva). Like many deposed Irish kings before him, MacMurrough was in search of a powerful ally, someone to lend their crown and their armies in the battle to regain his throne—a logical move on his part. But MacMurrough's act of seeking help from Henry II of England would prove disastrous for the land of Eire. It was like inviting a hungry wolf into a house of hens, and the feathers were about to fly.

Dermot MacMurrough arrived in Bristol, and then set out to find King Henry, a ruler who was often on the move in his sizable kingdom. Dermot found Henry in Aquitaine and poured out his troubles to the seemingly sympathetic ear about the abuse he had been receiving back home. Henry was a shrewd fellow, who recognized a no-risk, win-win situation when he saw one. Without offering any personal support or investment of his own, Henry "graciously" gave his permission for Dermot to solicit help from Henry's knights.

Henry even gave Dermot a letter of recommendation to assist in his recruitment. It read: "Know you that we have taken Diarmait [Dermot], prince of the men of Leinster, into the bosom of our grace and goodwill. Wherefore, too, whosoever within the bounds of our dominions shall be willing to lend him aid, as being our vassal and liegeman, in the recovery of his own, let him know that he has our favor and permission to that end."

If any of Henry's barons joined in Dermot's battle and lost, Henry would be none the worse for wear. On the other hand, if they helped secure any holdings in Ireland, Henry would be the overlord of those properties. It's little wonder he took the few minutes to write the letter, pat Dermot on the head, and send him on his way.

An Unholy Alliance

Dermot returned to Bristol and began campaigning with a vengeance. He liberally offered land and wealth that he didn't own; maybe Henry's knights were streetwise, because, at first, he had no takers. Then he threw his pretty daughter into the deal, and before he knew it, he had an ally *and* a son-in-law, Richard Fitzgilbert de Clare, the Norman earl of Pembroke from southwest Wales, better known in the chronicles of history as Strongbow.

In the fall of 1167, a more confident Dermot returned to Ireland and promptly received a thorough trouncing by his rivals, O'Connor and O'Rourke. Dermot's new allies rallied to his aid, though they didn't exactly roar across the sea in a fit of frenzy. When they sauntered over two years later, they brought a small expedition group that landed near Wexford. The group was led, not by Dermot's loving son-in-law Strongbow, but by another representative, Robert de Barry.

A Bard's Tale

When Strongbow finally decided to invade Ireland on Dermot's behalf, he sent a military detail ahead of him, about 90 men led by Raymond Le Gros. They landed on the rocky coast of southeast Wexford in a spot called Baginbun, where they camped behind a large double rampart. Fortunately for them, they had an excellent position, because approximately 2,000 angry Munstermen and Ostmen from Waterford attacked them. In spite of overwhelming odds, the smart Normans won the day by stampeding a herd of cattle into their attackers and breaking their ranks. The Normans killed several hundred of the Irish and took about 70 of them as prisoners. Sadly, they decided it would be easier to kill the prisoners, rather than continue to hold them, so they broke the prisoners' limbs and flung the prisoners over the edge of the cliff into the sea.

The Beginning of Erin's Great Woes

Strongbow didn't join the fight until May 1, 1170, when he and his troops arrived in southwestern County Wexford. Once on Irish soil, it didn't take long for Strongbow to figure out that Dermot had generously given him a title that he would have to fight for.

When Strongbow saw the relatively primitive battle weapons of the Irish and their lack of defense in the face of the Normans' more advanced weaponry, he decided to take what he wanted. In their simple, leather armor, bearing only slings and stones, the Irish were no match for the chain-mail-suited Norman warriors. Plus, among his 3,000 soldiers, Strongbow had archers, skilled in the use of the longbow as well as the deadly accurate crossbow. Once Strongbow's appetite was whetted, no tidbit was going to satisfy his cravings.

The Irish were courageous fighters, but courage made a thin armor. The Irish warriors were leveled like felled forests, along with their defenseless farmer countrymen. The Vikings had been fierce, but there had been a method to their madness and cruelty. Strongbow's men were completely without mercy, and entire communities were slaughtered as the army swept from one town to the next.

The Devils Won't Go Home

From 1169 to 1171, the Normans ravaged the island so savagely that, in an act of desperation, O'Connor offered to give Dermot the throne if only he would send the Normans back home. No doubt, Dermot would have loved to have accepted the offer, but by then he realized the horrible result of his inviting the Franks—as the Irish called them because they spoke French—into Ireland. The Normans had gained far too much ground for him to simply banish them. No one was going to be sending them home.

When Dermot MacMurrough died in 1171, Strongbow wasted no time claiming the kingship of Leinster. This upset King Henry, who realized that his vassal was doing quite well for himself on that neighboring island, well enough to become a threat.

King Henry Sets the Record Straight

Henry paid Strongbow a visit in 1171 and made sure he knew who was boss. Strongbow was cruel, but he wasn't a fool. He played the good lad and paid King Henry his due respect. By doing so, he kept his head, his crown, and his properties. Henry returned home, satisfied that all was well on Irish soil.

> **Gift of Gab**
>
> This 13th-century poem was written after the murder of Tighearnan O'Rourke by the Norman earl, Hugh de Lacy:
>
> Numerous will be their powerful wiles,
> Their fetters and their manacles,
> Numerous their lies, and executions
> And their stone houses
> Though great you deem the success of the foreigners
> You noble men of Ireland;
> The glorious Angel tells me
> That the Brefnians will avenge Tighearnan.

Six years later, in 1177, the conquest of Ireland by the Normans was official when Henry named his youngest son, a nitwit named John, "Lord of Ireland." When John inherited Henry's throne upon the death of his older brother, Richard the Lion-Hearted, he paid a visit to Ireland, where he promptly offended the chieftains by yanking on their beards. The relationship between Ireland and English kings was off to a rocky start.

A Castle in Every Back Yard

The Normans never really conquered Ireland, though they certainly gave it their best effort! At the most, over a 200-year period, they controlled three-quarters of the land, but even that control was only in theory. In reality, their sphere of influence barely covered the cities that they themselves had established and the immediate areas around their castles. In those regions, the people spoke French, paid homage to the barons, and lived according to English law. But outside those limited territories, the Irish did pretty much as they pleased, spoke Gaelic, and practiced the old brehon law. (See Chapter 1 for more on the nature of brehon law.)

There is an old Irish saying, "To breathe Erin's air, to drink her waters, is to become Irish." That's precisely what happened to the Normans. They intermarried and adopted many Irish customs. Before long, they were riding their horses bareback, wearing Irish garb, going barefoot, indulging in Irish foods and drink, singing Irish songs, and doing Irish dances. They built marvelous stone castles everywhere and more than a few equally impressive churches.

*Blarney Castle, home of
the famous stone.*

But grand buildings aside, all in all, the Normans had become proper Irishmen, much to the consternation of the rulers back home. Something had to be done, and something was. In the next chapter, you'll see just how much trouble the British caused.

The Least You Need to Know

➤ The Normans were a fierce, ambitious people who pillaged and plundered their way to Ireland.

➤ Rory O'Connor, one of the Irish high kings who succeeded Brian Boru, had his hands full trying to rule a rebellious country, especially the ambitious, brutal king of Leinster, Dermot MacMurrough.

➤ Dermot sought the help of Norman king, Henry II, and was offered the support of a fellow whom history would call Strongbow, who married Dermot's daughter.

➤ In May 1170, Strongbow and his men arrived in Ireland. The Norman invasion had begun.

➤ Although they never conquered all of Ireland, the Normans became firmly entrenched in Ireland, building stone castles and churches, taking Irish princesses as brides, blending and melding with the Irish culture until they were almost as Irish as English. The first Anglo-Irish had come to stay.

Chapter 8

Those Blasted Brits

In This Chapter

➤ Henry gives Ireland to son John—too bad John's an imbecile

➤ Edward I uses Ireland's wealth to finance his high life

➤ Ireland asks the Scots for help—big mistake!

➤ The much-despised Statutes of Kilkenny

➤ The Black Plague strikes the Emerald Isle

Henry II could have done a great deal for Ireland, but he didn't. He was cunning and powerful; he was a good king in the sense that he was such an awesome force that few even bothered to fight when he came calling. Therefore, his acquisitions were fairly bloodless. But he didn't care enough about Ireland to send the armies necessary to truly vanquish her.

Although this attitude might seem like a blessing, it wasn't in the long run, because it prolonged the battle between the Irish and the English. For the next 200 years, the Norman barons would continue to fight the Irish and each other. The Irish chieftains would do the same. The country was pretty much in a state of chaos, but then again, what else was new?

John Visits Ireland, Makes an Arse of Himself

Instead of ruling Ireland himself with his strength and skill, Henry II handed it over to his youngest and favorite son John. Why John was Henry's pet isn't clear to anyone who studies the lives of these two completely different men. The high degree of strength and intelligence of the father was a direct contrast to the foolishness of his weak son. When Prince John visited his newly awarded territory in 1185, pulling the beards of the noble chieftains was the least of his social blunders. He offended both Norman and Irish alike wherever he went.

Called John Lackland (though probably not to his face), his lack of territory had been a sore spot with the prince, who was the youngest of Henry II's four sons. He was eager to try his hand at ruling, and Ireland was his practice run. He began his princely duties by expelling Hugh de Lacy, one of his earls, from Ulster. Earl Hugh de Lacy had been a good Norman, sufficiently ruthless in his dealings with the Irish and a loyal subject of the Crown, even to the point of murdering Tighearnan O'Rourke, king of Breifne. But de Lacy had married an Irish princess, so John thought it best to strip him of his earldom. It wasn't one of John's more clever moves. De Lacy was a powerful enemy who would continue to cause problems for John behind the scenes.

A Bard's Tale

Hugh de Lacy had many powerful enemies, including Prince John of England, who would later become king. But when de Lacy met his ignominious end, it wasn't in a blaze of glory on the battlefield. The wealthy de Lacy had ordered the building of a new castle and was on site, inspecting the progress of its construction. Unwisely, he had instructed his builders to use stones from the ruins of an abbey that had been founded by St. Columba, a much loved and revered missionary of the early Irish church. One of the workers took offense at this sacrilege. When de Lacy bent over to examine the mortar in a freshly built wall, the worker swung his axe in the immediate vicinity of the earl's neck, and de Lacy was about a foot shorter.

John had worse things planned for another noble, William de Broase. John was perturbed that de Broase had been spreading vicious rumors about him. De Broase had dared to imply that John had murdered his nephew, Arthur of Brittany, with his own hand for political advantage. Although John's guilt in that matter was commonly accepted, most of John's subjects were intelligent enough to keep their opinions on the matter to themselves. But the outspoken de Broase had dared to voice his conviction aloud, and John wasn't happy. The petulant prince had de Broase's lands confiscated and had the man's wife thrown in prison, where she was starved to death.

John succeeded his brother Richard I (Richard the Lion-Hearted) on the British throne in 1199. After taking over the throne of England, he had little time for ruling Ireland, but he did leave his mark on her before he left:

➤ He began work on Dublin Castle, which would become the center of British government in Ireland.

➤ He introduced the English judicial system, which included traveling judges and trial by jury.

➤ The first coins were minted that bore the emblem of Ireland, the harp.

➤ Some of the counties were demarcated.

➤ He encouraged sea trading, and the Irish import/export commerce began to thrive.

Back in his own country, King John didn't do so well. He suffered a number of catastrophes during his reign. He lost all of the provinces of France that he had inherited, including Normandy. The cache that he always carried with him containing the crown jewels fell into a river as he crossed the bridge and was never seen again. He offended Pope Innocent III in an argument over the election of the new Archbishop of Canterbury and got himself excommunicated. His nobles rebelled and forced him to sign the *Magna Carta,* a document limiting his royal powers and those of his descendants. A civil war began during his reign and was still raging when John died a less than dignified death of dysentery.

After John, none of the succeeding English kings paid Ireland even a token visit for the next 200 years. Some historians say this was a mercy; others say it was a curse. Either way, the Irish were left to their own devices.

When the Cat's Away, the Peasants Steal the Livestock

The Norman barons and earls ruled Ireland, but loosely and ineffectively. Outside of the Norman castles and their immediate vicinities, the natives did as they pleased. In a letter, written in 1280, the residents of Saggart (near Dublin) protested that within a seven-year period, the Irish had stolen 30,000 sheep, 200 pigs, and 200 cattle from them.

Many of the English nobles returned home, abandoning their castles, which were then taken over by the Irish. Other such dwellings fell into ruin and decay. Such was the beginning of the depressing custom of the "absentee landlord."

The barons began to fight each other, much as the Irish chieftains had for centuries. Sometimes, rather than battle another Norman, the barons would encourage the Irish natives in their rival's domain

Speak Plain Irish

Some Irish chieftains who lived near the lands of Anglo-Saxon lords hired professional cattle thieves to do their stealing for them. Comically, these fellows were called **caterers.**

to revolt, saving the barons expense and bloodshed. As any study of the Irish people will show you, the last thing the Irish needed was someone to encourage them to fight.

O'Neill, the Last Ard Ri

In 1258, after John had died and his son, Henry III was on the throne, the Irish took a bold step. The powerful O'Neill clan proclaimed one of their own, Brian O'Neill, to be high king of Ireland. They must have thought it was time the Irish had an Ard Ri rather than some absentee king from across the sea.

But Henry III had other ideas. O'Neill's troops were defeated by Anglo-Norman forces at the battle of Downpatrick in 1260. In accordance with Henry's orders, Brian O'Neill was relieved of his head, which was sent back to Henry. No son of Erin ever laid claim to the title of Ard Ri again.

Edward I Drains Erin Dry

Henry III quickly lost interest in his emerald island and passed it along to his son Edward when the boy was 14. Edward I grew up to be a handsome fellow with expensive tastes. Holding the sort of elaborate courts he enjoyed took its toll on the family fortunes. He also loved to fight or, at least, to send his soldiers out to do it for him. He relished the role of conqueror. Unfortunately, the act of overthrowing other rulers required quite a bankroll, and Edward I turned to Ireland for finances to build his fortified stone castles and to arm his soldiers.

Since John had spent time in Ireland, encouraging her import/export trade, the island had grown prosperous. From England to the Irish ports flowed English iron, linen, salt, and beer. To England and the continent, the Irish sent their smoked salmon, corn, fine Irish horses (known to be small, fast, and agile), wool, and cowhides. Italian bankers had invested a great deal in the Irish economy, and it was booming. Edward began to drain his neighbor of her resources to support his lifestyle.

Then there was Ireland's other resource: her warriors. Edward pulled 5,700 men off the island to fight his war against Scotland between 1296 and 1301. Those soldiers were all armed and paid with monies from the Irish. It wasn't long before Ireland, the great money cow, had dry udders.

Edward II Means Well, But...

History hasn't been kind to Edward I's son, Edward II. Having succeeded his father in 1307, he managed a fairly nonproductive reign, and he has gone down in history as one of the weaker kings. But he was kinder to Ireland than his father, understanding that the island had been drained and needed to recoup. He wrote: "The funds left in Ireland have not been sufficient to preserve the peace there. The Irish burn, kill, rob, and commit other transgressions against the peace in an intolerable manner. Henceforth all Irish revenue is to be spent in Ireland to preserve the peace there and to carry out other arduous duties of government."

A Bard's Tale

The Normans considered the Irish to be barbarians of the first order. One of their chief complaints was that the Irish wore nothing at all under their heavy woolen mantles. Catching glimpses of the naked bodies of the "savages" was enough to turn an Englishman red with embarrassment and green with envy. One English traveler by the name of Fynes Morison described an Irish encampment this way:

> They sleep on the ground without straw or other thing under them, lying all in a circle about the fire with their feet towards it. And their bodies being naked, they cover their heads and upper parts with their mantles.

Surely, that must have been a strange sight for a dignified, if a bit prudish, English gentleman.

But the Irish chieftains and peasantry were out of patience. They were already fed up with the respective reigns of Henry, John, and the Edwards. So they once again invited a foreigner to help them overthrow their oppressors.

A Bard's Tale

The story of Roger Mortimer is a tale of betrayal, adultery, and murder. In 1317, he was made Lord Lieutenant of Ireland by King Edward II. One has to wonder if the good king would have given Roger such a fine promotion if he had known that Roger was dallying about with his wife, Queen Isabella.

Roger Mortimer worked hard at his job for 10 years, spending most of his time trying to rally baronial opposition to Edward Bruce. Then he and Isabella decided to torture and murder Edward II at Berkley Castle in 1327. Edward's son, Edward III, took exception to his father being slaughtered and had Mortimer hanged, like a common sheep thief.

More Wolves in the Hen House

Robert the Bruce had enjoyed a bit of success in Scotland, having been crowned King of Scotland in an act of defiance against the English crown. When Edward III came after him, intending to bring him back in line, Robert whipped Edward's troops rather soundly at the battle of Bannockburn in 1314. The Irish were quite impressed by this and asked Robert if he would like to help them cause some trouble for the English on Irish soil. Robert was engaged in his own activities at the time, but he liked the idea of giving his enemy grief whenever and wherever possible. So he sent his brother, Edward Bruce, along to do what he could to further the Irish cause.

Edward Bruce Makes a Bad Impression

Edward Bruce arrived in Ireland on May 25, 1315, with 200 ships and 6,000 soldiers. His ranks were soon broadened by the addition of Irish warriors and *gallowglasses*. With the support of some of the Irish chieftains, Edward made some progress, winning more battles than he lost against the barons. Many of the Irish thought the situation was on the mend; others eyed the Scottish foreigners with suspicion, waiting before they offered their support.

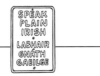

Speak Plain Irish

Gallowglass is a perversion of the Gaelic term *gall o glaigh,* meaning "foreign warrior." It was used to describe mercenary soldiers, who fought with the Irish (usually). Originally from the Western Isles, these foot soldiers were part Norse, part Gaelic, and well-armed with coats of mail, hefty helmets, daggers, and long-handled battle-axes that could slice through plate armor.

Edward returned home to Scotland long enough to convince brother Robert to visit Ireland with him. Robert did, and the two brothers conducted a march around the island for the purpose of strengthening Edward's position there. Edward's intention was to circle the country, making an impression on the natives, forcing submissions, and collecting tributes, in a display of power and authority. It might have worked had Edward's men been gentlemen.

But they weren't gentlemen, not by a longbowman's shot. Their circuit coincided with a famine, which effected most of Europe in 1317. As they made their rounds, they carelessly trampled precious crops, helped themselves to gardens, stampeded cattle, and even did a bit of burning and pillaging to show what mighty lads they were. In the end, the Irish, who had been plundered by far better fellows, proclaimed the Scots, "less noble than our own foreigners"—a lowly assessment, indeed.

Edward Versus Edward—Edward Loses!

Finally, the English government decided to intervene in Irish affairs and sent a bit of money over to the Normans, who used it to re-establish some semblance of order in Munster, Meath, and Leinster. Once again, the barons grew in strength. In October of 1318, Edward Bruce met English forces at the Battle of Faughart and was killed.

A Bard's Tale

One of Edward Bruce's most stalwart supporters sent a letter to the pope, protesting the treatment of the Irish by the English lords. In the document, called the *Remonstrance,* he complained that: "No Irishman may sue an Englishman. No man of this race is punished for the murder of an Irishman, even the most eminent; an Irishwoman, no matter how noble, who marries an Englishman is deprived at his death of her dowry; on the death of an Irishman, the English seize his property, thus reducing to bondage the blood which flowed in freedom from of old. The English say it is no more sin to kill an Irishman than it is to kill a dog."

The Hated Statutes of Kilkenny

Edward III couldn't find the time to visit Ireland personally to straighten out the mess, so like his fathers before him, he passed the problem of Ireland along to a son. He sent Clarence to Ireland in 1361 to slap the Anglo-Irish lords into shape.

Clarence was appalled to see how Irish, how "heathen," these Anglos had become. They were intermarrying with the peasants, playing Gaelic games, speaking a bit of Irish, and daring to even ride bareback like barbarians! This behavior was completely unacceptable for proper British gentlemen. Clarence's idea of a solution to the problem was the Statutes of Kilkenny, enacted in 1366. These statutes were some of the most despised laws ever to be proclaimed in Irish history.

These rules were among those that were decreed:

Gift of Gab

"Edward Bruce, the destroyer of Ireland in general, both foreigners and Gaidhi (Irish), was killed by foreigners in Ireland...and there was not done from the beginning of the world a deed that was better for the men of Ireland than that deed."

—From a less-than-complimentary obituary for Edward Bruce from the *Irish Annals of 1318*

➤ English were to have no formal contact with the Irish. This rule outlawed marriage between the two as well as adoption and concubinage.

➤ The English were forbidden to trade with native Irishmen.

➤ Only English names were to be used.

➤ Those of a higher level of income were to ride only horses that were saddled.

➤ The distinctly Irish sport of hurling was to be replaced with the genteel art of archery.

➤ No Anglo was allowed to keep, hire, or entertain any Irish musician, poet, or singer.

➤ Worst of all, the ancient code of brehon law, which had endured for centuries, was banned and replaced by English law.

These statutes were intolerable to the Irish, and they were unenforceable. All the Statutes of Kilkenny truly accomplished was to raise the level of Irish hatred for the English to new heights. According to the Irish Council in a report to Edward III, "Irish enemies…the king's Irish rebels…rode in hostile array…committing homicides, robberies, and arsons, pillaging, spoiling, and destroying monasteries, churches, castles, towns, and fortresses. The land is at a point to be lost if remedy and help are not immediately supplied."

The Grim Reaper Pays a Visit to Ireland

In a strange quirk of fate, another invader came from the continent to Ireland, this time, unbidden by the natives. This invader landed in the major cities of the Anglo lords and brought a massive amount of death and destruction to the English. But this invader didn't come in the form of foreign armies with swords, battle-axes, and screams of the attack. This dark invader, known as the Black Plague, came quietly.

Silently stealing across the waters on fleas and rats in the bellies of ships, the plague arrived in the port towns of Ireland and spread into the Anglo communities. The disease, also known as the bubonic plague, was loathsome beyond description. The afflicted died in agony; their symptoms included hideous boils in their armpit and groin areas, raging fevers, delirium, and then, mercifully, death. Carried by fleas, who transmitted it to rats and on to humans, the pestilence usually claimed many members of a family.

The urban areas of the Anglos were far more desperately affected by the plague than the rural areas of the native Irish. Few in the countryside suffered the affliction, but in the towns, as in Europe, a third of the population succumbed to this grimmest of reapers. The Anglos had been dealt a terrible blow, but it was such a dreadful event that only the most hard-hearted of Irishmen could have rejoiced in such suffering.

The Least You Need to Know

➤ Henry II made a gift of Ireland to his beloved, yet foolish, youngest son John. When Prince John visited Ireland, he alienated the whole island and got English/Irish politics off to a bad start.

➤ With Ireland in anarchy, many of the English lords high-tailed it back to the continent, leaving their lands, castles, people, and herds at the mercy of the Irish, who encroached, thieved, and all in all did what they bloody well liked.

➤ Taking advantage of the lack of leadership in the country, the Irish appointed Brian O'Neill as their Ard Ri, the high king of Ireland. Unfortunately, his reign lasted only two years before his head was lopped off and sent back to John's son, Henry III, for a souvenir.

➤ Fed up with the English, the Irish joined forces with Robert the Bruce of Scotland. Robert's brother, Edward Bruce, pillaged and plundered and made such a nuisance of himself that the Irish considered him worse than his ravaging predecessors.

➤ Worrying that the Anglo-Irish in Ireland were going to become more Irish than Anglo, the English passed the hated Statutes of Kilkenny, laws forbidding marriage between English and Irish and many other everyday practices such as trading. Worst of all, they outlawed the ancient, revered brehon law, replacing it with English law.

➤ A new invader hit Ireland: the Black Plague. Although the Irish in the countryside were hardly affected, approximately one third of the English in Ireland died of the horrible disease.

Chapter 9

The Earls and the Crown Duke It Out

In This Chapter

➤ Richard II forces allegiance from unwilling subjects

➤ The English civil war gives the Irish a break

➤ Irish chieftains run the country for a while

➤ Henry VIII declares himself Lord of Ireland

➤ The Irish revolt against their self-appointed "Lord"

The Norman conquest more or less trickled down the drain from the 14th century on. Harried by such carryings-on as the French War and the War of the Roses, the English monarchs didn't have much time or money to devote to the suppression of the Irish. With the British busy with other matters and baronial power on the decline, the Gaelic chieftains took advantage of the situation and stepped in to fill the gap.

Around the mid-1300s, things were on such an upswing that historians have proclaimed those days as the "Gaelic Revival." With some of the old Gaelic families running things again, it must have seemed as though the good old days had returned. The revival included poetry as well as politics. The traditional bards came forward as in the days of yore, singing the praises of their champions and reciting the lineages of which we Irish have always been so proud. It was cool to be Gaelic again.

Richard II Shows His Royal Face

No English monarch had set foot on Irish soil since 1210. The English monarchs had been so heavily involved in affairs with France they had given Ireland little or none of their time. So it was no matter of small import when Richard II paid Erin a visit in 1394.

Richard was 27 at the time and tall, fair, and foppish. At first, he displayed his most diplomatic persona. He wrote to the duke of York, saying of the Irish princes, "(They are) rebels only because of grievances and wrongs done to them on one side and lack of remedy on the other. If they are not widely trusted and put in good hope of grace, they will probably join our enemies." He promised "to do justice to every man."

But when he arrived, he wasn't exactly welcomed with open arms, but another kind of arms were awaiting his arrival. An English historian explained the situation thusly:

> In September, King Richard sailed for Ireland accompanied by the duke of Gloucester and the earls of March, Nottingham, and Rutland. The Irish were terrified by this huge force and did not dare to risk an open battle; instead, they subjected the king's army to numerous ambushes. In the end, however, the English overcame them, and many of the Irish chieftains were compelled to submit to Richard, who kept several of them with him, lest they should stir up any more trouble.

At a great Christmas feast held at Dublin Castle, 80 Irish chieftains vowed allegiance to him in return for having their titles to their lands renewed, but not all of the Irish leaders were willing to submit. For those holdouts, Richard had a persuasive way of recruiting supporters; he had a noose placed around their neck. With this sort of inducement, the chieftains swore their undying faithfulness.

King Richard felt it was also his duty to restore peace between two major warring factions: the Crown-appointed earl of Ulster, Roger Mortimer (not Queen Isabella's friend, he was dead by this point), and Niall Mor, or the "Great O'Neill," as he not-so-humbly called himself. O'Neill also claimed he was "Governor of the Irish in Ulster." This claim highly irritated Mortimer, and the two had been bickering over the issue of who was top dog until Richard ordered them to settle down, which they did.

When the king's back was turned and he had gone home to England, they were at each other again. Mortimer won his war against the Great O'Neill, but his was a short-lived victory. Some Leinstermen killed Mortimer in battle only three years later.

The English Battle Each Other for a Change

In 1399, when Richard III was ousted from office (or tossed off his throne, as the case may have been), it set off a chain of events that led to the War of the Roses, a bloody civil war in England between the houses of York and Lancaster. This war kept the British busy for quite some time, long enough for the Gaelic chieftains of Ireland to regain some of their power, but not long enough for them to make it a permanent state of affairs.

The chieftains might have taken over completely, but the Anglo-Irish who were deeply entrenched by this time weren't at all receptive to the idea of paying homage to a bunch of native barbarians. They tried to clamp down on the rebellious Irish, without much success. In a rare show of semi-unity, the Ulster chieftains joined forces and conducted raids, in some cases insisting that the Anglo-Irish pay *black rent.*

In the course of these wrangles, the Anglo-Irish power dwindled as the Gaelic chieftains' (who were calling themselves earls by this time) power increased. Before long, the area held by the Anglo-Irish, known as *the Pale,* had shrunk considerably. It extended only about 25 miles inland on the west coast, 25 miles north of Drogheda, and less than 25 miles south of Dublin. Even that land was subject to raids by disgruntled earls. All that raiding, robbing, and basically harassing the Anglos was about to pay off; the day of the Gaelic earls was at hand.

The Butler Did It

The fourth Earl of Ormonde, James Butler, was the first of the native Irish to take charge; he reigned over the greater part of the island in the early part of the 15th century. Because he was more of a diplomat than a conquering warrior, his rule was more peaceful than the Irish were accustomed to, which was a pleasant change of pace. Unfortunately, Butler's son married an Englishwoman and allied himself with the British. As a result, the Butler family lost its power in Gaelic government and faded from the scene for quite a while.

You Killed the Wrong Fella!

The Geraldines of Desmond were the next batters up. They were descended from the famous family of Nesta, who had come to Ireland on behalf of Dermot MacMurrough and Strongbow (see Chapter 7). Although the Geraldine leader, Thomas, Earl of Desmond, was of Norman descent, he ruled more in the old-fashioned style of a Gaelic chieftain than a Norman baron. As a result, he garnered faithful followers from both the Anglo-Irish rulers and the Irish natives.

It seems he did too good a job of playing the Gaelic chieftain, because he was arrested and beheaded for his troubles. The charge was that he had violated the Statutes of Kilkenny. Of course, no Irishman could live a day without violating some statute of those preposterous orders. The good earl had been

Speak Plain Irish

Black rent is a colorful name for extorted "protection" money.

Speak Plain Irish

The area around Dublin that was ruled by the Anglo-Irish was called **the Pale.** The phrase "beyond the Pale" means "outside of acceptable limits."

Gift of Gab

Although most English had little use for Erin's inhabitants, they admired the country itself. The following was written by the great English poet Edmund Spenser:

"And sure it is yet a most beautiful and sweet country as any under heaven, seamed throughout with many godly rivers with all sorts of fish most abundantly sprinkled with many very sweet islands and goodly lakes like little inland seas."

held in the highest esteem by his kinsmen, and the Geraldines reacted violently to his execution. The ruckus over the matter went on for nearly 100 years.

Henry VIII Throws a Royal Scepter into the Cogs

The earls continued running things with only occasional harassment from England, until Henry VIII ascended the throne. Henry took the Irish situation a bit more seriously and decided to do something about his wayward, uncivilized subjects across the sea.

According to the Tudor state papers written in 1515, Ireland was a barbaric place, out of control. Here's how the English described the country:

> More than 60 counties called regions inhabited with the King's enemies… where reigneth more than 60 chief captains wherein some call themselves Kings, some Princes, some Dukes, some Archdukes that liveth only by the sword and obeyeth unto no other temporal person…and every of the said captains maketh war and peace for himself. Also there be 30 great captains of the English folk that follow the same Irish order…and every of them maketh war and peace for himself without any license of the King.

How dare they! That "making war and peace for themselves" nonsense had to go. While Henry was contemplating what to do about the mess, the great earl Gerald Fitzgerald and his son, Silken Thomas (named after the fancy threads he liked to wear), decided to raise some rebel dust back home. That was all Henry needed.

The king sent his troops to put down the unruly lot, but as so many times before, it was no easy task. The English soldiers might have been better armed (much better armed), but the Irish knew the forests of their childhoods and could dart into the dark, dense woods where only a dimwitted Englishman would dare to follow.

For some reason, Henry seemed to think that the Irish, who wouldn't submit to English artillery, would fall into line if he uttered the right words. So he made it official, proclaiming himself Lord of Ireland. You can imagine how effective that was. A 1541 Act placed Ireland on the same ladder rung as England, in the sense that the country now absolutely, completely belonged to the Crown, at least according to Henry. The Irish weren't so easily convinced.

Henry's new rules required Ireland's nobles, whether they be Anglo-Irish or native Irish, to attend parliament in Dublin and to be ready at a moment's notice to perform military service on behalf of the Crown. Henry also admonished them to give their sons a proper English education and to stop demanding black rent. He might as well have told them to grow a second head and stand on it.

Henry VIII, self-proclaimed king of Ireland.

A Bard's Tale

Some of the better known Protestants included John Wycliffe, a divinity professor at Oxford; Jan Hus, who began a movement in Bohemia; and, of course, Martin Luther, who posted his 95 specific protestations on the door of the church in Wittenberg Germany in 1517. The Protestant movement had begun, and Ireland would never be the same.

A System Born to Fail

At least in his own mind, King Henry VIII had bent over backward to reach a peaceful solution with the Irish. Hadn't he allowed some of the native chieftains to remain on their own land as his tenants-in-chief? He thought the chieftains would be happy with an arrangement that gave them and their sons' sons recognition and limited powers in their appointed territories. Of course, this recognition was dependent on them behaving themselves as good subjects of the Crown.

Speak Plain Irish

During the time of the Gaelic Revival, the word **clan** was first used to denote the lordships that had sprung up to take the place of those English who had fallen by the wayside.

But Henry didn't know the Irish mind or understand the ancient Gaelic customs. The Irish chieftains weren't interested in owning the land as individuals; the very idea was incomprehensible. Every true Irishman knew that the land belonged to the *clan*, not the chieftain. Although the desire for power to govern is universal, the ambition to personally own property held no appeal for the Irish noble.

The two cultures varied also in another important respect. The English were big on passing titles and properties down according to *primogeniture,* the right of an eldest son to inherit that which belonged to his parents. Irish chieftains were elected from the strongest, most able "alpha" males among them. When a leader died, his son(s) could compete for the position, but there was no guarantee it would go to one of them.

These cultural differences between the English and the Irish and their inability or unwillingness to understand each other's ideals made any meeting of the minds difficult, peace impossible, and future relations bleak.

The Least You Need to Know

➤ England was having a tough time keeping the Irish chieftains in line, but when the War of the Roses began, the English were even more absorbed in their own affairs. The chieftains, or *earls* as they called themselves, took advantage of the situation and rose to power.

➤ When Henry VIII ascended the throne, he considered the Irish situation a disgrace and sent troops to subdue the earls, but the troops were unsuccessful.

➤ Henry decided that if military efforts hadn't worked, perhaps a royal edict would set things straight. He declared himself Lord of Ireland. Predictably, this declaration was most unacceptable to the Irish, who, as always, revolted.

➤ Basically, any arrangement between the English and the Irish was doomed to failure because of fundamental cultural differences.

Irish Domination, Tudor Style

When Elizabeth I, a Protestant, took the throne of England, her reign wasn't expected to last long. A number of powerful, European, Catholic monarchs could have risen against her, the most likely candidate being Philip II of Spain. But Elizabeth was used to living precariously; her older sister had been Mary Queen of Scots, or Bloody Mary, as she was not-so-affectionately called. With a sister like Mary and wondering every day if her head was going to be removed from her shoulders, Elizabeth had grown up in a state of controversy, suspicious of everyone. Considering how freely English kings and queens were coming and going in those days, one can scarcely blame her for looking over her shoulder.

Elizabeth had seemingly mixed ideas about how to handle the problem of Ireland. On one hand, she always preferred negotiation and diplomacy to military action. Elizabeth wasn't a pacifist, but she was renowned for her thrift (a nice way of saying she would skin a flea for its coat), and peace was cheaper than war. Although she wanted to keep things peaceful, Elizabeth was just as convinced that Ireland presented a threat to her reign and that her neighbor must be absolutely, completely under English control. She would settle for nothing else. Those Irish, who had been barbarians in desperate need of civilizing, were now heretics as well.

A Queen on the Chessboard

Henry the VIII was famous for, among other things, his many wives. He was also the first English king to secure a divorce (two of them). His daughter, Elizabeth I, was the product of one of his later unions. Divorce is not recognized in the Catholic religion, however, and neither is the offspring of any later unions. European Catholics, therefore, considered Elizabeth illegitimate and thus not a true heir to the throne.

True heir or not, Elizabeth was a true leader. She was a shrewd lady, a brilliant military strategist, and a cunning politician. She kept a tight hold on her purse strings, yet managed to maintain an effective army and navy. In part, she accomplished this by releasing prisoners from her jails and sending them abroad to fight her battles.

Elizabeth also knew the value of diplomacy and compromise, especially in the areas of religion. Having suffered under the influence of her older sister, Mary Queen of Scots, Elizabeth knew the sorrows caused by religious persecution. Under her father, Henry VIII, England had been Catholic and then Protestant. Under Mary, England turned Catholic. When Elizabeth came to power, England was Protestant again. She understood the damage that this religious switching had inflicted upon her people. She established a Protestant Church of England, but it was secular in personality. No mass was said; clergy was allowed to marry. The orthodox Catholic Irish didn't approve of this laxity, and they didn't like their new queen.

Like her predecessors, Elizabeth I feared that the out-of-control island to her west would provide a fertile breeding ground for rebellion against her (not an altogether unfounded paranoia). The lady had enough troubles at home trying to enforce Protestantism on subjects who didn't all want to convert to this "heretical" new faith.

Gift of Gab

Here's a little rhyme to help you remember what happened to Henry's six wives:

Divorced, beheaded, died
Divorced, beheaded, survived!

Gift of Gab

Do you recall this nursery rhyme?

"Mary, Mary, quite contrary,
How does your garden grow?
With silver bells and cockle shells
And pretty maids all in a row."

The "contrary Mary" in this poem was none other than the rather cranky Mary Queen of Scots. The pretty maids are her ladies-in-waiting.

In spite of her problems in England, her suspicious nature, and her sense of thrift, the harried queen somehow found the time, the troops, and the funds to cause grief on Irish soil. In the end, however, much of the suffering was experienced by her own soldiers. The problem was that Ireland was full of thick forests and soggy marshes, which wasn't so bad if you were Irish and knew how to navigate such obstacles. But if you were some English chap, ill-trained and poorly equipped for warfare, you could find yourself running face-first into a tree on a moonless night or struggling waist deep through a misty, cold bog.

Shane O'Neill, the Grand Barbarian

Seeing what difficulty the English were facing when trying to subdue the Irish, a Gaelic chieftain decided this would be a fine time to mount an even stiffer opposition to the Crown. Known as "The Proud," Shane O'Neill had been elected head of the O'Neill clan (a position simply called "The O'Neill") in 1559.

At that time, the Earl of Sussex was one of Elizabeth's advisors, and he put a bug in her ear that maybe it wasn't wise to allow a chieftain as powerful as Shane O'Neill to get ahead in the world. So Queen Elizabeth issued a royal invitation to Shane—actually, it was more like an arrest—to make a command appearance in her court. Shane was called on the Tudor carpet.

In court, Shane presented quite a sight with his long black hair and flowing yellow robes. His entourage was equally colorful: 200 gallowglasses dressed in wolfskins and toting battle-axes. So much for living down the stereotype of the barbaric Gaels.

Gift of Gab

"They were brought to such wretchedness as that any stony heart would have rued the same. Out of every corner of the woods and glens they came creeping forth upon their hands, for their legs would not bear them. They looked anatomies of death, they spake like ghosts crying out of their graves."

—Edmund Spenser, English poet, writing about the people of Munster during the reign of Elizabeth I

When he was presented to her royal majesty, Shane fell facedown on the floor at her feet and bellowed a long, wolfish howl. Then he identified himself by speaking in Gaelic, so neither the queen nor her nobles could understand a word he said. As he "negotiated" with Elizabeth, Shane, in typical arrogant, chieftain style, made it all too apparent that he considered himself on equal footing with her majesty. As an added little jab, he openly attended Mass at the Spanish embassy. Elizabeth insisted that Shane enjoy her hospitality, whether he cared to or not, for five months before allowing him to go home.

When the proud Shane O'Neill, chief of Gaelic chieftains, finally met his end, it wasn't with one of Elizabeth's soldiers or executioners, as any fortune teller might have predicted. A Scottish knife blade felled the Irish oak in a drunken brawl. Shane's head, however, was sent to Dublin where it hung on display outside the castle for years.

Hugh, the Next O'Neill to Cause Trouble

To the great chagrin of Elizabeth, she hadn't seen the last of the O'Neills. If Shane O'Neill had been a bombastic barbarian, his kinsman, Hugh O'Neill, was his exact opposite, a dignified Englishman of the highest order. He had been raised by the lord deputy of England, Sir Henry Sidney, reared in the new Protestant religion, and given a fine gentleman's education. He was perfectly comfortable in the English court and was made earl of Tyrone in 1585 by Elizabeth, one of his greatest admirers and supporters. Whether the Irish blood in Hugh O'Neill got the better of him, or whether he was simply ambitious and thought he could put one over on Elizabeth, we don't know. Either way, he led the last great Gaelic counter-attack against the English crown.

All in the Family

O'Neill allied himself with his neighbors, the O'Donnells, and won a major battle against the English at Yellow Ford in 1598. His English opponent in that contest was none other than his brother-in-law, Sir Henry Bagenal. The two men had been on bitter terms anyway because of Bagenal's ill treatment of O'Neill's sister.

In a later battle against the English, O'Neill wasn't so successful. At Kinsale, County Cork, he fought Elizabeth's Lord Deputy, Mountjoy, and lost. On that Christmas Eve in 1601, O'Neill was forced to meet Mountjoy's troops in open, traditional fighting and was unable to use his typical guerrilla, hit-run-duck tactics that had won the day at Yellow Ford. The battle lasted only three hours before O'Neill was defeated. He and his remaining troops retreated north.

It was two more years before O'Neill would formally surrender to Mountjoy. Little did O'Neill know, as he knelt before Elizabeth's Lord Deputy, that his nemesis, the queen herself, was dead. His defeat, though devastating, might have been a bit less bitter had he known the great lady wasn't around to enjoy the news of it. Many historians consider the moment of O'Neill's surrender, in March of 1603, to be the end of the great Gaelic chieftains of Ireland.

A Bard's Tale

Part of the English rationalization that allowed them to interfere so vigorously in Irish affairs was their conviction that the Irish were scandalously lewd people in need of civilizing. This conviction was a result of the vastly different social attitudes of the English and Irish. Gaelic marriages were far more flexible than English marriages, and Irish women were far more outgoing than their English counterparts. Englishmen were appalled that Irish females greeted individuals other than their husbands with a kiss. Irish women drank alcohol, presided over meetings and festivities, kept their own names after marriage, and divorced their husbands if they chose. These actions were unthinkable to the English and perfectly natural for Irish lasses.

The Flight of the Earls

After his defeat by Mountjoy, Hugh O'Neill was still allowed to retain his estates in Ulster. Though as time went on, he found that his powers were considerably lessened under the policies of England's latest monarch, James I. O'Neill and the other Gaelic chieftains (or earls, as they were called at that time) were being pressured even more to behave according to the Crown's wishes. They were being fined for not attending a mandated number of services at the Protestant-ruled Church of Ireland.

For these, and perhaps other reasons we do not know, Hugh O'Neill, Rory O'Donnell (the earl of Tyrconnell), and 99 other Irish lords did something that surprised, puzzled, and upset many: They left Ireland. Boarding a French ship on September 4, 1607, they sailed from Rathmullan on the west shore of Lough Swilly in Donegal and left their estates to the English. From there, they traveled to the Spanish Netherlands and then on to Rome. O'Neill died there—of melancholy, some say—at the age of 66.

Plant a Scot Here, and One There, and...

When the earls sailed away into the sunset, they left behind their lands and an enormous problem for the English. James I and his advisors thought long and hard about this dilemma, not wanting to make a bungle of it and cause the sort of riots and assorted mischief that had occurred in the past.

After two years, regulations were drafted that ordered the disbursement of those areas. In the interest of "fairness," 10 percent of the land went to native Irish (those who would pay twice the going rent for the privilege) and another 5 percent was awarded to English soldiers who had fought the Irish. The remaining 85 percent was to be used for the settlement or "plantation" of English and Scots who were sympathetic to the Crown.

The new English and Anglo-Scots needed cheap labor to work their fields, and the Irish continued to live on what they considered to be their land. A perfectly miserable and dangerous situation arose: Anglos living on previously Irish land used those angry, resentful, ousted natives as little more than slaves. Also, about 5,000 of the earls' abandoned, disgruntled soldiers were lurking in the bogs, waiting for something, anything, to happen. It was a breeding ground for more hate, exactly what the land of Eire didn't need.

The 1641 Uprising, an Explosion of Rage

By the year 1641, tempers were running hot, and fears had risen to new heights among the Gaelic Irish. They were being badly mistreated on many fronts, and they weren't the sort to take such abuse meekly. In October of 1641, the cauldron of resentment bubbled over its rim and a bloody rebellion was underway.

The Gaelic natives fully intended to destroy the Protestant ascendancy in Ireland, and they gave it a mighty and fearful effort. Turning on their masters, the dispossessed Irish killed as many as 2,000 Protestant settlers, and many more thousands were beaten, stripped, and driven naked into the wilderness.

One of the worst atrocities of the 1641 Uprising occurred in Portadown, County Armagh. Although there remains much debate about the number of victims, at least 100 Protestants—men, women, and children—were snatched from their homes by the rebels and thrown from a bridge into the Bann River. The barbarism of the event was compounded when the rebels bludgeoned those who managed to swim to shore. Some of the Irish even took boats into the water to reach their struggling, drowning victims, where they finished them off by bashing their heads.

A Bard's Tale

A victim of the massacre at Portadown, Elizabeth Price, had her five children torn from her and thrown off the bridge. She swore that she was "hanged up to confess to money, and afterwards let down, and had the soles of (my) feet fried and burnt at the fire and was often scourged and whipt."

Understandable or not, in the face of such cruelty, 'tis little wonder the memory of 1641 remained seared in the minds and spirits of the Protestants in that part of the world. The motto "Remember 1641," along with harbored grudges of so many other injustices on both sides became part of the fabric of the Irish culture.

The Least You Need to Know

➤ Elizabeth I worried that her enemies might assemble in Ireland and rise against her, so she sent troops to the island to keep the Gaelic "barbarians" in line.

➤ Fearing the power of the great Gaelic chieftain Shane O'Neill, Elizabeth ordered him to her court. She didn't allow him to return home until five months later.

➤ The next Gaelic chieftain to rise against Elizabeth was Hugh O'Neill. After a successful campaign against the English, Hugh O'Neill was defeated by Elizabeth's troops, led by Lord Deputy Mountjoy. Many historians consider his defeat to be the end of the great Irish chieftains.

➤ On September 4, 1607, Hugh O'Neill and a shipload of other Irish nobles left Ireland forever, abandoning their lands to the English in what was called "The Flight of the Earls."

➤ The new king of England, James I, decided to divide up the earls' land in a manner unfavorable to the Irish. The dissatisfied Irish rebels rose against the Protestant settlers in October 1641. Irish Catholics killed and exiled thousands of Protestants.

Chapter 11

The Curse of Cromwell

In This Chapter

➤ Cromwell wreaks havoc on the Emerald Isle

➤ The slaughter of Drogheda and Wexford

➤ Catholics meet secretly behind Mass rocks

➤ The English Crown goes Protestant, Catholic, and then Protestant, leaving the Irish in a tailspin

➤ The Penal Laws turn the Irish into less than second-class citizens

The terrors of the uprising of 1641 had been told from one end of Ireland to the other. The stories also crossed the sea, where they confirmed the worst suspicions of the English: The Irish were terrible, bloodthirsty savages who didn't deserve the air they breathed. The actual atrocities had been bad enough, but by the time the stories made it through the gossip mill, the tales of horror were dreadfully exaggerated.

The tales of war are never pretty. The new and improved version of the 1641 Uprising, however, took on a ghoulish tone. The following are just some of the stories that were told:

➤ The bodies of the murdered Protestants had been rendered for their fat, which was then used to make candles to be used in the Devil-Papist Masses.

➤ Every Irishman, barbarian that he was, could hardly wait to put his hands on an English gentlewoman and ravish her.

➤ Anglo-Irish children were in grave danger from the mad Gaels, who were waiting to snatch them and dash their little heads against the nearest wall.

The English considered the Irish barbarians before the uprising. After the uprising, the Irish were viewed as some sort of sub-species with evil origins and only wicked intentions. One of the biggest purporters of this myth was the Englishman Oliver Cromwell. This new-found bigotry of the English laid the groundwork for even more injustice toward their Gaelic neighbors.

Gift of Gab

If an Irish lad arises at the crack of noon with a mountain of a hangover, you just may hear him mutter the following:

"Surely Cromwell's armies and the auld devil himself has marched across me tongue!"

Speak of the Devil, and He'll Appear

To the Irish, the name of Oliver Cromwell is synonymous with the Old Horned One himself. One of the most vindictive curses uttered by the Irish is, "The curse of Cromwell on ye!" Indeed, Cromwell worked hard to receive this reputation. You'd be hard put to think of a soul more deserving of his infamy. Oddly enough, Cromwell thought of himself as a decent sort, an altogether good fellow on the right hand of God.

Before becoming a general in the English civil war, Oliver Cromwell had been a gentleman farmer. Like a lot of folks in his day, he got wind of the exaggerated accounts of the atrocities of 1641 in Ireland and believed them all. As a staunch Puritan and a religious zealot, he believed the best way to handle the problem of the Irish was to destroy every last one of them, and he certainly gave it his best effort!

King Charles Tumbles Off His Throne

Charles I of England had a couple of problems in common with his father, James I. They both had exaggerated self-images, thinking the scepter in their hand and the crown on their heads gave them the ability to do whatever they darned well pleased, and the common man be damned. Both demanded absolute power, what they called the Divine Right of Kings. Believing themselves emissaries of God, they felt no need to please the masses; as a result, the masses were most displeased with them. They basically ignored their Parliament, a tendency which Parliament viewed rather dimly.

Second, they both had love relationships with a troublemaker named George Villiers. James I had been so infatuated with Villiers that he made him Duke of Buckingham. Before James's death, the opportunist Villiers decided that the younger prince would make a better pawn than an aging king, so he cast his web for Charles and caught him. Like his father before him, Charles allowed the Duke of Buckingham far too much power in his court. When an outraged parliament decided to impeach the duke, the king came to his lover's aid by dissolving parliament. Who needed them anyway, what with divine right and all that?

Too late, Charles realized that even kings need the loyalty of their subjects. Without parliament to raise funds for him, Charles had no money for necessities, such as an army. So when he decided to persecute the Scots for being Presbyterian—he wanted them to be proper Anglicans, like himself—they rose against him. Having no respectable army with which to defend himself, Charles was in deep trouble. His problems were about to multiply, because his enemies had a powerful weapon on their side: Oliver Cromwell, a lad with a deadly mission that he considered to be a directive from God. A brilliant soldier and a ruthless opponent, Cromwell considered it his personal calling to destroy Charles I, and he did exactly that.

Cromwell Leads the Charge Against Charles

Oliver Cromwell had a way with words, and when he became a member of parliament in 1628, his rousing speeches to that already disgruntled gathering heated their blood and their tempers. When civil war broke out in 1642, Cromwell proved himself an even more remarkable soldier than orator, leading a cavalry on behalf of parliament and against the king. Charles fled to Scotland, for some strange reason, forgetting how little love the Scots had for him. They trussed him up like a cooked goose and sent him back home to his parliament.

For a while, confusion, not the king, reigned. Charles managed to escape, but he was recaptured. He negotiated with the members of parliament, who seemed reluctant to kill him now that they had him. But he broke enough of his promises and caused enough problems that in the end they decided to be rid of him. On January 30, 1649, they relieved Charles I of his crown by removing it right down to his royal neck.

The Irish watched all this from Erin's shores, wondering what it would mean to them. In general, they had supported Charles I, hoping that because of his Catholic wife, Henrietta Maria, sister to the king of France, he would cut the Irish some slack. Certainly, Charles I wasn't as horrid to the Irish as some of his predecessors had been. But by allying themselves with Charles, the Irish made a formidable enemy in Oliver Cromwell. He wouldn't forget that Ireland's allegiance had been placed against him, and he would make Ireland pay a terrible price.

Oliver Earns His Bloody Name

After King Charles I was duly dealt with, deposed, and beheaded, Oliver Cromwell became the Lord Protector of the new Commonwealth, and England was considered to be a republic rather than a monarchy. Firmly ensconced in England, and having put down an uprising in Scotland, Cromwell decided it was time to whip those devil Irish Catholics into shape. In light of the atrocities of 1641, Cromwell saw himself as an avenging agent of God, punishing His enemies. Because the Irish had sided with Charles and against him, they must be God's enemies, too, or so he decided.

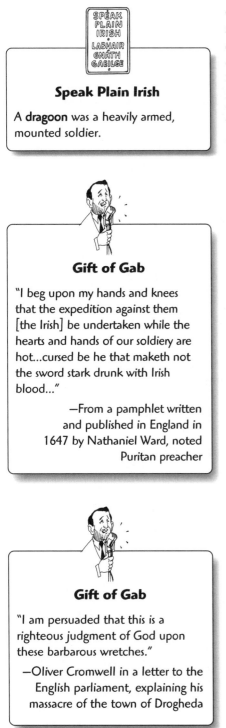

Speak Plain Irish

A **dragoon** was a heavily armed, mounted soldier.

Gift of Gab

"I beg upon my hands and knees that the expedition against them [the Irish] be undertaken while the hearts and hands of our soldiery are hot...cursed be he that maketh not the sword stark drunk with Irish blood..."

—From a pamphlet written and published in England in 1647 by Nathaniel Ward, noted Puritan preacher

Gift of Gab

"I am persuaded that this is a righteous judgment of God upon these barbarous wretches."

—Oliver Cromwell in a letter to the English parliament, explaining his massacre of the town of Drogheda

Cromwell assembled his troops: eight regiments of foot soldiers, six regiments on horseback, and several more *dragoons*. All total, there were about 17,000 of the most able-bodied and well-equipped soldiers on the planet, ready and willing to invade Ireland. They also had no great love or respect for the Catholic religion. All of these soldiers were of the papist-hating kind and truly believed that Ireland was their rightful property. Erin didn't know what had hit it.

Of Cromwell's many sins against humanity, the worst is his slaughter at Drogheda in September 1649. He and his troops stormed the well-fortified city, which lies north of Dublin. At first, they couldn't break through the city's protective barrier, and Cromwell's army suffered much higher casualties than they were accustomed to.

Enraged, Cromwell and his men attacked again and again. Finally, they broke through Drogheda's wall, and 7,000 to 8,000 of them poured into the doomed city. They mercilessly slaughtered several thousand men, women, and children, most of whom were completely defenseless. A number of Catholic priests were killed also, in spite of their taking refuge in a church. One group of unprotected townspeople was herded into a second church, the doors were barred, and the place was set afire.

Cutting a Swath of Death

From Drogheda, Cromwell and his army marched across the island, burning, destroying, and conquering as they went. Having heard of the horrors of Drogheda, many towns submitted without resistance in order to avoid any more of Cromwell's savage slaughter. The city of Wexford wasn't so lucky. Although its inhabitants did submit, apparently they didn't do it fast enough to suit Cromwell. While the negotiations of Wexford's submission were still going on, he ordered his soldiers to kill 2,000 of the citizens of that ill-fated town.

Priests Wanted Dead or Alive, Preferably Dead

Cromwell's policies also included the persecution of the "devil papists," and the efforts focused on the priests. They were wanted men, but no one wanted them alive. They were hunted down and killed as though they were vicious animals; after all, that was how Cromwell saw them. He seemed to think that if he could get rid of the priests, the "evil" would be nipped in the bud.

The simple act of saying Mass to a group of parishioners could cost a priest his head, so many Catholics assembled at rural landmarks, called *Mass rocks*, to celebrate Mass. Some of the most distinctive sites in any community were particularly large or unique rocks in solitary spots. The Catholics would congregate at these well-known places and conduct their religious rites while lookouts kept a watchful eye.

To Hell or Connacht!

The last few areas to resist Cromwell's forces, Waterford, Limerick, and Galway, were eventually beat into submission, bringing Ireland completely under British rule. By the time Oliver Cromwell was finished with Ireland and "peace" was declared, one-third of the Irish Catholics had been killed.

After Cromwell brought Ireland into submission and returned home to England in May 1650, the tyranny continued. The military he left behind enforced his policies of persecution, including a new horror: transplantation. In 1652, under Cromwell's direction, the British parliament proclaimed the Cromwellian Act of Settlement, which forced Irish landowners to relocate. Upon threat of death, they had to leave their more fertile lands in the eastern part of the island and move to areas west of the river Shannon, specifically the barren lands of Connacht. The British divided the now-vacant, fertile lands among themselves.

The transplantees were given such short notice that many had no chance to harvest their crops, so they trudged through the cold, wet winter weather, many starving along the way. The catch phrase, "To Hell or Connacht," showed the narrow distinction between the two destinations for Cromwell's

'Tisn't So!

To this day, some claim to hear the screams of the mothers and the cries of the babies who were burned in that church in Drogheda when walking at night near its ruins.

Speak Plain Irish

Mass rocks were landmarks known to locals where persecuted Catholics would gather to secretly celebrate Mass. The penalty for a priest saying Mass was death.

'Tisn't So!

Under Cromwellian law, rewards were paid for anyone who presented the proper authorities with the head of a wolf or of a Catholic bishop.

victims. Such was Cromwell's legacy, and such are the memories he left behind that would continue to sear the hearts and minds of the Irish people for generations.

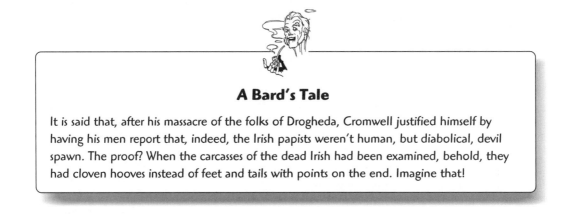

A Bard's Tale

It is said that, after his massacre of the folks of Drogheda, Cromwell justified himself by having his men report that, indeed, the Irish papists weren't human, but diabolical, devil spawn. The proof? When the carcasses of the dead Irish had been examined, behold, they had cloven hooves instead of feet and tails with points on the end. Imagine that!

Anyone for a Round of Musical Religions?

Ireland had endured the swing of England's political pendulum in the past, but it hadn't experienced anything like the wide sweeps that occurred from 1660 to 1700. By the time of Cromwell's death in 1658, the English had realized that having a Lord Protector like old Ollie wasn't any better than having a king. So they decided to set Charles II on the throne. He was the son of Charles I, who had been executed.

Remember, Charles I was the closest thing to an ally the Irish had enjoyed in an English monarch, and they were hoping his son would prove equally supportive. Charles II's wife was Catholic, and many Irish had given their lives to fight for his father's cause. They hoped they would be rewarded by a grateful son. There was also a lot of speculation and tension about whether the Irish land that had been granted to the Cromwellian supporters would revert to its previous owners. Would the dispossessed Irish be brought back from the rock-infested fields of Connacht and resettled on their old, more fertile land?

But Charles II had seen what had happened to his father when the old man had gone against the favor of the masses, and the English weren't happy with the Irish Catholics at that time. Charles wasn't about to alienate the majority of his British subjects by making life easier for some Irishmen across the sea.

Charles did make an effort, of sorts; he returned about one-third of the Irish Catholics' property that had been confiscated under Cromwell. So at least some of those sent "To Hell or Connacht" were able to return home to their fertile lands in the east. Also, Charles halted the persecution of the Catholics so that the hunting and killing of priests ceased. The result was a compromise of sorts, called The Restoration of 1660, and things settled down a bit. Although Charles II sought what he called "justice" for all, he reserved his "favor" for his British subjects, and life for the Irish was only marginally better during his reign.

James II, Better Times on the Way?

In 1685, Charles II died, and his brother, James II, took the crown. James was a Roman Catholic and favored the Irish. The native Irish rejoiced, thinking their troubles had ended at last. The Protestants, however, got testy; they worried that it was their turn to suffer bloody eviction. Their concerns were not without cause.

In his eagerness to return Ireland to Catholicism, James II sent Richard Talbot, the earl of Tyrconnell, to Ireland to act as his Lord Lieutenant. Immediately Talbot began to oust the Protestants from public offices, including the Irish parliament, and replace them with Catholics. You can imagine how that was received. Talbot also organized an army for the king's use, should he need it, to enforce these changes.

Protestants, especially those in the city of Derry, began to recall the horrors of 1641, and they quarreled among themselves about the best way to handle the possible threat. When the earl of Antrim, nicknamed "Redshanks," arrived with an army (13 boys to be exact) to garrison the town, the Derry Protestants slammed the city gates in the army's face. Although this action might have been heroic, it wasn't wise, as time would tell.

Back home in England, the Houses of Lords and Commons were as unhappy with James as the Irish Protestants. They were calling for him to step down and demanding that James's son-in-law, William of Orange, be placed on the throne. As things heated up, James decided to take his stand on Irish soil, where he had the most loyal subjects. In March 1689, he and Richard Talbot led an army to the city of Derry (already on James' bad side for the gate-slamming incident).

The siege of Derry began in April 1689, when James led a ramshackle army against the town. To say that James' army was ill-equipped is complimentary. He had only one cannon and didn't have any shovels or spades to dig under the city walls. The army couldn't attack the town of 30,000 people; the best the ragtag oppressors could do was hold their captives inside the city until the poor souls starved to death.

And they did. When the food ran out, people ate every four-legged mammal they could get their hands on: cats, dogs, rats, and mice. It was said that one particularly plump fellow was afraid to leave his house because of the hungry looks from his famished neighbors.

In the middle of June, six weeks into the siege, the English (William of Orange supporters) sent a fleet of ships laden with supplies to relieve the suffering. But James' troops blocked the river Foyle, refusing to let them pass and laying a boom across the water. On July 28th, three of the English ships rammed the boom and forced their way through. At the same time, Protestant troops won an important battle against an Irish Catholic force at Newtownbutler, meaning that James had lost his hold on the north of Ireland.

The decisive battle in the war between James and William of Orange occurred in Ireland in the lush, beautiful Boyne river valley in 1690. Called by historians "The Battle of the Boyne," the fight was the point at which the tide turned against James and the Irish Catholics. James was defeated, and Ireland was solidly in the power of the Protestant Ascendancy.

The Harsh Penalties of the Penal Laws

Eighty percent of the land in Ireland had changed hands within 100 or so years, so it's no wonder that the country was filled with ill will and the Irish were a tad uneasy about their future. Their suspicions were confirmed when the English parliament passed the hated *Penal Laws.*

In these statutes, Irish Catholics were restricted in many ways, including the following:

Speak Plain Irish

The **Penal Laws** were nasty statutes passed to "penalize" Catholics for their Catholicism. These hated laws were first written in 1695, and they continued to be revised until 1727. Irish Catholics suffered under them for more than a century.

➤ Catholics were excluded from holding office.

➤ Catholic priests and bishops were banished, and thus Catholic worship was forbidden.

➤ Catholics were forbidden to marry Protestants.

➤ Catholics could not carry weapons.

➤ Catholics could not teach school.

➤ Catholics were forbidden to purchase or lease land or take land settlement disputes to court.

➤ Catholics were excluded from working in any field of scientific study (leading to the stereotype that the Irish are sentimental fools with a talent only for myth, governed by superstition).

One petty and humiliating rule prohibited a Catholic from owning a horse worth more than £5. This was a particularly cutting law against the Irish, because they are a people who have always adored horses.

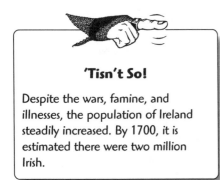

'Tisn't So!

Despite the wars, famine, and illnesses, the population of Ireland steadily increased. By 1700, it is estimated there were two million Irish.

The one penal law that was to have the most devastating effect on the Irish people was that which governed the inheritance of land. Protestants were allowed to leave their estate intact to any one of their children, whomever they chose, but Catholics were forced to subdivide their property among *all* of their children. Because Irish families tend to be on the large side, this law meant that the parcels of land became smaller and smaller as they were divided among each successive generation. With the estates cut into tiny pieces, many of the Irish who had formerly been well-to-do sank into poverty. Those who had already been poor were now wretched.

Meet You Behind the Hedgerow

The result of the Penal Laws and the Protestant Ascendancy's rule was disastrous for Irish culture. More and more, English became the language of the land rather than the Irish Gaelic. In addition, Irish Catholic children were forbidden to receive an education under the Penal Laws.

As they had many times throughout Irish history, the bards came to the rescue, preserving the national identity. Forbidden to teach openly, the poets and scholars of the day taught in "hedgerow schools," classes held secretly behind hedges, rocks, and in old, abandoned buildings across the countryside. They kept the Gaelic language alive, as well as the legends and myths of the ancient Celtic culture. The scholastic level of their teaching was high, including not only poetry and literature, but also mathematics and astronomy. The children of poor, Catholic tenant farmers were receiving excellent educations at the hand of these dedicated masters. As always, when the spirit of Erin was threatened, her poets and bards carried the torch of enlightenment through the dark times.

The Least You Need to Know

➤ Believing the exaggerated stories of the 1641 Uprising atrocities, the new leader of England, Oliver Cromwell, attempted to wipe out Ireland's Catholics. In his effort to do so, he cut a swath of death and destruction as he marched across the island.

➤ Cromwell was best known for his ravaging of the town of Drogheda, where his troops killed 1,000 men, women, and children in an act of violence that made Cromwell's name synonymous with evil.

➤ During Cromwell's wrath, priests were hunted and killed, forcing Catholics to gather secretly behind stones, called Mass rocks, to practice their religion.

➤ During a civil war in England, the Crown shifted from Protestant to Catholic and back to Protestant. Tensions ran rampant, and violence was widespread.

➤ With Protestant William of Orange on the throne, the hated Penal Laws were enacted, forbidding Catholics to hold office, to marry Protestants, to carry arms, to take a land dispute to court, or even to own a horse valued at more than £5.

➤ As the Irish language was being replaced by English, and other aspects of Irish culture began to wane, the national pride was carried on by the bards, who secretly taught the children of the poor tenant farmers in "hedgerow schools."

Chapter 12

The Price of Freedom: Blood and Imprisonment

After the Protestant William of Orange had toppled his father-in-law, Catholic James II, from the throne of England, the Protestants in Ireland were determined to rise in power as quickly as possible and to never be on the bottom of the heap again. The period of time from 1690 to 1800 is known in Ireland as the Protestant Ascendancy, marking an era of Protestant rule on the island. To make things a bit confusing, those who were in power at the time were also called the Protestant Ascendancy. In this chapter, you'll see how the Protestant Ascendancy tried to quash the Irish spirit but quickly learned one thing: You can't keep a good Irishman down.

Oppression 101

The *Protestant Ascendancy* and the English government had a pretty tight partnership in Ireland in the 18th century. The Ascendancy kept the native Irish under control, and in return, England used her power to make sure the Protestants retained their position of power on the island of Gaelic "barbarians."

Speak Plain Irish

The **Protestant Ascendancy** is a period of time between 1690 and 1800 when the Protestants ruled Ireland. The term also applies to that ruling class of people.

Catholics were subjugated at every turn as even more acts of parliament made life difficult for them. Catholics, who greatly valued education, were still unable to teach their young or even send their children abroad for an education, keep schools, become teachers or tutors, or earn degrees.

Being Catholic meant you couldn't buy or lease more than two acres of land. Because the Irish peasantry lived off the land, this law meant they were assured a meager living at best. A peasant's rent was fixed at two-thirds of the crops or livestock raised on his property. This meant that if he worked harder or smarter and produced more, he was penalized for his ingenuity and labor.

Although a sword was a common accessory of menswear at that time, Catholics were forbidden to carry one or even to own a gun. A Catholic blacksmith could be executed for smithing a *pike* (spear), the simple but effective weapon of Irish peasantry throughout the ages. As before, Catholics could not own a horse worth more than £5. Catholics and Protestants were still forbidden to marry, and anyone performing one of these illegal unions was hanged.

Even more disheartening, no Roman Catholic could inherit land—only Protestants would be considered rightful heirs. As might be expected, even among the devout Catholics of Ireland, there were some who converted, at least in name, to Protestant-

Speak Plain Irish

The **agrarian sects**, or secret societies, were underground terrorist groups made up of common folk, mostly peasants. The word *agrarian* means "one who favors the equitable distribution of land." Originally, agrarian societies were formed with the intention of putting pressure on the Protestant landlords, forcing them to abandon their hold on formerly Irish lands.

ism as a means of keeping their land in the family—and keeping their families alive. Some attended Protestant services, as the law required, and then celebrated Mass behind closed doors in their own homes or barns. Others became "Protestant" so they would be allowed to send their children abroad to get a Catholic education. All in all, under the prosecution of the Ascendancy, the Catholics lost much, and much of what they lost was the joy and richness of their Catholicism.

In retaliation against this oppression, the Catholic peasantry organized into *agrarian sects*, or secret societies, underground terrorist groups who inflicted covert punishments on Protestant landlords, such as mutilating livestock, burning houses, and beating and even killing the aristocrats themselves. These groups included the following:

➤ The Whiteboys, so named because they blackened their faces and wore white smocks over their clothes

➤ Hearts of Steel and Hearts of Oak, who distinguished themselves by the sprigs of oak in their hats

➤ The Carders, who were known for an especially wicked method of torture: They raked wire carding combs across the faces of landlords, scarring them horribly

The actions of these groups were bold, violent, and sometimes cruel, a direct reflection of the horrors inflicted upon the peasant populace they represented.

In addition to these agrarian rebels, other freedom fighters dreamed of shedding the chains of British rule and unifying Ireland by peaceful means. Two of those visionaries stood out among the rest: Theobald Wolfe Tone and Daniel O'Connell. Respectively, they would become known as the Father of Irish Nationalism and the Great Liberator.

Theobald Wolfe Tone, Father of Irish Nationalism

When the Irish heard of the successes of the French Revolution, they were intrigued. If the French peasants could overthrow their rulers and establish a government of their own design, the Irish reasoned that maybe they could follow in the Frenchmen's footsteps. As the Catholic peasantry watched the French monarchy tumble, they began to consider what such a revolution of their own might mean.

One fellow who was particularly interested in the French peasant uprising was Theobald Wolfe Tone. A powerful character with a highly ideological philosophy, Wolfe Tone believed the day would come when the words Catholic and Protestant could be exchanged for the all-inclusive "Irish." An agnostic, raised a Protestant, Tone was one of the founders and most active members of a group called the United Irishmen. They favored parliamentary reform with the ultimate goal of complete freedom for Ireland and the breaking of all ties with Britain. The idea of Irish nationalism had been born, and many considered Wolfe Tone its father.

Unlike their more violent agrarian brothers, the United Irishmen lobbied peacefully, putting their grievances before the Protestants and the British government. But they made small headway in a country filled with segregationist strife. The majority of Protestants feared the Catholics, and their fear fed their hatred. They weren't ready to accept ideas of one nation, one people.

Tone and his United Irishmen gained notoriety for their novel notions of unity. He wrote a number of pamphlets that were widely read, which advocated the idea of a united, independent Ireland gained through peaceful, parliamentary reform. Although

'Tisn't So!

Many people believe that all underground Irish groups are violent in their methods and their philosophy. But the primary goal of The Society of United Irishmen (later called simply the United Irishmen) was to bring all Irishmen, Catholics, and Protestants together. This group believed that the common love of Christ would be enough to unite Ireland's Christians. Sadly, this wasn't to be. Fear proved stronger than love.

Gift of Gab

"Ireland would have been free long ago, were it not for the bloody informers!"

—An old Irish saying

Speak Plain Irish

Pitch is a thick, dark, sticky substance formed from the distillation of coal tar, wood tar, or petroleum. It is generally utilized for less cruel purposes than the one mentioned in the text. Mostly, pitch is used in waterproofing, roofing, and paving.

Wolfe's intentions and those of the United Irishmen were peaceful, not violent, they were still considered a threat by the British authorities. Anyone who espoused Irish freedom was considered a dangerous radical.

The British infiltrated the group, planting spies to keep an eye and ear on things. The British still remembered the bloody rebellion of 1641 and were determined that such a thing would never happen again. Anything and anyone who smacked of rebellion was considered an enemy to be watched and, if necessary, eliminated.

Fraught with informers, the United Irishmen organization was forced underground by the unrelenting harassment of the English soldiers. Troops who represented the Crown searched for rebels from house to house and administered floggings at will, as well as committing other hideously cruel acts to discourage the United Irishmen and to display their power.

One of the most common forms of torture was pitch-capping, which involved covering the top of a person's head with a paper bag and a "cap" of *pitch* (a black, tar-like substance), and then setting it on fire. The cap could only be removed by tearing it away, which the victim usually did, along with their hair and a portion of their scalp. Another form of torture was that of half-hanging. The victim would be hanged, but only until he or she lost consciousness. Then the noose would be loosened until the victim revived, and the horrible process would begin all over again.

A Bloody Rebellion

The Catholics weren't the only ones who formed secret, terrorist groups. The Protestants had their own gangs who roamed the countryside, using violent means to achieve their goals. The Presbyterians were avenged by the Peep o'Day Boys, who paraded through Catholic areas to the beat of marching bands, flying flags, brandishing weapons, shooting out windows, and smashing property right and left. Their objective was to drive the Catholics from their homes; sometimes it worked.

In September 1795, the Peep o'Day Boys reformed their group into a new organization, which they called the Orangemen. The orange color of their banners symbolized the victory of Protestant William of Orange over the Catholic James II. The tradition of wearing orange sashes and marching through Catholic areas continues even today, as does much of the animosity spawned during those harsh times.

Between the Orangemen attacking Catholics, the Catholics terrorizing the Protestants, and the British soldiers hunting, torturing, and killing the "rebels," Ireland soil absorbed a great deal of blood in those last years of the 1700s. In 1795, the governor of Armagh wrote: "No night passes that houses are not destroyed, and scarce a week that some dreadful murders are not committed. Nothing can exceed the animosity between Protestant and Catholic at this moment in this country."

An estimated 50,000 persons died before the rebellion was crushed. In the end, having achieved nothing with his organization's peaceful lobbying, Wolfe Tone, the idealist and peacemaker, had to relocate or face arrest. Incriminating letters written between him and revolutionaries in France had been found. Freedom fighters had been hanged for far less, so Tone left Ireland and headed for France.

In France, the articulate, impassioned Wolfe Tone was well-respected as a champion of Irish nationalism, even by Napoleon himself. While there, he began to see that he might need more than peaceful words to fight the British, and convinced the French that by striking a military blow against Britain on Irish shores, they would benefit both countries. France agreed.

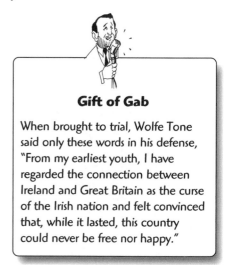

Gift of Gab

When brought to trial, Wolfe Tone said only these words in his defense, "From my earliest youth, I have regarded the connection between Ireland and Great Britain as the curse of the Irish nation and felt convinced that, while it lasted, this country could never be free nor happy."

The French Get in the Act

Accepting Wolfe Tone's point of view that Ireland would provide a good base from which to attack Britain, the French sent 10 ships with 2,800 men to the northern coast of Donegal. Tone was aboard the flagship. Unfortunately, the British intercepted the fleet, and having much better guns, they captured several of the ships, including the one Tone was riding. Tone was arrested, tried, and found guilty of treason. He asked no mercy except to be shot, like a soldier, rather than hanged like a criminal. His sentence? Hanging.

A Sad Demise for Erin's Son

On the night before he was to be hanged, Tone cut his own throat. Unfortunately, all he had was a penknife, and he merely succeeded in putting himself in a state of agony. After a week of unspeakable misery, he overheard a doctor say that if he were to speak or move he would die. He whispered, "I can yet find word to thank you, sir. It is the most welcome news you could give me." Referring to his botched attempt to cut his jugular, he added, "I find I am but a bad anatomist." As predicted, he died. Wolfe Tone, the Father of Irish Nationalism was gone at the age of 35. But his dream of an independent Ireland would be handed down from one generation to the next of freedom fighters.

The Act of Union, a Doomed Marriage

The unruly Irish were the bee in Britain's bonnet, and the Crown wanted to find a way to quash their nationalist efforts once and for all. So the British government, led by their prime minister, William Pitt, decided on a new plan for handling the problem with the Irish. At that time, there was a token Dublin parliament in place, giving the illusion of some degree of Irish self-government, but operating under the power of the British parliament. With a great deal of coercion and an enormous amount of bribes, the British parliament convinced the Dublin parliament to, in effect, vote itself into oblivion. With the Irish parliament committing involuntary political suicide, Ireland was now governed solely by the British parliament.

The Catholics Lose Again

All this talk about Ireland becoming an independent country, completely unfettered from Britain, upset the British prime minister, William Pitt. With Britain at war in a desperate battle with France, the possibility of a close neighbor, Ireland, providing a base for the enemy was unthinkable. Pitt decided to make Britain's hold on Ireland more binding and legal than ever before.

In the beginning of the 1700s, the Protestants in Ireland had asked England to declare Ireland officially part and parcel of England, but had been turned down. Now the British saw the advantage of such an arrangement. On January 1, 1801, the United Kingdom of Great Britain and Ireland was born under what Britain called the Act of Union. The Brits presented the merger as something akin to a marriage. The Irish considered it forcible rape.

At first, the British propaganda used to sell the bill of goods to the Catholics was convincing, so much so that the Protestants protested, thinking they would get the short end of the royal scepter, and the Catholics supported it. Some of the attractive features of the union included these promises:

➤ Ireland was to be awarded 100 seats in the British House of Commons and 28 peers (nobles) and 4 bishops in the House of Lords.

➤ Free trade would exist between Ireland and Britain.

➤ Catholic emancipation was guaranteed. Pitt agreed to introduce a bill to that effect as soon as the union was final.

But problems arose almost immediately when the Irish Catholics found out that those Irish who took parliamentary seats would be forced to take an oath of allegiance that would exclude Catholics. Also, in spite of William Pitt's full intentions to write an emancipation bill for the Catholics, King George III felt that emancipating the Catholics would contradict his coronation oath to support the Protestant church in England. Pitt resigned over the issue, and the Catholics were left high, dry, and unemancipated.

Once again, the Irish Catholics felt they had been given empty, broken promises. They still could not have any say in their own government, as had been suggested in the beginning to gain their support. In parliament, majority ruled. Although the Irish Catholics were the majority in Ireland, Catholicism was a minority religion in the United Kingdom as a whole.

Ireland One with England? Never!

It didn't take too long for a nice brew of trouble to boil over after the Act of Union was passed. Irish Catholics became extremely *agitated* and called for their immediate emancipation. As before, peaceful, parliamentary methods, like those of Wolfe Tone's supporters, were not effective in bringing about change, but that was before a young Catholic lawyer from County Kerry appeared on the scene. He was Daniel O'Connell, and he was destined to be called Ireland's Great Liberator.

Speak Plain Irish

In the Irish culture, **agitation** means the arousal of public opinion. It implies that incitement is through relatively peaceful means, such as rousing speeches, rather than violent methods. At different times in Ireland, more than one agitator cooled his heels in the *gaol* (jail) for his crime.

Daniel O'Connell, the Great Liberator

Daniel O'Connell was a peace-loving man, a skilled barrister, a gifted orator, and a brilliant mind with radically inventive ideas. He founded the Catholic Association, a political machine that was organized by the clergy within their own parishes. The Catholic Association depended upon small, monthly donations from its members. All but the very poorest could afford the penny-per-month dues, and its membership was enormous (a quarter of a million Irish peasants), bringing the organization all the funds it needed to be effective. Its dual purpose was O'Connell's own: to gain emancipation for Ireland and to repeal the Act of Union.

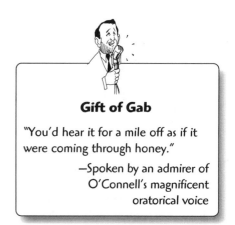

Gift of Gab

"You'd hear it for a mile off as if it were coming through honey."

—Spoken by an admirer of O'Connell's magnificent oratorical voice

Any banding together of Catholics alarmed the Protestants. They could recall the bloody rebellions and were afraid this organization would start another. In March 1825, the Catholic Association was outlawed. O'Connell had boasted that if the authorities tried to ban his organization he would "drive a coach and four" through the legal restrictions placed on it. Using his verbal skills and knowledge of the law, he restructured the Association, calling it a "public and private charity" that stood for "public peace and tranquillity as well as private harmony between all classes." He expressly stated that all of its purposes were "not prohibited by law." O'Connell the brilliant barrister had done it. Legally, the authorities had no basis to ban the new association.

The Catholic Relief Act of 1793 had given most Catholics who owned property the right to vote in Ireland. Until O'Connell's movement, the Catholics had mostly voted as their landlords instructed them to. But the Catholic Association and the local priests who were the energy behind it encouraged the Irish to vote however they pleased. In the general election of 1826, they were pleased to cast their votes for candidates who supported emancipation. Days before the election, members of the Catholic Association paraded up and down the streets of their towns wearing the color green, the symbol of Irish nationalism. On polling day that year, a number of Protestants lost important political offices they had held for decades.

Our Man O'Connell Takes His Parliamentary Seat

Catholics hadn't been elected to parliament. It wasn't exactly illegal; it just hadn't been done, but that was the next goal of the Catholic Association. The same priests who had organized the locals to elect other politicians began to work toward seating O'Connell in parliament. Again, they paraded in the streets, wearing green and chanting emancipationist slogans in support of their man, O'Connell. He won in a landslide. Although the British were afraid of this rabble-rouser from Kerry, the masses had voted him in, and the British were afraid to do anything other than seat him in parliament.

In 1829, a Catholic Emancipation Act was passed. Catholics could now be judges, admirals, generals, and members of parliament. Their goal fulfilled, the Catholic Association dissolved itself. O'Connell then began his campaign to fulfill his other dream for Ireland: the repeal of the Act of Union.

Gift of Gab

"Not for all the universe contains would I, in the struggle for what I conceive my country's cause, consent to the effusion of a single drop of human blood, except my own."

—Daniel O'Connell, stated during a speech in 1843

Captivator of the Masses

O'Connell was a whiz at organization, as were those local priests who had supported him in the Catholic Association. They put together mass assemblies called "monster meetings" where O'Connell expounded the virtues of his political agenda, specifically the movement to force dissolution of the union between Ireland and Britain. Although he stressed that these rallies were to be peaceful, the enormous crowds were a source of anxiety for the officials. Through the sheer weight of its numbers, his movement gained momentum.

O'Connell rallied for more freedoms for the Irish, still seeking that elusive goal of a repeal of the Act of Union. He conducted one of his monster meetings at Tara, a spot near Dublin dear to the heart of the native Irish because it had been the seat of ancient Irish kings. But when O'Connell planned a meeting at Clontarf, the place where the great Brian Boru died (see Chapter 6), the British government banned it.

Older and a bit weary of the repercussions, O'Connell thought it best to cancel the event. Some of the Irish, including a group called Young Ireland, criticized O'Connell, claiming he had gotten soft in his old age. Their tactics and philosophy tended to be more dramatic and violent. Many of the Irish were growing impatient waiting to achieve their goals through peaceful means. Violent action seemed faster, more effective, and efficient. O'Connell was losing some of his support.

Gift of Gab

When the great O'Connell stood before the assembly at Tara, he spoke these eloquent words: "We are at Tara of the Kings—the spot from which emanated the social power, the legal authority, the rights to dominion over the furthest extremes of the land...Step by step we are approaching the great goal of Repeal of the Union, but it is at length with the strides of a giant."

A Bard's Tale

A group of energetic, passionate young fellows fought to repeal the Act of Union by organizing a group called Young Ireland. One of its leaders, Thomas Meagher, explained the group's philosophy in this way: "I do not disclaim the use of arms as immoral, nor do I believe (it is the truth to say) the God of Heaven withholds his sanction from the use of arms...be it for defense, or be it for the assertion of a nation's liberty. I look upon the sword as a sacred weapon."

Young Ireland opposed O'Connell at the end of his career, believing his political, peaceful methods too slow and ineffective. Later, in 1848, they organized a small "revolt" that ended in humiliation and defeat. But they had set a precedent of paramilitaristic resistance against the British, and such resistance continues even today.

Imprisoned for His Troubles

Even though he had canceled the meeting in Clontarf, O'Connell was arrested. Refusing to ride in a hackney cab to jail, he insisted on walking through the streets so that everyone could witness his captivity. An all-Protestant jury convicted him of conspiring to alter the constitution by force. He was given bail for a three-month period before serving his sentence. He spent his remaining time of freedom holding public meetings in major English cities, including London.

While he was incarcerated for five months in mid-1844, Daniel O'Connell's following grew, and public opinion was so passionate on his behalf that the House of Lords decided that O'Connell's jury had been illegally manipulated by the prosecution. O'Connell was sent home to Dublin, where he was met by marching bands, the glow of bonfires, adoring crowds, and houses decked with laurel wreaths. He had served only five months in prison, but his incarceration took a toll on the 70-year-old hero. In 1847, he embarked on a pilgrimage to Rome, but he didn't arrive at his destination. He died in Genoa, Italy. The Great Liberator's heart was sent on to Rome, where it was interred in the Church of St. Agatha. His body was returned to Dublin and buried in Glasnevin Cemetery on August 5, 1847, amid the largest funeral Dublin had ever known.

The political concerns of O'Connell and his followers were soon to be left in the ditches in view of a much greater threat. On the horizon was a terrible catastrophe and the darkest chapter in all of Ireland's black history. The people of Erin didn't know it yet, but the Irish Potato Famine, otherwise known as the Great Hunger, was nearly upon them. In O'Connell's last speech delivered to the House of Commons on February 8, 1847, he gave this chillingly accurate prophecy: "Ireland is in your hands…your power. If you do not save her she can't save herself. I predict that one quarter of the population will perish unless you come to her relief."

The Least You Need to Know

➤ Dreaming of a unified Ireland, Theobald Wolfe Tone and his fellow patriots formed an organization called the United Irishmen. They lobbied peacefully for an Irish free republic, but with no success.

➤ British soldiers hunted the rebels down, torturing and killing anyone who even appeared to sympathize with the Irish cause. The United Irishmen were forced to go underground, and Wolfe Tone had to flee to France.

➤ Tone returned to Ireland with help in the form of a fleet of French ships and nearly 3,000 men. The flagship was captured by the British with Tone aboard, and Tone was tried and convicted of treason. He is called the Father of Irish Nationalism.

➤ On January 1, 1801, England dissolved Ireland's parliament and passed the Act of Union, stating that Great Britain and Ireland were one country.

➤ The unhappy Irish found a liberator in the form of a young Kerry lawyer, Daniel O'Connell, who organized the Catholic Association, a group dedicated to the peaceful lobbying for Catholic emancipation and the repeal of the Act of Union.

➤ Worried about O'Connell's growing power, the government banned his last assembly that was to be held at Clontarf. Obediently, O'Connell cancelled the meeting, but he was arrested anyway and imprisoned. He died in exile in Genoa in 1847.

Chapter 13

The Great Hunger

> **In This Chapter**
>
> ➤ Fungus-infected potatoes leave millions of people without food
>
> ➤ Starving peasants are evicted from their homes in the bitter winter
>
> ➤ Fevers and other grim diseases add to the misery
>
> ➤ The British government tries to help, then abandons Ireland
>
> ➤ Millions board "coffin ships" bound for America

Before the year 1845, Ireland had endured numerous invasions, each bringing more death and destruction than the one before. Usually death arrived in a cacophony of war cries, the clanging of swords and axes, or the roar of artillery. But when the most malignant of all enemies appeared, it did so silently aboard American ships docking in Irish harbors. This time the Grim Reaper took the form of a tiny fungus, an infestation that would destroy a main food source of eight million people and the sole food source for two million others. The world would name this catastrophe the Irish Potato Famine, but those who endured the horror and their children's children would call it the Great Hunger.

Disaster, 'Tis Sure to Strike

In the 1800s, Ireland was Europe's most densely populated country. In spite of war, poverty, isolated famines, and the assorted massacre, the Irish peasantry was flourishing. As a result of the laws regarding the division of Irish estates to heirs (see Chapter 11), most of the Irish lived on tiny patches of not-so-great land where they scratched a simple existence from the stone-laden ground.

Fortunately, potatoes were an easy crop and grew well just about anywhere. Some of the farmers who had slightly better soil raised other vegetables, which they turned over to their landlords to pay their rents. Others paid rent with their excess potatoes. In turn, the landlords used what they liked for themselves. Since some were living in England (known as
absentee landlords), the majority of vegetables were exported, and the profits from the sale of vegetables were used to support the landlords' abundant lifestyles.

As a diet, the humble potato was a wonderful staple. For those peasants fortunate enough to also have a glass of buttermilk a day, their nutritional needs were nicely supplied. Even though the Irish lead a substandard existence under an oppressive system that had been forced upon them by the power-hungry Brits, life in Ireland continued without great human suffering. Then "the blight" struck.

A Bard's Tale

Many a joke has been made about the Irish and their love of potatoes. It seems they may have been ahead of themselves with the spud-a-day diet (even if it wasn't by their choosing). Some of the more sallow English nobles, who would have benefited from a day in the sunshine cutting turf, noted upon visiting Ireland how attractive, robust, and healthy the natives were, despite their extreme poverty.

The Blight, Where Is It Comin' From?

No one could imagine what caused the blight, which made perfectly beautiful potatoes turn into a foul, watery, black mush within a day or two after digging. Britain's *Tory* prime minister, Robert Peel, appointed a group of scientists to study the problem and propose a solution. These scientists, however, did more to add to the problem than to fix it. Acting on the commission's worthless advice, the peasants tried to correct the problem in various ways by "making large holes in the sides of the pits to admit air and by scarcely putting any covering on top of the pits but the dry stalks." These efforts and a number of other home remedies did nothing to stop the putrefaction.

Who or What Is to Blame?

As the mystery of the famine continued to baffle farmer and scientist alike, a number of outlandish possibilities were considered to be the cause of the problem:

➤ The smoke from those new inventions, locomotives

➤ Vapors from "blind" volcanoes hidden deep inside the earth

➤ The electricity from a summer of more-than-average lightning storms

➤ The recent use of fowl manure for fertilizer

These are but a few of the explanations for the inedible potatoes. In truth, it was the nasty little fungus, *Phytophthora infestans,* that polluted first the soil, then the plant itself. None of the peasants' attempts to redeem their doomed crops would have worked. But even if they had known this, they probably would have still tried. What else was there to do, when your only source of food was disappearing before your eyes? Lie down and die? Sadly, that's what they did eventually, by the hundreds of thousands.

Empty Bellies and Heavy Hearts

So virulent was the infestation that by 1846 the blight had covered the entire island. For a while, the Irish were able to eat their seed potatoes (those set aside to "seed" next year's crop), but when the entire harvest of 1846 turned putrid, the situation quickly became desperate. With their staple gone, the Irish ate the few other crops they had previously grown to exchange for rent. But even those soon disappeared. Though the Irish were forbidden by law from hunting on the landlords' estates, "poaching" became widespread, and soon there was even a shortage of game in the woods.

Human beings wasted away to mere skeletons. These emaciated people roamed the countryside looking for something to eat; their mouths were stained green from trying to eat grass. Nursing mothers were unable to produce milk to feed their babies, and infant mortality skyrocketed. Those same mothers eventually perished as well.

Those who survived suffered with the horrible smell of rotting potatoes that permeated the island. It was burned into the memory of anyone forced to endure it. Sometimes the first hint of disaster was that awful stench. Some claimed the rancid, sulfuric, sewer-like smell was strong enough to keep the weary awake at night and cause the dogs to howl in protest.

Speak Plain Irish

Of the two major political parties in England, a **Tory** is a member of Britain's Conservative Party. Ironically, before the late 17th century in Ireland, a Tory was an Irish outlaw who favored the killing of English soldiers and settlers and who survived by means of plunder.

'Tisn't So!

When the Irish began to die from lack of food, some Protestant clergy preached from the pulpit that the Almighty had brought this curse upon the barbarian papists as a punishment for their sins.

A Bard's Tale

One of the many legends to come from the Great Hunger is that concerning *hungry grass,* which is a site where people perished during the Famine, where they would eat grass because they had no food. To this day, some of the locals will warn you that it is bad manners, not to mention bad luck, to walk across a field of hungry grass without some sort of food in your pocket. A bed-and-breakfast mistress might even offer you a bit of bread for your journey. If she does so, take it graciously. The horrors of the famine are still all too real to the Irish for these matters to be treated lightly.

The Wagons Roll By, Filled with Food

Perhaps the cruelest irony of the time was that there was plenty of food being raised on Irish soil, more than enough to feed her starving masses. Wagons loaded with produce traveled the roads on their way to the harbors, where the bounty was transferred to ships for exportation. The peasant tenants handed the crops over to the English landlords to pay the exorbitant rents being charged at the time. The one thing Irishmen feared more than starvation was eviction. To be without a roof over your head meant sure death, and they forestalled that consequence as long as possible by handing over whatever they had.

More than a few landlords lived high lifestyles solely supported by this bounty from their Irish tenants. Many a cartload of life-giving grain left the harbors of Ireland for no other reason than to pay some British landlord's gambling debts.

A Bard's Tale

Some have asked why the destitute victims of the famine stood by and allowed the wagons filled to the brim with food to ramble by on their way to the docks for export. Why didn't they attack the wagons and take the food? A few did. But the majority had the ancient Celtic mindset, the long held value that honor was greater than life. A virtuous man refused to steal from another, even if it meant death. Those who question their inaction have mistaken integrity and nobility for passivity and cowardice. The famine may have taken many Irish lives, but it did not break their spirit, nor change their basic character.

If Starvation Weren't Enough: Evictions

When the Irish ran completely out of food and had nothing to eat and nothing with which to pay the rent, a number of landlords seized the opportunity (some considering it heaven-sent) to rid themselves of the "pestilence that has invaded the land." The poor tenants couldn't provide as much revenue as farming and cattle-raising, so when the famine victims fell behind in their payments, they were evicted from their humble homes. Evictions were widespread in Ireland, with more occurring each year as the famine deepened. In the year 1850 alone, an estimated 104,000 tenants were evicted. In many cases, the cottages were burned and leveled, making room for more efficient agricultural use.

1846–47: The Coldest Winter in History

Those who had been cast from their homes huddled together in ditches in masses, seeking warmth and shelter. They gathered in caves, ruins, and any sort of shack they could find. As cruel fate would have it, the winter of 1846–47 (the middle of the four-year famine) was one of the coldest in Irish history. Although snow rarely falls on that mild, temperate island, it did in great abundance that winter, and it fell on souls who, heaven knows, had misery enough. Many of those who were evicted froze to death, or their sickness and physical depletion were made worse by having to face the harsh elements. For a peasant family, being evicted that winter was the same as receiving a death sentence.

Fevers Rage

To add to the agonies of starvation and eviction, disease thrived in the cramped quarters where evicted peasants crowded together, trying to escape the miserable cold. Typhus, relapsing fever, dysentery, and cholera were rampant. Fever hospitals were set up to care for the afflicted, but there were far too few of those institutions, and they were far apart. Many of these "havens" even became places of infection. What starvation and the cold didn't kill, the raging fevers did. In fact, many believe that more perished from contagious diseases than starvation.

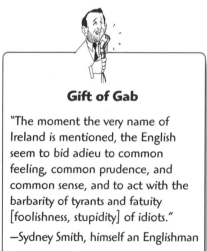

Gift of Gab

"The moment the very name of Ireland is mentioned, the English seem to bid adieu to common feeling, common prudence, and common sense, and to act with the barbarity of tyrants and fatuity [foolishness, stupidity] of idiots."

—Sydney Smith, himself an Englishman

So many died so quickly that coffins became scarce. As a solution to this problem, caskets were made with hinged or sliding bottoms. The deceased was placed inside, the coffin was held over the grave, the bottom was moved so that the corpse was deposited in the earth, and the casket was set on the cemetery wall for the next user. These were the lucky dead; many of the less-fortunate were interred in mass graves.

British Efforts: Too Little, Too Late

In spite of the prevalent opinion among the British aristocracy that the Irish were whiners who always exaggerated their own problems, the English were more than aware of the desperation of the famine victims. Long before the blight had hit in 1845, studies had been conducted in England that underlined the dangers of having a nation so dependent on one staple, such as the potato. It had been a disaster waiting to happen, but no one did anything before the worst occurred, and they did pathetically little more after it did.

Speak Plain Irish

Laissez-faire is a French phrase, literally meaning "let people do as they please." In economic terms, it is the doctrine that government should not interfere in any way with commerce.

You Call It Maize; We Call It Inedible

British Prime Minister Robert Peel did take some steps to alleviate the suffering, to his credit. According to the rules of *laissez-faire* (the economic doctrine that government should not interfere in any way with commerce) to which England adhered, Peel wasn't allowed to distribute free food to the peasants because this action might upset the balance of the British economy. But he stretched the rules as far as he could and ordered large shipments of maize (Indian corn) from the United States.

The maize was stored in depots, held until the prices of other foods reached their peak, and then distributed for low cost to the starving. By then, it was too late. The destitute had no money, not even enough to meet the modest price being asked. Besides, the Irish were potato eaters, not bread bakers. They had very few mills to grind the corn, a grain that was completely foreign to them and extremely difficult to grind. To make it digestible, it had to be ground twice. But Trevelyan (head of the Irish Famine Relief, see the later section) was unwilling to pay this extra expense. He wrote: "I cannot believe it will be necessary to grind the Indian corn twice…dependence on charity is not to be made an agreeable mode of life." The charity-dependent Irish had no idea how to make the maize edible, and many died of horrible digestive problems from trying to eat it whole and uncooked.

Gift of Gab

"Deaths…innumerable from starvation are occurring every day….the pampered officials, removed as they are from these scenes of heart-rending distress, can have no idea of them and don't appear to give themselves much trouble about them."

—A Mayo priest, 1846

Building a Road to Nowhere

Public work was offered to the famine and eviction victims. In March 1847, as many as 728,000 were put to work, building stone fences with no purpose and roads that led to nowhere. But making weak, starving, deathly ill men work at hard labor in the bitter cold was inhumane, not to mention impractical. This form of "relief" was ineffective to say the least.

Yet the peasants scrambled for the opportunity to do the work and earn the payment of one meal a day for a family of six. "The whole laboring population seems to be seeking employment on the Public Works," a Board of Works officer wrote. He claimed that he had "poor, wretched, half-clad wretches howling at the door for food."

Trevelyan: With His Help, We're Dyin'!

When the Tories lost the leadership of England to the *Whigs* in the summer of 1846, things went from bad to much worse for the Irish. A fellow named Charles Edward Trevelyan was put in charge of the Irish Famine Relief, which was a disastrous appointment for the Irish. The British could have hardly picked a chap less sympathetic than the bigoted Trevelyan. He stated, "Ireland must be left to the operation of natural causes." Translation: "If they die, they die."

Trevelyan subscribed to the belief that the Irish were lazy, irresponsible lie-abouts. He stated, "If the Irish once find out there are any circumstances in which they can get free government grants, we shall have a system of mendicancy [begging] such as the world never knew." As a result, Trevelyan was reluctant to develop any programs that would give the Irish too much relief, as though too much were possible under the dire circumstances of their misery.

Basically, Trevelyan and many others in powerful positions at that time believed the famine was the result of a combination of two things:

1. The moral bankruptcy of the Irish

2. Their natural, biological inferiority

Speak Plain Irish

The **Whigs** were the other major political party in 18th and 19th century England. Now known as the Liberal Party, Whigs championed reform and parliamentary rights.

Gift of Gab

"The great evil with which we have to contend is not the physical evil of the famine but the moral evil of the selfish, perverse, and turbulent character of the people."

—Sir Charles Trevelyan

Either way, Brits like Trevelyan believed that the misery the Irish were experiencing was their own fault. Having decided that, any sense of responsibility the English might have felt to help them was relieved.

Friends, Indeed!

One group who rallied to the aid of the famine victims and relieved a tremendous amount of suffering was the Society of Friends, otherwise known as the Quakers. Many members of the British government believed that, although things weren't all that nice for the Irish, conditions couldn't possibly be as bad as they were claiming. After all, the Irish were prone to exaggeration, or so they believed.

But the Society of Friends did their own investigation as independent observers of the situation in November 1846. The leader of that expedition into the rural, badly stricken areas of Ireland, William Forster, claimed that he saw children, "like skeletons, their features sharpened with hunger and their limbs wasted, so that there was little left but bones, their hands and arms, in particular, being much emaciated, and the happy expression of infancy gone from their faces, leaving the anxious look of premature old age." He also noted that all signs of livestock had disappeared entirely. Everywhere he went, he heard one cry, "The hunger is upon us!"

With great compassion and organizational skills, the Quakers gathered boatloads of food and transported it to Ireland. From the harbors, they effectively did what the British government claimed was impossible; they distributed the supplies to the remote areas of the island that needed it most.

The Price of a Bowl of Soup? Your Faith

The Quakers' example was so sterling that it embarrassed the English into making a somewhat larger effort on behalf of their Irish subjects. The English established soup kitchens to feed the starving Irish. But, as with the rest of their efforts, this program was poorly thought out and sometimes more of a hindrance than a help. The famine victims waited, sometimes all day, in the cold for a bowl of thin, watered-down soup. Here's the kicker: The price of this sustenance in some of the soup kitchens was conversion. Any Catholic receiving soup in one of these lines was required first to renounce his faith and accept Protestantism.

Speak Plain Irish

Souperism was the betrayal by a Catholic of his or her religion by converting to Protestantism in order to receive food from the English soup kitchens.

By doing this, the "convert" believed that he condemned his immortal soul, thinking as he did that eternal salvation could only be found inside the Catholic faith. So most refused, choosing death over what they were convinced was heresy and everlasting damnation for their souls. But some wretched persons took the oath, drank the soup, and were ostracized by their community. Not only were they outcasts because of their actions, but their children and grandchildren for generations to come were outcasts as well. *Souperism* was considered a vile sin, a blatant betrayal of one's faith and fellow Catholics.

By 1847, with the worst part of the famine still to come, Trevelyan decided that already "too much had been done" and halted all forms of relief: the kitchens dispensing watered down soup, the inedible Indian corn, and the work programs that were more cruel than useful. He was fully supported by the Whig prime minister, Lord John Russell, who stated, "I do not believe it is in the power of this House to prevent the dreadful scenes of suffering and death now occurring in Ireland." In truth, he considered it too costly to try. As Trevelyan wished, the Irish were left to the operation of natural causes.

'Tisn't So!

Charles Trevelyan was knighted for his so-called service in "helping" the people of Ireland through the Great Hunger.

Help from Unexpected Benefactors

To suggest that all Englishmen and women were as callous as Trevelyan would be inaccurate and grossly unfair. Many of the British landlords in Ireland went bankrupt, spending fortunes that had been in their families for generations, to care for their tenants and those of other, less compassionate landlords. Some risked their own lives by turning their beautiful estates into fever wards and nursing the sick themselves.

One such benevolent absentee landlord, Nicholas Cummins, filled a ship full of food and sailed from England to Ireland to make a present of the food to his own tenants and others in need. He took along a company of armed guards, expecting to be besieged by mobs of hunger-crazed peasants upon docking in Ireland. What he found were masses of victims, dying on the roads and in dreadful hovels, far too weak to present any sort of threat to anyone. The horrors he witnessed so scarred his soul that he returned home and did everything in his power to alert the average citizen of Britain to the extent of the catastrophe.

A Bard's Tale

A Cork magistrate, Nicholas Cummins, related what he saw when visiting Skibbereen in December 1846: "I entered some of the hovels...and the scenes that presented themselves were such as no tongue or pen can convey the slightest idea of. In the first, six famished and ghastly skeletons, to all appearance dead, were huddled in a corner on some filthy straw, their sole covering what seemed a ragged horse-cloth, and their wretched legs hanging about, naked above the knees. I approached in horror and found by a low moaning they were alive, they were in fever—four children, a woman, and what had once been a man."

In England, many great ladies campaigned tirelessly, raising relief funds and organizing drives to supply food for the masses. They wrote heart-rending letters to newspapers, begging for help on behalf of the victims and, in many cases, getting it.

A Million Emigrate Aboard Coffin Ships

With nowhere left to turn, the famine victims began a massive emigration. They fled the starving island in ships bound, mostly, for America. Seizing the opportunity to bilk the destitute, profiteers pulled ancient, decrepit ships out of mothballs and filled these "coffin ships" to the brim with the poorly nourished, often desperately ill escapees. The food aboard was inadequate even for healthy people, let alone these wretched individuals. Crammed together in rat-infested holds below deck, they died in great numbers. So many perished and were "buried" at sea that it was grimly stated, "The floor of the Atlantic is littered with Irish bones." By 1900, four million Irish men and women had emigrated to the United States. They took with them the memory of the famine and the bitterness it engendered against Mother England.

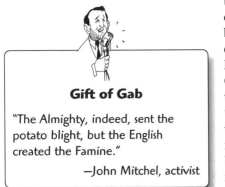

Gift of Gab

"The Almighty, indeed, sent the potato blight, but the English created the Famine."

—John Mitchel, activist

The Memory of "This Monstrous Thing"

Irish author Hugh Dorian wrote in *Donegal Sixty Years Ago*, "In a very short time there was nothing but stillness, a mournful silence in the villages, in the cottages grim poverty and emaciated faces…The tinkers fled to the cities; the musicians disappeared and never returned. Many of the residents too made their escape at once, finding employment or early graves elsewhere. There were no more friendly meetings at the neighbors' houses in the afternoons, no gatherings on the hillsides on Sundays, no song, no merry laugh of the maidens. Not only were the human beings silent and lonely, but the brute creation also, for not even the bark of the dog or the crowing of a cock was to be heard."

Indeed, much has been said and written about the Great Hunger. As with many catastrophes throughout world history, debate has raged about who or what was to blame. Obviously, no one wants to shoulder the responsibility for such human suffering. No doubt there is enough blame and misery to burden many shoulders. Who knows how many more lives could have been saved had more compassion been shown? Who knows how many were saved through loving, charitable deeds? There is only one answer to the last question: Not enough.

There are those who say it is ludicrous to blame Britain for the infestation of Irish potatoes by a fungus that arrived from America. They claim that England did all she could at the time, pointing to the efforts of Robert Peel and the monetary donations of Queen Victoria herself. Some say it is only bitter radicals who keep the mythology of the famine alive to serve their own hate-driven agendas.

On the other side, those same accused nationalists believe the Great Hunger was nothing short of genocide on the part of the British government. At least one million people died needlessly in a land filled with food raised by Irish hands on soil that, rightfully, should have been Irish. They point to the fact that the dependence of the peasants upon potatoes was the direct result of enforced British policy. They say the extreme neglect and inaction on the part of the English when the blight struck was deliberate and calculated, and the deaths caused by that deliberate passivity were intentional.

Perhaps the truth lies somewhere in the middle. Who can know the thoughts, feelings, and intentions of men like Charles Trevelyan 150 years after the fact? We can only judge them by their words and their actions, or lack thereof.

'Tisn't So!

A nasty rumor was circulated that when Queen Victoria was asked to donate money personally for the relief of Irish suffering during the Great Hunger, she offered a measly 5 pounds, but official records show that she gave 2,000 pounds.

The Least You Need to Know

➤ Because of the unfair laws governing land inheritances, the Irish were living off tiny plots of land and were almost completely dependent upon the potato.

➤ A fungus arrived, borne on ships from America, and began to infest the potatoes, turning them into a foul-smelling, black, inedible mush.

➤ The emaciated peasants roamed the countryside in search of something, anything, to eat. Hundreds of thousands died in ditches and along roadsides, their mouths stained green from trying to eat grass. Meanwhile, shiploads of food raised by those peasants were being exported to put money in the landlords' pockets.

➤ Under the leadership of the Tory party, the British government took some steps to help the Irish. But then the Whigs took over, and a heartless fellow named Charles Trevelyan was appointed head of the Irish Famine Relief. He decided that too much had been done already and cut off all aid to the starving masses.

➤ The Irish were given some help by the Society of Friends (the Quakers), by English gentlewomen who raised funds in England on Ireland's behalf, and from a number of sympathetic British landlords who spent their fortunes trying to save their tenants.

➤ At least a million Irish perished and even more boarded ill-fated "coffin ships" bound for America. These ships were so dreadful that many died before reaching their destinations.

Chapter 14

Emigration: 'Tis You Must Go and I Must Bide

In This Chapter

➤ Waves of poor and tired arrive in America, and the cities fill with Irish

➤ "No Irish Need Apply!"—the struggle of the Irish immigrant looking for work

➤ Healthy folks leave cities and head for the hills

➤ Bridget has all the work she can handle

➤ Irish labor builds the great cities

As we've seen in the last several chapters, the spirit of rebellion and the need for freedom was strong in Ireland. Some Irish, however, grew weary of the struggle at home and chose to find their freedom elsewhere. From 1800 to 1921, as many as 40 million emigrants came to the United States from all over the world. But of those, 7 million—that's 20 percent—were from Ireland, which was a rather large contribution from such a geographically small island. Although emigration from Ireland to the United States occurred in several waves, none had as large an impact as the Irish immigrants who came through Ellis Island in the years before the turn of the 19th century. True, the hardships they faced in America's cities sometimes rivaled those they had left in the Emerald Isle, but their presence was vital to building this new country.

Wave After Wave

The Irish have been emigrating to the United States since the country's early beginnings. The first wave of Eire's sons and daughters washed onto American shores during

Gift of Gab

Memories by Thomas D'Arcy M'Gee

I left two loves on a distant strand,
One young, and fond, and fair, and
bland;
One fair, and old, and sadly grand—
My wedded wife and my native land.

the Colonial period of the 17th century. Most of those folk were Scotch-Irish Protestants who left because of economic hardships in Ireland. The second wave was the largest, a great exodus of sick and starving Catholics fleeing the horrors of the Irish Potato Famine of the mid-1800s (see Chapter 13, "The Great Hunger"). In the post-famine years, the numbers of Irish immigrants coming to the United States steadily decreased, though it has always been and continues to be a significant amount. The sons and daughters of Erin continue to cross the great ocean in search of the American dream.

Each new swell brought Irish immigrants with their own special gifts and own set of needs, hoping to give of their talents and receive aid from their new country. Their value to America was incalculable. While they were rebuilding their own lives, they built America.

Early Arrivals

Even before the Potato Famine of the mid-1800s, Protestants from Ulster had been arriving in America and settling in Pennsylvania and Virginia. British-imposed economics had been difficult even for them, and they left to find a better, easier life for their families in the more affluent United States. Tough, hardworking, no-nonsense folk, they soon became successful, productive citizens of their new country. Some even pioneered their way into the Appalachian area, where they created comfortable homesteads for themselves.

In addition to the Protestants, Catholics by the thousands flocked to America's shores. Maryland was established as a refuge for English Catholics in the 1600s, a century filled with threats to Catholics in Ireland as well, including the terror of Cromwell and the confiscation of Catholic lands. More persecutions from the British brought another wave of Catholics to the United States just before the Famine of the 1840s. As many as 40,000 a year were making the ocean trek to a new home in America throughout the 1830s when Ireland was in a state of virtual civil war between the Irish peasants and their British landlords.

The Great Famine Exodus

Of course, far more Catholics came across during the Potato Famine. From 1846 through 1852, between 200,000 and 250,000 Irish left Ireland each year. After that, the amounts increased or decreased, depending upon the economy in Ireland. Few Irish wanted to leave their soft land with its green fields and blue lakes for the cement walls and asphalt streets of America's industrial cities. They reluctantly did so when the wolves of poverty, starvation, and oppression were howling at their doors.

Those who escaped the Potato Famine often just barely did so. They arrived on the shores of America by the shipload; they were starving, sick, and traumatized. After they landed, their lots weren't much better as they were crammed into the squalid tenements of New York City, Boston, and Philadelphia. Some weren't so lucky and wound up in the basements of those tenements. Diseases such as typhus, tuberculosis, cholera, typhoid, and dysentery were rampant. Boston was one of the worst cities because many of the poor lived in damp, filthy cellars, which were breeding places for contagious illnesses.

Even though at this time the burden of a large family was great, the birth rate among the Irish immigrants also was high, as was the number of infant mortalities. Many babies died shortly after birth, and countless children never reached the age of five. During the 1850s, the life expectancy for the Irish in Boston was an appalling 22! Philadelphia was a bit better, but it also had its areas that were unfit for human habitation, yet served as "home" to thousands of unfortunates. Those who arrived in the United States already sick and physically depleted had little chance of surviving. Quickly, sadly, the weak fell by the wayside, the death toll among them being virtually as high as it had been in rural famine Ireland.

Liberal, compassionate cities such as Boston—who had originally welcomed the emigrants openly in a great spirit of humanitarianism—were soon overwhelmed as certain parts of the towns became slums almost overnight. With disease running rampant through those sections of the cities, crime rising, and property seriously devalued, the quality of life for those living there plummeted. It was hard for those who had opened their doors to the immigrants not to become resentful. Yet without resources, without steady work and a living wage, without basic health or the nutrition and medical care to rebuild their depleted bodies, the Irish were hard put to improve their lot. Elevating their social and economic status to that of their nonimmigrant neighbors was hardly a priority to a people struggling to survive day to day.

'Tisn't So!

In 1855, New York City's Irish (those born in Ireland) accounted for 28 percent of the population. Five years later, New York was called "the largest Irish city in the world." Around the same time, Boston's population was 31 percent Irish, and Philadelphia's population was 21 percent Irish.

No Irish Need Apply!

The people of those fair cities soon changed their attitudes about welcoming the poor, tired masses, and their generosity waned. Before long, it was quite unpopular to be Irish, and "No Irish Need Apply" signs hung in the windows of businesses and boarding houses. Segregation was practiced in every walk of daily life, and the Irish found themselves on the outside of society.

Speak Plain Irish

The term **Paddy** was given to the Irish by the Americans, who probably thought every male in Ireland was named Patrick. Whether the term is derogatory is debatable, depending upon who is using it and in what context. It can be an insult or a term of endearment. Like many racist terms, it is safer to use it if you are a Paddy yourself.

At that time, outside was a dangerous place to be. It meant no job, and therefore no food, no room, or any of the other basic necessities of life. It could also prove dangerous if a gang of hoodlums decided you weren't welcome in their hallway or alleyway. Plenty of tough fellows, Anglos who were native to their cities, as well as members of other immigrant minority groups such as the Italians, decided early that they didn't like *Paddys*. Not that their bigotry bothered the Paddys all that much; they were accustomed to not being liked. If hatred and discrimination had been fatal, the Irish would have disappeared from the earth long ago. But this attitude certainly made things more difficult for a people who had, heaven knows, faced challenges enough.

The Irish Catholic had fled Ireland to escape the oppression of bigotry, specifically that of British Protestants, only to find more of the same in America. The United States was, after all, primarily Protestant, and the "natives," or well-established, previously immigrated peoples, harbored much of the same prejudices as the Anglos in Ireland. The "tired, poor, huddled masses" had been welcomed to their new land, only to be quickly demoted to second-class citizens.

Gift of Gab

Grateful for his emigrant ancestors, John F. Kennedy told a crowd in Country Wexford, "It took 115 years to make this trip and three generations. If my great-grandfather hadn't left New Ross, today I would be working over there at the Albatross Company [a fertilizer plant]."

They Scatter to the Four Winds

Not all Irish came to America with little more than a dream. Some stepped off the boat strong and healthy and with a bit of money to spend. These folks quickly sized up the situation in the cities as less than ideal (to say the least) and struck out for a more pleasant place to settle. Many cut a path west to California (specifically the San Francisco area), some went south, and others made their homes in the industrial areas of the midwest. Michigan, Indiana, and Illinois received vast amounts of Irish settlers, as did New York, Massachusetts, Pennsylvania, Ohio, and New Jersey.

Grandpa Was a Trader, Grandma Had Braids

Years ago in the southern United States, many newly transported Irishmen became traveling traders. According to Cherokee law, they were not allowed to conduct their business with the Cherokee nation unless they were "part of the family." So out of practicality and in the name of capitalism, the Irishmen took Cherokee brides (not such a bad deal, considering the beauty of the Cherokee people) so that they could freely trade with all the relatives.

The result of such couplings of Irish paternity and Cherokee maternity created offspring with an interesting combination of physical features. These folks are frequently tall, lean, and broad-shouldered. Although their hair is dark and straight, their skin is very pale and often their eyes are light-colored in hues of blue, green, or gold. They have high cheekbones, strong jaws, and fiery dispositions to match. (In case you were wondering, yes, there are some redheads with dark skin and black eyes!) To this day in the south, you can still find descendants of this blending of Irish and Cherokee.

> **'Tisn't So!**
>
> There exists a mistaken notion that all Irish Americans are Catholic and that all of their ancestors came over during the Potato Famine. That's true of many Irish Americans, but only partially. Between 40 and 50 percent of Americans with Irish ancestry are Scotch-Irish Protestants. Is a Scotch-Irish person any less Irish for not being Catholic? Not at all. If you're Protestant and Scotch-Irish, congratulations, you're a Paddy, too!

Lasses Fare Better Than Lads

The experience of adapting to a new country is a daunting one for any immigrant, who must find a place in society to work, live, and socialize. But Irish men and Irish women experienced vastly different situations upon arriving in America. For the men, life was extremely difficult and dangerous, and it took some time to adjust as well as find work. The skills the women brought with them allowed them to find a workplace in which to thrive.

Irish Lasses Find Their Niche

Irish women had been quite industrious back home in Ireland. With large numbers of children growing around their fires, they worked night and day to care for their families. From an early age, Irish girls were taught the domestic skills of cooking, sewing, cleaning, and dandling babies on their knees. Often older sisters spent more time carrying the youngest child around and keeping him occupied than the harried mother of the baby. Many of the Irish women had also worked outside the home, serving the British and Anglo-Irish on their estates. They were quite familiar with the workings of a staff inside a great house and the personal needs and desires of its mistress.

All of these skills were instantly marketable when an Irish woman disembarked in the United States. At that time in the eastern seaboard cities, even middle-class Americans had at least one female domestic to help with the housework and to care for the children. Unlike their rambunctious men, Irish women had a reputation for having gentle, quiet spirits. Irish women soon developed a reputation for being excellent domestics, and every New York lady and Boston socialite was raving about her Irish help.

Irish Lads Have a Tough Time Adjusting

Before coming to America, Irish men had mostly been farmers. With the tiny parcels of land allowed them, few had enough space to grow anything other than potatoes, which were a low-maintenance crop. Other than the planting and harvesting (a fairly simple process), little was involved in raising them. These skills were basically useless to the poor Irishman when he arrived in the great cities of America.

'Tisn't So!

The stereotype of the lawless, quarrelsome Irish did have a bit of truth to it; there were high levels of crime among the Irish. But note that the offenses were mostly minor violations such as petty theft, which are common among any low-income group. Although fists frequently flew in barroom brawls, the murder rate among the Irish was lower than most demographic segments of the population.

Speak Plain Irish

Mick is a derogatory word for a person of Irish heritage, coined because the first two letters of many Irish last names begin with the letters *Mc*. **Papist** is a derogatory term for one who ardently supports the pope.

Another problem of a public relations nature plagued immigrant Irishmen. The Irish have always enjoyed hefting a pint, the consumption of alcoholic beverages being an important part of the culture for both men and women. This cultural difference between the Irish and their Anglo-American neighbors, plus the lack of employment earned the Irish men a reputation for being drunken and lazy. Considering the degree of misery in their lives, it is little wonder some attempted to drown their troubles in brew, but it could hardly be said of the lot of them.

The Irish men's reputation for violence didn't help them either. Back home, many had been politically active, and that activity had been in the form of agrarian societies, underground terrorist groups who conducted secret raids against their landlords and those who persecuted them. Under the oppressive circumstances in which these societies were spawned, illegal actions and violent measures may have been understandable. But the Irish fellows had a difficult time realizing that in America there was a justice system for handling disputes, and it wasn't necessary to settle quarrels with your fists.

All in all, times were tough for Irish men. Jobs were scarce, and the ones they could find usually involved hard, dangerous labor, such as construction, and paid low wages. For the most part, in their new country they were poorly regarded and ill-treated. Sadly, the stereotype of the drunken, violent, lazy Irish *mick* or *papist* was established during these post-famine immigrant times in American culture, and the young Irishman would have quite a time overcoming it. Work did come eventually, and it was the kind with which heroes are made; this young American nation needed to grow, and the Irish lads were ready to build.

The Building of America

Modern America was mostly built by the labor of its immigrants, and many of those immigrants were Irish Americans. Their hands, sweat, strong backs, blood, and sometimes their lives were the gifts they gave to their new country as they worked on her railroads, bridges, buildings, dams, and canals. Simply put, no one worked harder at the building of America than her Irish sons.

Tracks as Far as You Can See

The largest number of Irish immigrants came to America between the years 1840 and 1860. During that same period, the miles of railroad track in the United States went from 3,000 to 30,000. This was no coincidence. Irishmen laid ties and rails from one end of the nation to the other, and although the work was horribly difficult and infinitely dangerous, many Irishmen chose that life over one in the city tenements. At least they had fresh air to breathe (except in the tunnels) and clear, open spaces. Many men died blasting mountains and digging tunnels through solid rock. Unfortunately, the life of an Irishman was a cheap commodity in those days, and many were lost while linking the transcontinental rails.

Another mighty effort that involved Irish workers was the digging of the labyrinth of subway tunnels below and around New York City. Miles and miles of subway passages were hollowed from the earth by these laborers, providing for 710 miles of track. (If stretched end to end, the rails would reach from New York City to Fort Wayne, Indiana.) Today, one out of nine of all Americans using mass transit to reach their workplaces ride through tunnels dug by Irish laborers.

Those Breathtaking Skylines

One of the engineering wonders of its day was New York City's beautiful Brooklyn Bridge, which was built chiefly with Irish labor. Many Irishmen died in its construction, but because of the Brooklyn Bridge, the city of New York was able to expand through Brooklyn, into Queens, and onto Long Island, raising both the city's population, as well as its work force and economic status.

When the city center of Chicago was nearly destroyed by fire, it was Irish hands that rebuilt it, raising a line of glorious skyscrapers that can still be appreciated today. The magnificent skyline of New York City, considered to be one of the most beautiful in the world, was also largely built with Irish labor.

Gift of Gab

Am I Remembered? by Thomas D'Arcy M'Gee

Am I remembered in Erin?
I charge you, speak me true—
Has my name a sound, a meaning
In the scenes my boyhood knew?
Does the heart of the mother ever
Recall her exile's name?
For to be forgot in Erin
And on earth is all the same.

Whether building the railroads, skyscrapers, or bridges, the Irish laborers were not protected, as workers are now, by legal standards guarding their safety. Many died in construction-related accidents; some were even entombed in cement graves, their bodies forever a part of the structure they were building.

The American Catholic Church to the Rescue

Many of the immigrants had families to greet them when they arrived in America, but many did not. For many of the lonely, displaced Irish, their only link with home was the local parish. Frequently, the Church also aided in welcoming the new arrivals. Often they assisted in making arrangements for even more Irish relatives to join their American families. For discouraged souls who had lost everything and everyone, the church provided a network, as well as a new family, based on faith.

The local parish provided a place, outside of the local pubs that sprang up everywhere the Irish congregated, where displaced Irish could socialize, meet folks from the old country, practice their holiday customs, and celebrate their culture. Parties, complete with singing, dancing, traditional music, and Irish food bolstered the spirits of the parishioners and revived fond memories of home. These gatherings also served as meeting places for young people searching for mates, long-lost relatives searching for their loved ones, and those who simply longed for the sight of a friendly, Irish face and the soft sound of the Irish lilt. The church provided a taste of home to the lonely Irish; it is no wonder they supported their local parishes so faithfully with their time, energies, and money.

'Tisn't So!

When St. Patrick's Cathedral, that mighty gothic structure in midtown Manhattan across from Rockefeller Plaza, was first built, people objected to its location, complaining that it was inconvenient to attend as it was too far out of town!

In a society where they were common laborers and servants and the objects of bigotry and discrimination, Irish people had little in which they could take pride. But they donated their hard-earned money generously to build churches, which were sometimes the first churches in their areas. Although the donations were meager, they were plentiful, and some of the structures were magnificent, such as St. Patrick's Cathedral in New York City. Not only were the monetary donations Irish, but much of the labor involved in building the structures was done by Irish hands as well. After a day's work of cleaning house or pouring cement, an Irish woman or man could enter one of these elegant buildings for a quiet hour of prayer and know that, at least in part, it belonged to them.

Full Steam Ahead!

By the 1860s, ocean-going vessels powered by steam were in full swing, and tickets aboard these ships were affordable to more of the emigrants. Often the money for the journey was provided by a relative in the United States who had previously made the crossing. Also, the trip, which had once been a grueling four weeks at sea, was reduced to a comparatively short 10 days. The journey was more comfortable, safer, and more sanitary; it also offered better food. All in all, it was an agreeable way to transport oneself to a new life. The Irish continued to make the trip until there were more of us here than there. The flood of Irish immigrants gradually slowed to a steady stream, but Irish still continue to come to the United States, where they have added and continue to add so much of their particular magic to our melting pot.

The Least You Need to Know

➤ The first wave of emigrants to cross from Ireland to America arrived during the Colonial times. They were hardworking, no-nonsense, Presbyterian Scotch-Irish, and they fit right into the fabric of the new country.

➤ The massive exodus of Potato Famine victims filled up American cities along the eastern seaboard. By 1855, New York City was 28 percent Irish, Boston was 31 percent Irish, and Philadelphia was 21 percent Irish.

➤ The Famine refugees arrived sick, starved, and unskilled, with little but the rags on their backs. Almost overnight, they turned areas of cities into slums, making them unwelcome to the native population. Signs reading, "No Irish Need Apply," were posted in shop windows everywhere, and jobs were difficult to find.

➤ The healthier and heartier immigrants quickly moved through the cities and on to other areas of the country: the West, North, South, and Midwest.

➤ Irish women were skilled domestics and quickly found employment as maids in American homes.

➤ Irish men had a tougher time finding jobs, as their main occupation in Ireland had been growing potatoes. Eventually, though, thousands of them labored at backbreaking jobs, building the skylines of cities such as New York and Chicago and laying miles and miles of railroad track.

➤ The Catholic church provided a home away from home for its displaced, lonely parishioners. Although they had little money, the Irish generously donated what they could and helped build churches in their areas. Some were magnificent, such as St. Patrick's Cathedral in midtown Manhattan.

➤ With the advent of inexpensive steam ship tickets, more American Irish sent tickets to those back home, making it possible for them to emigrate, too.

Chapter 15

The Blood of the Martyrs

In This Chapter

➤ More rebel groups spring up; revolution is in the air

➤ Parnell for Home Rule; Parnell the adulterer

➤ The Gaelic Revival celebrates everything Irish

➤ Sinn Fein appears, along with new hopes

➤ The Easter Uprising of 1916: "A terrible beauty is born"

As a result of the bitterness that multiplied during the Great Hunger, rebel nationalist groups in Ireland gained strength and purpose. The affiliation known as Young Ireland (those who had become disillusioned with O'Connell's peaceful methods) attempted an uprising, as did a number of other such groups. But these uprisings were failures, mostly due to problems of disorganization, betrayal by informers, and a lack of support on a grassroots level. These failures were difficult to bear for the Irish, but they took away some hard lessons with these missed attempts at independence, and a new revolution was in the air.

The Fires of Rebellion Flare Again

The growing spirit of rebellion in Ireland led to the formation of several groups that pushed for Irish freedom. The *Fenians* were born from a tangent group of the Young Ireland organization. The Fenians' goals were straightforward: a democratic republic, governed independently, the right to vote for all adult males, reform in laws regulating landownership, and separation of church and state.

Speak Plain Irish

One of the leaders of the **Fenians**, John Mahony, was a student of Gaelic mythology. He named the group after the Fianna, a legendary class of warriors from ancient times.

Gift of Gab

This is the sacred oath of the Fenians: "I, (name of member), in the presence of Almighty God, do solemnly swear allegiance to the Irish Republic, now virtually established, and that I will do my utmost, at every risk, while life lasts, to defend its independence and integrity, and finally, that I will yield implicit obedience in all things, not contrary to the laws of God, to the commands of my superior officers. So help me God! Amen."

From within the Fenians, another, far more militant group was to come: the Irish section of the Irish/American Fenian organization, known as the Irish Republican Brotherhood or IRB. Little is known about its origins; this group was sometimes known only as "the brotherhood" or "the organization" because its members were better than most at maintaining their secrecy (although they, like most Irish rebels, had problems with informers). In general, the members of the IRB were better educated than other militant groups and enjoyed higher standards of living, and some were even well-trained military men. Therefore, the British authorities found the IRB more intimidating than the Fenians.

The most effective tool the British had against the underground groups such as the IRB was the ability to infiltrate the sects with spies. Sad to say, the British seemed to have no trouble finding traitors within those groups who would sell their brothers for pieces of silver by informing on them. Covert operations provided the British with more than they needed to know about most republican organizations. Even though the IRB had an elaborate system of organization—nine privates reported to a sergeant, nine sergeants reported to one captain, and nine captains reported to a "center" to shield those at the top of the organization—they, too, were infiltrated, even at the highest levels.

Another Irish uprising was attempted in 1867; as before, it amounted to little. The Fenians in Ireland and their supporters in America would continue to be active, but their next big effort would occur after the Easter Uprising of 1916 under the reorganization and leadership of a lad named Michael Collins. For now, another sort of revolution was brewing beneath the surface. Once again, it was time to try the peaceful, political approach to reform.

The Fall of Charles Parnell

A Protestant landlord from County Wicklow, Charles Stewart Parnell, was to lead the next agitation: the battle for *Home Rule*. Parnell's American mother had been staunchly anti-British, and she had imparted her political views to her son at an early age. Parnell supported the Fenians, at least in principle. Both he and that group wanted Home Rule for Ireland, the ability for Ireland to have a governing body separate from British parliament that could make decisions on her behalf. The Fenians intended to achieve this goal through whatever means necessary, even violent ones; Parnell favored more peaceful, political revolution.

Along with a few Irish members of parliament in Westminster, Parnell was successful in having two bills concerning Home Rule introduced. Neither was passed, but the government did make some concessions in the form of land bills that made the distribution of Irish property more fair to the Irish Catholics. Even though Parnell had not made Home Rule a reality for Ireland, his forceful personality, brilliant political mind, and tireless efforts in search of his goal brought the issue to the forefront of British politics and public awareness.

Although Parnell rose to the top of Irish politics and lead the Home Rule Party, he was never to achieve his goal of Home Rule for Ireland. A scandal brought his career to an ignominious end. He was publicly exposed for an affair with a married woman, Katherine O'Shea, when Mrs. O'Shea's husband, William, named Parnell as co-respondent (a nice way of saying Parnell was his wife's lover) in a divorce filing in 1889. Although William O'Shea had known about the affair for years, he had remained quiet to safeguard the money he thought he would be receiving from Katherine's wealthy aunt. When the aunt died and William O'Shea didn't receive the expected inheritance, he filed for divorce.

Parnell's adversary, Prime Minister Gladstone, jumped at the opportunity to denounce Parnell as a morally bankrupt individual who should be ousted by his party. Parnell was deeply in love with Katherine O'Shea and welcomed the divorce, because it would afford him the opportunity to marry her. Their marriage may have been satisfying to Charles and Katherine, but it didn't satisfy his political critics, who demanded he step down from leadership of the Home Rule Party.

Refusing to be dismissed, Parnell resisted, but he lost the fight when the Catholics and members of his own party rallied against him. His health had been failing for some time, and he died in Katherine's arms on October 6, 1891. They had been married less than four months.

Speak Plain Irish

Home Rule is the idea that Ireland should have an Irish parliament based on the British Commons and Lords. The reigning monarch of Britain would still rule over Ireland, but all domestic affairs and most taxation issues would be handled in Dublin, rather than London. The Home Rule Party was the political organization headed by Charles Stewart Parnell, whose primary agenda was to bring about Home Rule for Ireland.

Gift of Gab

"Parnellism is a simple love of adultery and all those who profess Parnellism profess to love and admire adultery."

—Quote by one of Parnell's contemporaries, an Irish Catholic clergyman, to his parish

More than anything else, Parnell and his Home Rule Party showed Ireland, Britain, and the rest of the world that Ireland could create and maintain a political machine with a clearly defined agenda. Before Parnell, Irish movements had been sporadic and often fraught with violence. But Ireland was capable of systematic, sustained political organization and was therefore capable of self-government. In spite of his scandalous end, Parnell showed that Irish politics were a serious matter and that the Irish were a political force to be reckoned with.

'Tisn't So!

It would be a lovely thing to say that all Irish everywhere enjoyed and benefited from the Gaelic Revival, but it was primarily a product of the middle-class Irish. For the most part, the Irish peasantry was too busy trying to find a bite to eat and keep a roof over their head to worry about such things as poetry, mythology, and great Celtic literature.

Speak Plain Irish

The Gaelic language is difficult for those not born to it. What you see written on paper bears little resemblance to what comes out of an Irishman's mouth when he's speaking it. To avoid making a complete fool of yourself at your local pub, don't pronounce *Sinn Fein* "Sin Feen." It's said "Shin Fain." Ye mustn't ask why. 'Tis just the way 'tis.

Gaels Revive!

In the wake of Parnell's scandal, Home Rule for Ireland was delayed for another generation. Disillusioned by their hero's fall from grace, the Irish turned their attention to other endeavors. New organizations appeared with reform on their mind, but this time, the reforms were cultural, not political.

The Irish had a deep yearning to appreciate and encourage their own Irishness. In this time, known as the Gaelic Revival (yes, this was only one of several), every area of Irish heritage was cultivated. From the Irish language to Celtic mythology, to the poetry of the bards, to traditional music and dancing, the natives celebrated their heritage. The Gaelic League concentrated on the arts, and the Gaelic Athletic Association resurrected such Irish games as Gaelic football and hurling. Once again, Erin's sons and daughters considered it a fine thing to have been born Irish.

Thanks to Parnell's work, the British had lost a great deal in the arena of public opinion in the way they treated their Irish subjects. British citizens and the rest of the world were putting pressure on the British government to loosen their stranglehold on the Irish and their culture. This pressure enabled the Gaelic Revival to occur with a minimal amount of persecution of its supporters.

The Birth of Sinn Fein

In 1905, a journalist named Arthur Griffith formed an organization that was destined to be around for quite some time: Sinn Fein. Gaelic for "Ourselves alone," Sinn Fein's goal was to establish an Irish parliament in Dublin and to persuade the Irish members of parliament to boycott Westminster.

Like some of the nationalist groups before them, Sinn Fein was fighting an uphill war against grassroots empathy. The same Irish who claimed to abhor British oppression turned out in throngs to cheer Queen Victoria when she visited Ireland in 1900. Most of them were less concerned about politics than what they were going to put in their mouths come dinner time.

A Bard's Tale

Have you wondered what the big deal is about the colors green and orange in Ireland? Those two hues are most meaningful in Erin's land. Believe it or not, red was the color of choice through the centuries for the ancient Celts. But when the idea of Irish nationalism became big, so did the color of green. If you look around you at an Irish landscape, that's what you see: green, green, and more of that same beautiful color. Orange is the symbol of the Protestants of Ireland, harking back to the very Protestant king of Britain, William of Orange. Throughout the years, wearing a simple green shamrock in your lapel or an orange sash around your neck was a clear symbol of your politics.

The Emerald Isle Is Lookin' a Wee Bit Orange

The Protestants were banding together in organizations of their own. The Orange Society, named after the Protestant British king, William of Orange, and created back in 1795, came forward to oppose Home Rule and to preserve the Union. They even called themselves Unionists. The last thing they wanted was for a primarily Catholic Ireland to break away, in any way, from the Protestant England. As Protestants themselves, they relied heavily on the British government's protection and support. Without that umbrella, they would be an exposed minority at the mercy of the Catholics. Having been there at fateful times in the past, they would do anything to keep it from happening again.

The Protestant Unionists' zeal was a sharp contrast to the apathy of the Irish Catholics. Having had the wind blown from their sails during the Parnell scandal, the Home Rule supporters weren't up for the fight, but the Unionists were. Happy to have the tide turning their way for a change due to the inactivity of the Home Rule supporters, the Protestants of the northern province of Ulster got together and on September 28, 1912, almost 75 percent of them over the age of 15 signed an oath that they would use all means necessary to defeat Home Rule. Many etched their signatures in blood.

To back up their promise with substance, the Ulster Volunteer Force was formed the next year, an organization of 90,000 armed and ready soldiers—not a good omen for a peaceful solution to the struggle between the Protestants and Catholics. The Union between Ireland and England would be dissolved only over their cold corpses.

The Lines Are Drawn for Civil War

It was no great surprise that when a Home Act Rule was finally passed in 1914 at the prompting of the Irish Nationalist Party, led by John Redmond. But it was a law with no teeth. Even before it was affirmed, the Brits were considering excluding four counties in Ulster from its provisions. Such an amending bill would seriously dilute the Act's effectiveness for the Irish. But just as it seemed the country might rip apart at her seams over the issue, a far greater concern surfaced: war in Europe.

The Home Rule Act was placed on the back burner for the time being, and some mourned its absence and probable demise. But most agreed that even if World War I hadn't interfered, Home Rule in Ireland would not have become a functioning reality. As a man named Roy Foster said, "There seems no good reason to doubt that Home Rule would have been greeted in Ulster with armed rebellion."

'Tisn't So!

British government officials didn't always have a full grasp of the Irish situation, or they pretended not to have. Prime Minister Benjamin Disraeli said, "I want to see a public man come forward and say what the Irish Question is... It is the Pope one day, potatoes the next."

The Easter Uprising of 1916

The Easter Uprising of 1916, one of the most bloody and politically important revolts in Irish history, very nearly didn't happen. Some say it would have been better for all if it hadn't. Others believe that without that ill-fated rebellion, Irish freedom would never have been won. Whatever its influence on later events, the revolution got off to a shaky start.

A Fight Doomed Before It Began

With Britain fighting the Germans, the staunch, Irish republican rebels figured it was an opportune time to rise. Home Rule had been offered to them and then postponed, like a post-dated check. Now it looked as though there would never be sufficient "funds" to "cash" it. When the disillusioned and angry Irish asked Britain's enemies, the Germans, for help, the Germans offered 20,000 rifles, which would be transported aboard a German ship, the *Aud*. The ship and its cargo were to dock on the Kerry coast April 20, 1916, and would be led to shore by an Irish pilot boat.

All the plans were set, but at the last minute, the rebels' military council decided it would be best for the guns to arrive after the rising, rather than before. (Go figure.)

They sent a message to the Germans, requesting the delay, but the communication was intercepted and never delivered.

The *Aud* arrived, as originally planned, on April 20 and was not met by the prearranged pilot boat. She cruised up and down the coast until she was finally intercepted by British ships. The German captain sank her, rather than allow her and her cargo to fall into enemy hands, and the 20,000 badly needed rifles succumbed to a watery grave.

The Rebels Put Up a Hellish Fight

Leader Padraig Pearse and his compatriots in the Irish Republican Brotherhood (IRB) decided to go ahead even without the weapons. The plan was to take control of central Dublin, beginning with the magnificent Dublin Post Office, where they would set up headquarters.

The General Post Office in Dublin.

Although the British responded immediately and gave it all they had, they were surprised at how valiantly and skillfully the Irish rebels fought. Strongholds, manned by only a few rebels, held their positions for long, bloody periods, taking far more casualties than they suffered. At Mount Street Bridge, the British troops honestly thought they were battling 200 rebels; there were 17.

The English shelled the Post Office, severely damaging the once handsome building and killing more than a few civilians in the process. When the Post Office was set on fire, Pearse surrendered in the interest of preventing further bloodshed.

Gift of Gab

At the Dublin Post Office, Pearse made his famous proclamation:

"In the name of God and of the dead generations from which she receives her old tradition of nationhood, Ireland through us summons her children to her flag and strikes for her freedom."

A Bard's Tale

The magnificent General Post Office in Dublin (known to locals as the G.P.O.) that was so badly damaged during the Uprising of 1916 is standing today in fine form. Although the building was mostly destroyed during the battle, the original facade remains, and inside a monument commemorates the uprising.

In the end, the death toll for the day was 64 rebels, 130 British, and approximately 300 civilians. Irish nationalism had existed before that day, but the blood of its martyrs would make the ground even more fertile for patriotic fervor. The uprising and the executions that followed would change the way the Irish saw themselves forever. As the great poet William Butler Yeats would later describe the events of that day, "All is changed, changed utterly. A terrible beauty is born."

Executions, Day and Night

Although the rebels had thought themselves fighting for the common Irishman, the Irish weren't all that pleased about their efforts. Dubliners were angry with the resulting heavy civilian casualties, not to mention the ruin of their beautiful city. In some cases, the rebels were even bombarded with rotten tomatoes! Although the Dubliners used the mayhem and confusion as an opportunity to do a bit of "free shopping" in the local stores, they mostly cursed their would-be benefactors. The rest of the country wasn't enthralled with their actions, either. For the most part, the general public either considered the IRB fools or showed a marked apathy about the whole bloody affair—until the executions began.

Britain took a very hard stand against the rebels; little or no mercy was shown. Beginning on May 3, 1916, and continuing for a week, they executed 15 rebels. Some of the cases were particularly pathetic or were considered unjust. Willie Pearse was shot only because he was unlucky enough to be Padraig Pearse's brother. An Irish rebel named James Connolly, with gangrenous wounds in his legs from battle, had to be carried to his execution site and tied in a chair before being shot.

When the Irish heard of the gruesome details of the executions, they sided with the rebels, and the dead leaders became martyrs, sacrificed on the altar for Erin's freedom. Suddenly, what had been an ill-fated, badly organized, unpopular uprising was an event to rally around. Without the 1916 Uprising, unsuccessful as it may have seemed at the time, the Irish might never have gained their independence. Maybe those heroes didn't die in vain after all.

The Least You Need to Know

➤ From the bitterness about the Great Hunger, a number of rebel organizations regrouped, and others were born, including Young Ireland, the Fenians, and the Irish Republican Brotherhood (IRB). They had differences of opinion on some issues, but they all had a common goal: to break the power England had held over Ireland for so long.

➤ The various rebellions were getting nowhere. Then along came a brilliant statesman named Charles Stewart Parnell, a Protestant landlord from County Wicklow and the unlikely champion for an Irish republic. He succeeded in having a couple of bills passed through parliament, but his career ended ignominiously when he was named a contributing party to a divorce after a long-term affair with a married woman.

➤ Discouraged and disillusioned about the hopes of political reform, the Irish began to take pride in their culture, resurrecting ancient Gaelic literature, song, dance, and the Irish language. This period was called the Gaelic Revival.

➤ A new party by the name of Sinn Fein appeared on the scene. This group was as dedicated to an Irish free republic as its enemy, the Orange Society, was opposed to the same.

➤ In 1914, a Home Rule Act of sorts was passed, but it was so full of holes as to be worthless. Then World War I began, and the whole issue was temporarily swept aside.

➤ The Easter Uprising of 1916 failed dismally. Not even the Irish supported the rebels until the conquered leaders were pathetically and systematically executed over the course of a week. The Irish in Ireland and in America were outraged. Their anger propelled the rebel forces into the next battle, a political one, but no less turbulent.

Chapter 16

The Irish Free State Is Born, but It's a Difficult Delivery

In This Chapter

➤ Sinn Fein declares Ireland's freedom and the War of Independence begins

➤ Michael Collins fights guerrilla style

➤ Sunday, Bloody Sunday

➤ Collins signs the Treaty, his death warrant

➤ The Irish stop fighting England and turn guns on each other

➤ Independence at last, but not for all

The Easter Uprising of 1916 succeeded in swinging public opinion to the side of those fighting for Irish independence from Britain, but the actual separation didn't come right away. Home Rule was still an unfulfilled dream for the Irish Catholics, a goal that seemed to move farther out of sight with every passing day. But in 1917, a glimmer of hope appeared on the horizon in the form of a tall, charismatic fellow named Michael Collins.

In this chapter, you will see how the soldier/politician Collins seduced both militant and peaceful factions to his cause. With the help of others, such as the war hero, Eamon de Valera, Collins would achieve independence for a large part of Ireland. But for some, part wasn't enough. The success of Michael Collins and others was considered a defeat by some, and that opinion would cost Collins his life.

The Players on the Giant Green Chessboard

Many different rebel groups had a hand in fighting for Ireland's independence, and a few other groups were opposed to Erin's sons and daughters breaking out from under British rule. Before we go any further, it might be helpful to recall some of the groups who have been active up to this time on both sides of Irish politics. The following is a short list of those organizations and a few new ones:

Gift of Gab

"The Irish emigration into Britain is an example of a less civilized population spreading themselves, as a kind of substratum, beneath a more civilized community; and without excelling in any branch of industry, obtaining possession of all the lowest departments of manual labor."

—A section of the *Report on the State of the Irish Poor in Great Britain*

➤ **Young Ireland.** Founded in the early 1840s by Thomas Davis, an intellectual and Trinity College graduate, this group practiced uncompromising, defiant Irish nationalism and the veneration of heroes of past rebellions. It opposed Daniel O'Connell and his peaceful, political methods of reform, arguing that only force would bring about the desired independence of Ireland from England.

➤ **The Fenians.** Named after the ancient Irish warriors, the Fianna, and formed in 1858 by James Stephens after the tragedy of the Great Famine, this group wanted Ireland to permanently sever all ties with England. From 1858 on, the Fenians had two branches: the Irish Republican Brotherhood and the Fenian Brotherhood (later called Clan na Gael in America).

➤ **The Irish Republican Brotherhood (IRB).** Founded in 1858 and lead by former Fenian Tom Clarke, the IRB was considered the most effective of all Ireland's revolutionary national movements and was largely supported by American sympathizers from its inception. Under the leadership of poet/teacher Padraig Pearse, this group launched the Easter Uprising of 1916. A number of its members were among those executed by the British after the failed revolt.

➤ **The Irish Republican Army (IRA).** Created around 1918 by followers of Michael Collins and others fighting for Irish independence, this group was the right arm of Michael Collins during the War of Independence. Experts at guerrilla warfare, the members of the IRA waged covert battles against the British authorities.

➤ **Sinn Fein.** Formed in 1905 by journalist Arthur Griffith, Sinn Fein means "Ourselves" or "Ourselves Alone" depending on which expert in the Gaelic language you ask. This group originally supported the idea of Ireland having a separate parliament in Dublin, rather than being ruled by England's Westminster parliament. It also supported reforms that were as cultural as political, advocating a revival of the Gaelic language, Gaelic literature, and music. Sinn Fein was restructured around 1917 to include the IRB.

➤ **Royal Irish Constabulary (RIC).** These British military-style police enforced law in Ireland on behalf of the British Crown.

➤ **Black and Tans.** Recruited from England to supplement the RIC, these soldiers/police were hastily outfitted and wore uniforms that were half-military, half-police (part tan, part black). They were selected for their toughness and known for their brutality when dealing with the Irish public.

Mr. Collins Uses His Considerable Talents

In the struggle for Ireland's independence, a new warrior entered the fight by the name of Michael Collins. He was a brilliant organizer, with a quick, shrewd mind and a talent for getting business done.

Born in 1890 to a Catholic tenant farmer in Cork, the young Collins had worked as a clerk, a secretary, and accountant. Those skills would prove useful to him later, as he managed the finances of the Irish Army battling the British for Irish freedom. But Michael Collins wasn't your stereotypical conservative accountant type. He was fiercely passionate about his country, and he quickly climbed the ranks in the freedom movement.

As a member of the Irish Republican Brotherhood, he joined those who revolted in the Easter Uprising of 1916 and was arrested with them. One of the lucky ones who escaped execution, he took up the battle for independence as soon as he was released from prison. Collins realized the folly of armed rebellions and uprisings that would only be squelched by the superior military of the British. He had other methods up his sleeve when it came to dealing with the British.

The newly formed Irish Republican Army (IRA) became Collins's primary weapon in his guerrilla assault against the Royal Irish Constabulary (the RIC). "The Big Fellow," as Collins was called by his compatriots, thought nothing of ordering the execution of RIC intelligence officers if they refused to heed his warnings and desert their post.

Sinn Fein on the Rise

In spite of his tactics, Collins had the support of the non-violent Sinn Fein members, including its founder, Arthur Griffith. At that time Sinn Fein was a soup kettle with many ingredients: the Irish Republican Brotherhood (IRB), the Irish Volunteers, as well as their regular members. In 1917, Sinn Fein had grown to a quarter of a million and was a power to be reckoned with. They were largely supported by funds donated by Americans who had been appalled by the executions following the 1916 Uprising.

At Last, the Cord Is Severed

If there was truly a moment that marked Ireland's long overdue separation from Great Britain, it was the election of December 1918, when the Sinn Fein party won by an avalanche. Having won 73 seats to their opposition's (the Nationalists) 6, they could write their own agenda, and they did. They announced the separation of Britain and Ireland. Ireland would have her own parliament in Dublin, called Dail Eireann, which means Irish Assembly, and Eamon de Valera, a patriot who had fought as a rebel in the Easter Uprising of 1916 and lived to tell about it, would be president.

A Bard's Tale

If you're wondering why a lad who was such a prominent figure in Irish politics had a name like de Valera, here's the answer: Eamon de Valera was born in 1882 in the United States to a Spanish father and an Irish mother. The fact that he was American born just may have saved him from execution when he was imprisoned for his participation in the Easter Uprising of 1916.

Independent? Says You!

The British weren't about to take Ireland's declaration of independence lying down, and the War of Independence began. It would continue until 1921. Once again, Ulster wasn't of the same mind as the rest of the island. Her Protestant majority, especially the Orangemen (see Chapter 12), wasn't at all interested in becoming the minority members of an Irish Catholic republic. They hadn't even wanted Home Rule, let alone a severance of all ties with England.

The War of Independence began in Tipperary, a county in south-central Ireland where a couple of constables (policemen) from the Royal Irish Constabulary were shot by Irish Volunteers. Although it is believed that their actions were *not* ordered by Michael Collins, we can suppose that he was supportive. Thus began the executions of British figures of authority at the hands of the IRA.

Before the war, Michael Collins had spent much of his efforts raising funds for the republican movement, but now he turned that brilliant mind toward organizing the guerrilla war against the RIC. The IRA laid ambushes, raided police stations and stole the weapons stored there, and attacked patrols. Considering the brutality of the RIC, as well as their auxiliary force called the Black

'Tisn't So!

When the Orangemen first came into being in 1795, they were known to swear to this motto: "In the awful, presence of Almighty God, I do solemnly swear that I will to the utmost of my power support the King and the present government and I do further swear that I will use my utmost exertions to exterminate all the Catholics of the Kingdom of Ireland."

and Tans (excessive violence, burnings and looting, unwarranted beatings, questionable killings, unjust imprisonments, and, worst of all, punishing the Irish civilians for the activities of the rebels), Collins and his followers suffered no attacks of conscience over their killings. The British saw these killings as murders, but the IRA called them executions.

Between the RIC, the Black and Tans, and the British army, the Crown's troops numbered approximately 40,000. The IRA had only 3,000 to 5,000 members. Although he could easily be criticized for his terrorist tactics, Michael Collins believed he was evening the odds the only way he could.

Gift of Gab

"These Irish are really shocking, abominable people—not like any other civilized nation."

—Queen Victoria

A Bard's Tale

If you sidle up to a bar, you might see the publican pouring a drink called a Black and Tan. Yes, the drink was named after those notorious British police auxiliaries in the early 1900s. The beverage is a concoction made of a pale ale (the Tan part) topped with Guinness (a dark ale, which constitutes the Black part).

Bloody Sunday

On November 21, 1920, 14 British officers, all believed to be covert British intelligence, were executed by an armed IRA detail dispatched by Michael Collins. Some of the Brits were murdered in front of their wives, a fact that didn't sit at all well with the IRA's critics. Collins would later defend his actions by stating his belief that those who were killed had been plotting the death of IRA members. He explained: "I found out that those fellows we put on the spot were going to put a lot of us on the spot, so I got in first."

But the killing wasn't over. Later in the afternoon, the Black and Tans retaliated in a particularly barbaric fashion, mowing down 12 people with machine guns at an All-Ireland Gaelic football game in Croke Park. Firing indiscriminately into the crowd, they also wounded 60 others. That evening two IRA men and a completely innocent Sinn Feiner, who had mysteriously been brought in for "questioning," were killed in Dublin Castle for "attempting to escape."

'Tisn't So!

When the Black and Tans were dispatched to Drogheda, they posted notices that read: "If in the vicinity a policeman is shot, five of the leading Sinn Feiners will be shot.... Stop the shooting of the police or we will lay low every house that smells of Sinn Fein."

In the days that followed, the violence escalated as the IRA carried out more attacks against the Black and Tans, and the British police retaliated. In Cork, 11 officers were killed in an IRA ambush. In retaliation, the Black and Tans burnt the city center of Cork and cut the hoses of the firemen who were trying to extinguish the blazes. In Balbriggan, County Dublin, an RIC officer was killed, so the British set the town afire, burning several creameries—a common practice for the Black and Tans because creameries provided both food and industry for a town. Again, the common folk of Ireland were paying for the activities of the IRA.

From Bloody Sunday on, the war escalated, enveloping the country. The Irish folk were in a terrible spot, caught in the violent cycle of terror and counter-terror. The war was a no-holds-barred misery with all rules of "civilized warfare" abandoned. Anything went. Even though not all of the Irish supported the IRA (some were put off by their hard-fisted tactics), the British troops assumed all native Irish were IRA sympathizers. No one felt safe in their beds at night, because they could be raided by troops at all hours looking for IRA members under the beds.

Michael Collins Signs His Own Life Away

By the time 1921 rolled around, the battle had proven long and difficult, and Michael Collins could see that the IRA was losing. They couldn't hold out much longer. Fortunately, the Brits didn't know how rag-tag they had become. Had the British known how close they were to winning the battle, they might never have invited the Irish to come to England and "negotiate" an agreement. De Valera decided, for reasons that are still being debated, to stay at home and send Collins in his stead. Collins agreed, but reluctantly, stating that he was only going as a representative of the IRB, not for Ireland.

Once he arrived, Collins realized that the English were not in a bartering mood. After all the centuries of bloodshed between the two countries, Mother England still wanted things her way. Ireland could be independent, but on British terms. They insisted that Ireland be called a "free state," not a republic, and that the six Ulster counties (Antrim, Down, Armagh, Londonderry, Tyrone, and Fermanagh) be allowed to opt out and remain part of Britain, if they wished. Of course, they would wish, so Ireland still would not be completely free.

Even though the IRA had fooled the British, Collins knew that his forces were sorely weakened and felt he had no choice. He could accept the deal, flawed though it was, or return home and continue a battle they were sure to lose. He signed the agreement, saying, "I have signed my death warrant."

Back at home, the treaty passed the Irish parliament by a narrow margin of seven votes. De Valera walked away from the debate in tears and gave up his presidency. The IRA saw Collins as a traitor to their cause, because, in their eyes, he had surrendered part of Ireland to the British, rather than insisting on unity. In hopes of still achieving their goal of complete freedom from Britain for all of Ireland, they decided to continue fighting.

Brother Against Brother

Having just won a somewhat empty victory against Britain, the Irish now took up arms against each other. Those who had wanted to continue fighting until all of Ireland was free now considered themselves the adversaries of the "traitors" who had given the six northern counties to Britain. Collins's own IRA was now his enemy. Strangely enough, Collins and his new followers (those who defended the treaty) were supported by the British, who had been their bitter enemies before. The Brits were even supplying Collins's men with guns, which were being used against his old IRA comrades. The irony was just too cruel.

'Tisn't So!

Before journeying to County Cork in August 1922, Michael Collins was warned about the lack of security afforded by driving in an open-topped vehicle. "Sure, they won't shoot me in my own county," he said. He was wrong.

On a trip to County Cork in August 1922, Collins was warned about his safety when riding in a Rolls Royce with an open top. He was shot in the head during an ambush in Bealnamblath and died. He was 32 years old.

The Bitter Taste of Victory

In the end, the better-armed Free Staters, as they were called, won over the anti-treaty IRA forces. The Irish had their hollow victory; the treaty would stand, with Ireland divided. But even with the civil war ended, the IRA wouldn't accept their defeat. They wouldn't accept the new Free State or the Unionist government in Belfast. As far as they were concerned, Irishmen were still in bondage to England, and violence would continue to be used until Erin was free. It's apparent from the front page of any current Irish newspaper that many people continue to feel this way.

The Least You Need to Know

➤ Sinn Fein passed the act that finally severed Ireland's bonds to England, or so it seemed. Not only did Britain object, but the Orangemen of Ulster and the Ulster Protestants also wanted to remain part of England. The War for Independence began.

➤ Michael Collins led his IRA to conduct guerrilla warfare on the Royal Irish Constabulary and the British soldiers. Although they had a number of victories in the form of assassinations and so on, Collins knew they were going to lose the battle in the end.

➤ On a day known now as Bloody Sunday, Collins's IRA squad killed 14 British intelligence officers, some in front of their wives. A British auxiliary group called the Black and Tans retaliated by spraying a crowd at an All-Ireland football game with machine guns and killing 12 people. Two IRA prisoners in Dublin Castle were killed, as well as an innocent Sinn Feiner.

➤ Eamon de Valera, the president of the Irish Assembly, or Dail Eireann, sent Michael Collins to England to negotiate an agreement to end the conflict. Believing it was the only thing to do, Collins signed a treaty that gave most of Ireland independence as a "Free State" but kept Ulster under British control.

➤ The treaty was extremely unpopular back home with the IRA and other nationalists, spawning a civil war. Collins was seen as a traitor to his own cause. On August 1922, he was ambushed and shot to death.

➤ The Civil War between the Free Staters and the anti-treaty IRA ended with the Free Staters victorious, but it was an empty victory. Many IRA members refused to give up the fight until all of Ireland was "free of British tyranny." To this day, many *still* fight and believe their cause to be holy and just.

Chapter 17

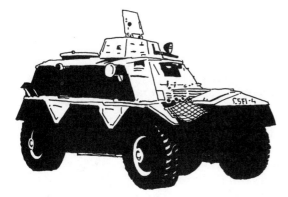

Eire's Growing Pains: The 20th Century in the Emerald Isle

In This Chapter

➤ Paramilitary activity increases as the Anglo-Irish Treaty brings more strife than peace

➤ With so much hate and violence, how can Ireland ever unify?

➤ World War II gives Northern Ireland the chance to show its loyalty to the Crown

➤ Abortion, divorce, birth control and other volatile issues

➤ The Peace Agreement, a new chance for peace?

You'd be hard-pressed to find a nation that didn't experience growing pains during the twentieth century. Ireland is no exception. The birth of the Free State was certainly a leap in the right direction for Irish independence, but not everyone was satisfied with this deal, and they showed their disappointment. In addition to the never-ending struggle between the North and the Republic, hints of a new, modern world began washing up the island's shores. Issues were debated that this Catholic nation never dreamed would be in question: divorce, birth control, and abortion. A woman became president of Eire. Finally, talk of peace became the subject of many a newspaper's front page. In this chapter, I'll take you through the events of this past century in Ireland and see where the Emerald Isle stands as we approach a new millennium.

The North Wants to Keep the Crown

Throughout history, the province of Ulster had consisted of nine counties. While negotiating the Anglo-Irish Treaty, which separated the southern Free State of Ireland from Northern Ireland, the British offered the Unionists those nine counties. But they chose to take only six, the six with the highest percentage of Protestants. If they had elected to keep all nine of the ancient counties, the Catholics would have constituted 43 percent of the populace. This was too high a percentage for Protestant comfort, hence, the decision to go with six. As the ruling majority, they could be assured of maintaining control over the area and remaining the Protestant "Ascendancy." Although there was a Belfast parliament, the British Westminster parliament held the reins and would still make all-important decisions regarding finance, foreign policy, defense, and external trade for Northern Ireland.

The British had never intended for the separation of Northern Ireland and the Free State of Ireland to be permanent. They had foreseen this separation as a temporary measure that would be reversed further down the line with Northern Ireland being peacefully absorbed into the Free State. But the Unionists vehemently opposed any action in that direction. If they were joined to the Free State, they would become the minority in a primarily Catholic country, subject to the will of those they considered to be their long-standing enemies. As subjects of the Crown, they enjoyed the privileges of British protection and financial assistance, as well as the prestige of being part of Great Britain, historically one of the most powerful forces in Europe and beyond. As the Protestant Unionists saw it, they had everything to gain by staying part of England and nothing to achieve by joining the Irish Free State.

The Blood Still Flows

The Catholics were far less happy about the new arrangement. So many lives had been lost and so much suffering had occurred in the fight for Ireland's complete independence from England that traditionalists were bitter, believing those losses to have been in vain because part of Ireland still remained under British control. In protest, the IRA escalated its violence, but their efforts only served to make their lot worse in the end.

Northern Ireland's first prime minister, Sir James Craig, formed a specific branch of the police force, the "B Special" constabulary to deal with the problem. Their tactics were particularly heavy-handed, and the Catholics hated them. Safeguarding the rights of the Catholic minority was not high on the list of the British authorities. The Unionist government also passed the Civil Authorities Act of 1922, otherwise known as the Special Powers Act. This act gave the authorities even more control, allowing them to flog republican suspects and making the possession of firearms a capital offense.

'Tisn't So!

Although the Irish Republican Army (IRA) has been known for its boldness, a few critics during the 1920s said the letters "IRA" should stand for "I Run Away." Though if these critics were wise, they wouldn't have said this to the IRA lads' faces. Certainly, running away is not the way they gained their fiercely passionate reputations.

Traditional republicans became all the more determined to oust the British from "their land." Their covert activities became blatant rioting. Between 1920 and 1922, 450 people, mostly Catholics, were killed in the clashes between republican sympathizers and authorities. Things were so bad that many Catholic families fled across the border into the Free State.

The Gap Becomes a Chasm

The deaths, injuries, and suffering caused by this fighting caused the gap between the Catholics and the Protestants to become an ever-widening chasm. The idea of gradually absorbing the six northern counties into the rest of the Irish Free State by peaceful, constitutional means became less and less plausible. Patriotic passions flared, and the paramilitary groups responded with attacks and counter-attacks. The violence peaked in 1935 when 11 people were killed in Belfast riots and hundreds of Catholic families were driven from their homes.

Troubles at Home in the Free State

When Eamon de Valera was elected in 1932 to lead the Free State, the Unionists in Northern Ireland became even more nervous. De Valera was known for his determination to make Northern Ireland one with the rest of the island. He made his intentions even clearer when drawing up the 1937 Constitution of the Free State, in which Article 2 stated, "The national territory consists of the whole island of Ireland, its islands, and the territorial seas." The Constitution also claimed a jurisdiction over 26 counties pending the "reintegration of the national territory." These were fighting words to the Protestant North.

In 1939, the IRA conducted a particularly bold raid of a government arsenal within Free State territory itself, in Dublin's Phoenix Park. They scored a massive amount of weaponry. This robbery against the Free State itself caused a reluctant de Valera to pass an Offenses Against the State Act so that IRA suspects could be interned. A Treason Act was also passed, which later resulted in four IRA men being executed.

'Tisn't So!

Although some may think of flogging as nothing more than a serious spanking, flogging was a deadly serious business to the British, who were experts at administering them. Most flogging victims, which included suspected republican sympathizers, would go unconscious during the beatings from shock and/or blood loss. The person being flogged sometimes died as a result of the terrible injuries the whips caused. Those who survived were often permanently maimed, with severed nerves and muscles.

A Bard's Tale

The famous lion who roared at the beginning of MGM movies lived in Dublin's Phoenix Park zoo. Well, he didn't do the actual roaring, but he was the one who opened his mouth so wide and impressed several generations of moviegoers with his incisors. In fact, he was yawning. A proper African lion supplied the roar after the fact.

'Tisn't Easy North of the Border, Either

Besides worrying about their neighbors to the south absorbing them and unifying them against their will, the Northern Ireland Protestants had internal pressures of their own: They were suffering an economic depression. Between 1920 and 1940, unemployment rates hovered at a high 25 percent. During that time, the Ulster slums were some of the worst in Europe:

➤ Eighty-seven percent of the rural houses had no running water.

➤ Tuberculosis ravaged the communities, killing many under the age of 25.

➤ The infant mortality rate was shockingly high, as was the number of mothers who died during childbirth.

Although, certainly, a wide cross-section of the populace was in misery, the Catholics were in much worse straits than the Protestants, and their woes were made more difficult by the bigotry against them. Even Sir Basil Brooke, who would serve as the prime minister of Northern Ireland from 1943 to 1963, proudly boasted that he didn't employ Catholics, none whatsoever! Unfortunately, his opinion was shared by a large percentage of the Protestant populace. Protestants weren't all that popular with the Catholics, either. Loving thy neighbor wasn't widely practiced at that time in Northern Ireland.

The Irish War Effort

During World War II, Northern Ireland had the opportunity to show its loyalty to the Crown. It provided an important sea base, and its aircraft and shipbuilding industries made a valuable contribution to England's war effort. Northern Ireland suffered for its allegiance, though. Germany bombed it in several raids. In 1941, 700 citizens of Belfast were killed, and 100,000 were rendered homeless in bombing raids.

On the other hand, the Free State under Eamon de Valera remained decidedly neutral. The Unionists pointed to this "disloyalty" as proof of the lack of character of the Catholics and their Free State. The factions became even more clearly polarized.

When the war was over, Northern Ireland, as well as the rest of the United Kingdom, received new benefits from Britain for its war efforts. Northern Ireland received free health care and welfare benefits for its citizens, as well as funding for secondary schools and universities.

The economic status of Northern Ireland greatly improved after the war. Modernizing agricultural practices resulted in greater exports of livestock and grains. Britain provided generous grants to develop industry in Northern Ireland, and the province flourished. Among the Catholics, however, unemployment rates remained high. The majority lived well below the poverty line, as they continued to suffer from exclusionary hiring practices.

Speak Plain Irish

The **Irish Free State** was created in 1922 and continued until Eire seceded from the Commonwealth in 1948 and proclaimed itself the **Republic of Ireland.** The new constitution suggested this act was a step toward ending the separation of Northern Ireland from the southern Republic, but that wording was only rhetoric. The separation still exists today.

Republican Fervor Flares Again and Again

In 1956, the IRA began a new movement to end the partition of Ireland. Within the next six years, 19 IRA members and several British authorities were killed. Property damages amounted to more than a million *pounds*. The majority of the Catholics were too consumed with their own financial problems to offer active support to the rebels. In 1962, the IRA halted their campaign, citing the apathy of their own people as the reason for its failure.

Speak Plain Irish

The unit of currency presently used in Ireland is the Irish **pound,** or **punt.** A million pounds would translate into (at the time this book was written) about $1,500,000.

The lull in patriotic passions was temporary and short-lived. In 1968–69, several incidents occurred that incited yet another wave of republican insurrection:

➤ The prime minister of Northern Ireland from 1963 to 1969, Terence O'Neill, attempted to appease the Catholics by visiting a few of their schools. This small gesture of reconciliation was met with extreme hostility from certain Protestants.

➤ O'Neill also met with the prime minister of the Irish Republic, Sean Lemass. Both of these moves were called "moving towards Rome" by a Presbyterian minister named Ian Kyle Paisley.

➤ In 1968, a group of Catholic students created the People's Democracy Movement, based on the Civil Rights Movement in the United States. Some Unionists accused the People's Democracy Movement of being nothing more than a front for the IRA. The B Specials were used to put down demonstrations by the People's Democracy Movement, and they did so with great enthusiasm.

Protestant Protest

On January 30, 1972, Ireland was to suffer yet another "Bloody Sunday." That day in Derry, 13 unarmed Catholics were killed by soldiers of the First Parachute Regiment during a march protesting the internment of Catholic prisoners.

On the other side of the political fence, the hard-line, brilliant, and highly energetic spokesman for the anti-Catholic movement, Reverend Ian Kyle Paisley, formed the Democratic Unionist Party, a group as ardent in its unionist ideology as the rebel organizations were in their republican attitudes. At one point, the police stood by, refusing to intervene, when a mob of Paisley's followers stoned Catholic demonstrators outside Londonderry. Unrest increased as B Specials terrorized Belfast Catholics. The vicious cycle escalated as more rebel uprisings were met with heavier-handed tactics by the military. With each episode of violence, Paisley's party grew in numbers and strength. The more he preached against the Catholics, the more they rose to oppose. Blood flowed, once again staining Eire's green land an ugly red.

The IRA Split

Around this time, a change occurred in the ranks of the IRA. A new Chief of Staff, an intellectual fellow named Cathal Goulding, favored the use of political activity instead of violence to achieve their ends. The more traditional IRA members disagreed with this stance, which they saw as weak and ineffectual. In 1970, these members left the IRA, formed what they called the Provisional IRA, and declared their goal: to raise arms against the British forces in Northern Ireland.

The Provisional IRA, also called the PIRA or the Provos, didn't have the support of the majority of the Northern Irish Catholics for quite some time. But continued aggression on the part of the British army and the B Special forces toward the Catholics pushed them to the Provos' side.

Random acts of violence, shootings, and bombings became commonplace. Attacks and retaliations occurred with ever increasing frequency and brutality. A tragic cycle had begun that would continue decade after decade and is still going on today.

Abortion, Divorce, Birth Control, and Other Touchy Topics

Since Ireland had received the Christian religion from St. Patrick, the Irish had adhered more strictly to its commandments than many peoples who had converted. Some historians attribute this high degree of obedience to the ancient Celts' reverence for law, originally brehon law, which transferred to the precepts of the Catholic Church. Although many societies are Catholic in name, but don't feel especially obliged to follow the teachings of the church to the letter, the Irish traditionally have been ardently faithful to the rules handed down by Rome. This faith has never been more obvious than in the issues of abortion and divorce. During the 1980s and even into the '90s, these and other highly controversial issues tore at the already tattered fabric of Irish society.

'Til Death Do Us Part and Not Before

The church's position on divorce has always been clear and simple: No divorce! Marriage was not to be dissolved unless there were strong grounds for an annulment. According to the Catholic law, you may receive an annulment if the marriage was proven to have never truly existed in the eyes of the Church and, therefore, God.

The largely Catholic population of the Free State, later to become the Republic of Ireland, wrote this position into law, making divorce illegal. As a result, those who no longer chose to live together as husband and wife and could not obtain an annulment from the Church (a difficult process to be sure) had only one choice: to remain separated, but still legally married. People could not divorce one individual and marry a second time.

No doubt this "no divorce" law resulted in some couples working through difficult times and healing a wounded marriage, but the law had other, less positive results, forcing people to live in loveless marriages and stay with mates who were physically and emotionally abusive. Those who decided to live separately did not have the opportunity to form another, more successful union with some new love interest. Because the Church was equally opposed to intimate relationships between unmarried people, a separated person who was unable to reconcile with their mate was denied the joys of sexual companionship for the rest of their lives.

Most Irish Catholics embraced this law, believing it strengthened family bonds and prevented the frivolous disposal of one's mate and the breaking of one's sacred matrimonial vows. North of the border, where divorce was legal, the Protestants pointed to the divorce prohibition as evidence of Rome's "stranglehold" on their neighbors. They argued that even if divorce were legal and therefore an option for Protestants and other non-Catholics living in the Republic, the Church's ruling would still be in effect for the Catholics.

On June 26, 1986, a referendum was presented to the people of the Republic of Ireland, which would have lifted the ban. At first, the polls indicated that it might pass. But the opposition campaigned vigorously and the referendum was soundly defeated by a 63 percent majority voting against it. The Irish people had made their wishes clear on the matter: No divorce.

Pro-Choice Versus Pro-Life in Eire

In the early 1980s, in the wake of the U.S. Supreme Court's ruling that upheld a woman's right to have an abortion in America, the Republic of Ireland's government became nervous that such an action might be taken in their country. Adamantly opposed to abortion under almost any circumstance (most elected officials agreed, at least unofficially, that abortion would be acceptable in the case of an ectopic pregnancy or uterine cancer), government officials wanted to assure that the anti-abortion laws couldn't be undermined in any way. They wrote an amendment to their Constitution, which read:

> Nothing in the Constitution shall be invoked to invalidate or to deprive of force or effect a provision of the law on the grounds that it prohibits abortion.

The referendum to add the amendment was passed by a two-thirds majority. Although the wording of that amendment might be as clear as a mudhole in a Killarney road, the meaning was plain: The Irish government had no intention of changing the Constitution's anti-abortion law.

'Tisn't So!

Although some might think that Ireland's anti-abortion laws prohibit all Irish women from receiving abortions, this isn't so. An estimated 4,000 Irish women per year travel to Great Britain to receive abortions.

The world became aware of the Irish stance against abortion and its ramifications in 1992. That year, the Irish Attorney General took out an injunction against a 14-year-old girl who had been raped to prevent her from going to England for an abortion. Even in Ireland, there was an outcry on the girl's behalf, and the case was referred to the Supreme Court. As the girl had threatened to commit suicide if she was forced to continue the pregnancy to full term, the injunction was lifted on the grounds that the mother's life was in danger. Also, they decided that the European Community law, guaranteeing freedom of movement between countries, superseded Ireland's anti-abortion laws and amendment. The girl could go wherever she chose, including to Britain for her abortion.

In November 1992, three referendums concerning abortion were presented to the voters. They addressed the following issues:

➤ The right to receive information about abortion services

➤ The right to travel somewhere to receive an abortion

➤ The mother's right to life, should the pregnancy present a mortal threat to her

The first two passed, while the third failed, because all sides were dissatisfied with the wording.

Birth Control: A Bitter Pill to Swallow

In the Republic of Ireland, contraceptives were illegal, as was giving of advice about birth control methods. After waging a vigorous battle with feminists, the government did relent slightly in this area, allowing contraceptives to be sold to married people. Then in 1985, a bill was passed that legalized the sale of condoms without prescriptions to people over the age of 18, but only through chemists and health boards. New laws, enacted in January 1993, allowed the sale of contraceptives, regardless of age, and lowered the age of sexual consent to 17.

'Tisn't So!

Who says the Irish aren't keeping up with modern life? Another milestone that occurred in this Catholic nation in June of 1993 was the legalization of homosexuality between consenting adults.

A Lady in the President's Seat

In 1990, the feminists, the trade unions, and the Labour Party scored a resounding victory by electing one of their champions, Mary Robinson, to the office of president. The daughter of two doctors who holds a master's degree from Harvard Law School, Mrs. Robinson was an accomplished academic lawyer and Labour Party member of the Senate for 20 years. The mother of two was married to a Protestant banker, who had also been a political cartoonist for the *Irish Times*. An outspoken supporter of women's issues, she actively campaigned for divorce, contraception, and women's rights. The first female president of Ireland, she was elected by a 52 percent majority.

Speak Plain Irish

In Ireland, the office of president is a highly prestigious position, but it isn't the highest office in the land, as it is in the United States. In the Irish government, the prime minister (in Gaelic, the *Taoiseach*) wields the most power, not the president.

A Bard's Tale

Although Mary Robinson was the first woman president to be elected in Ireland, it isn't so surprising that the modern Irish, descendants of the ancient Celts, would place a woman in a high position of leadership. Thousands of years ago, their forefathers (and foremothers) had no problem with female warriors and leaders. Some of the most ruthless, effective warrior-leaders in Irish history were women. Mary Robinson stood in company with the likes of Grace O'Malley, the pirate queen who ruled the Clew Bay area of northwestern Ireland during the same period as her chief rival, Elizabeth I, ruled England.

Peace After So Long?

Just when some were believing there would never be peace on Eire's fair island, a glimmer of hope glowed in the darkness. As of the writing of this book, it appears that the goal of a peaceful solution may be within reach for the Irish people.

In mid-1997, the IRA declared a cease-fire for the purpose of seeking a peaceful settlement. In September of that year, representatives of Sinn Fein (still the political wing of the IRA) sat at a negotiation table with Great Britain, the Republic of Ireland, and Northern Ireland. A month later, for the first time in 76 years, a British prime minister, newly elected Tony Blair, met one-on-one with the leader of the Irish Republicans, Sinn Feiner Gerry Adams.

The Americans Lend a Hand

Hoping that outside help might aid the peace talks, the prime minister of the Republic of Ireland, Bertie Ahern, met with U.S. President Bill Clinton in December 1997 in Washington, D.C. Clinton agreed to "stay personally involved…in however ways I can be helpful."

Another prominent American with a passion for Ireland, U.S. Senator George J. Mitchell of Maine, chaired the ongoing meetings. As always, when Irishmen sat down to agree on something they felt passionate about, several major issues seemed impossible to resolve. Hopes were not high; the situation seemed difficult.

But the peacemakers surprised everyone. On April 10, 1998, representatives of several political parties (including the Ulster Unionist Party, Sinn Fein, the Ulster Democratic Party, the Labour Party, and the Social Democratic Party) crafted what would later be known as the Good Friday Agreement. The basics of the agreement were as follows:

➤ The political institutions of Northern Ireland would be reorganized to include a new, 108-member assembly to be called the Northern Ireland Assembly. They would govern Northern Ireland, thus ending 26 years of direct rule from Britain.

➤ The new Northern Ireland Assembly would assume the form of a governing cabinet. The majority political party would endorse a prime minister.

➤ A North-South Ministerial Council would form an assembly of legislative leaders from the Republic of Ireland and Northern Ireland.

➤ The Council of the Isles, another newly formed group, would meet twice a year and would consist of representatives from the parliaments of Britain, Ireland, and the new assemblies established in Northern Ireland, Wales, and Scotland.

➤ The Republic of Ireland would delete all references from its Constitution that made claims on Northern Ireland.

When the agreement was offered as a referendum to the Irish voters on May 22, 1998, 85 percent passed it (71 percent of voters in Northern Ireland, 95 percent in the Republic of Ireland).

Gift of Gab

As the Good Friday Peace Agreement negotiations drew to a close, the articulate Irish Prime Minister Bertie Ahern said, "Today's agreement is a victory for peace and democratic politics. We have seized the initiative from the men of violence. Let's not relinquish it, now or ever."

Undoing the Final Knots

Agreeing to peace and implementing it are two different things. Transforming the precepts written on paper into workable policy has proven to be a highly difficult task, especially in such sensitive areas as police reform, disarming militants, and freeing prisoners in Northern Ireland.

Recently, a number of horrible bombings have caused some to wonder if the "troubles" will ever be over in Ireland. But the Irish people declare they have had enough of killing, vengeance, and suffering. With their votes, they have spoken to those revolutionaries who want to continue the war. They have asked them not to fight on their behalf. Peace is more dear to the war-weary heart of the average Irish person than the dream of unification.

The hopeful, opening words of the Good Friday Peace Agreement state: "We, the participants in the multiparty negotiations, believe that the agreement we have negotiated offers a truly historic opportunity for a new beginning. The tragedies of the past have left a deep and profoundly regrettable legacy of suffering. We must never forget those who have died or been injured, or their families. But we can best honor them through a fresh start, in which we firmly dedicate ourselves to the achievement of reconciliation, tolerance, and mutual trust and to the protection and vindication of the human rights of all."

The Least You Need to Know

➤ After the Anglo-Irish Treaty that Michael Collins and others signed, there was more strife than peace in the newly divided Ireland.

➤ When World War II arrived, Northern Ireland provided valuable assistance to Britain's war effort, gaining the Crown's loyalty for years to come. This loyalty was repaid later in the form of welfare, health, and education benefits, among others.

➤ Faithful to the teachings of the Catholic Church, the Republic of Ireland has faced difficult decisions on how to handle the subjects of divorce, abortion, and birth control.

➤ The Good Friday Peace Agreement, drafted on Good Friday in 1998, has given the Irish new hope that, perhaps, a lasting peace can finally be achieved.

Part 4
Erin's Hall of Fame

Part 4 introduces you to a cast of characters who make up the Irish Hall of Fame. Policemen, politicians, and soldiers, who exemplify Irish courage, honor, and sacrifice, have earned their place in this distinguished gallery. And then there are the bards. From the ancient Celts who spun their heroic legends and snared their listeners' imaginations to the modern playwrights whose work is being produced on New York's Broadway today, the Irish have always been master storytellers. Their tales have touched the hearts of the world for thousands of years and will continue to do so for as long as people gather together during the hours between sunset and sunrise to enjoy the bards' art.

Chapter 18

Making Their Way American Style: Politicians, Soldiers, Police, and Boxers

---

In This Chapter

➤ The Irish knack for politics

➤ Labor unites under Irish leadership

➤ Irish lads fight and die valiantly in America's battles

➤ That swaggering lad with the badge and the billy club

➤ Those fighting Irish boxer boys

For hailing from such a gentle and unassuming land, the Irish have certainly had their share of strife and struggle. But as the saying goes, that which does not kill you will make you stronger. Indeed, the Irish are a hearty bunch. Despite the many invaders that tried to obliterate or subjugate this nation of people, the Irish have survived and thrived through the most difficult of toil. You may find an Irish lad or lass to be quick with a smile and joke, but don't let this easy-going nature fool you: The Irish are a strong, proud, and driven nation of people. The sons and daughters of Erin accomplished great things, not the least of which occurred in their new country, the United States. In this chapter, we'll take a look at the contributions of the Irish to that melting pot they dove into.

Politics: Blarney Took Them Far

If ever an occupation required a laddie's silken tongue it was politics. Not only did the Irish have an advantage over many other groups of immigrants because they already spoke English when they arrived in America, but having virtually "swallered the Blarney stone," most Irish could talk circles around their non-Irish opponents.

Some of America's finest politicians boasted Irish heritage, including members of congress and mayors of major cities. Five of our early presidents hailed from Irish stock: Andrew Jackson, James Knox Polk, James Buchanan, Chester Alan Arthur, and Woodrow Wilson. Ireland also gave us powerful union leaders, who strove for the rights of the common laborer, a cause always close to the Irish heart.

Whether president, ward boss, or labor organizer, the gift of gab served the Irish well in their new country. Having seen the tragic lot of a people without power, the Irish knew all too well the importance of having some degree of control over one's own existence. In the old country, a man could seize power only by risking his life and often the lives of others in war or rebellion. But in the United States, a person who had a way with words and people could rise to the top of the world and maybe even make society a better place for himself, his family, and community.

Bardic Tools Serve Them Well

If the Irish had a talent for anything, it was the ability to negotiate between warring factions. Coming from a land with a long history of clan wars and the arbitrations necessary to end them armed the Irish with mediation skills far above average. When Irishmen landed in America, they saw a shining opportunity awaiting them: Just make peace between some lads who were banging their heads together, and you had yourself a fine job!

The Irish were also good at interceding on behalf of the new waves of immigrants. They understood all too well the unique problems of those who had recently arrived in a strange country. As politicians, they were in an ideal situation to both assist the newcomers and to gain their undying loyalty and, of course, their votes.

Another advantage of having Celtic bards for grandfathers was the ability to insult your enemy with grace and acerbic wit. In political debate, an articulate Irishman could cut his opponent off at the knees with one verbal blow, usually much to the amusement of everyone present (except, of course, the fellow kneeling).

To Attention, Boys! Here Comes the Ward Boss!

Gaining a political office meant power, and keeping that office meant job security. With such a carrot dangling in the air, not all Irish politicians maintained altruistic motives like improving the world and serving the public.

In the major cities of the United States during the mid-1800s, the concept of the Irish "boss" was emerging. Called "ward bosses," these fellows controlled much of daily life within their wards (election districts of a city). These fellows weren't particular about how they gained the top position in their ward, nor were they picky about how they kept the office. The more powerful of them wielded an enormous amount of control over their constituents; they decided which jobs went to whom and who lived where. They charged handsomely for these so-called "services." Often they extorted protection money and collected bribes to overlook the graft, vice, and crime going on in their districts.

A Bard's Tale

Thomas "Tip" O'Neill, Speaker of the U.S. House of Representatives and member of Congress for 34 years, was as Irish as American Irish get and proud of it. When his grandfather and two great-uncles came to America in 1855, they were so emotionally traumatized by the horrors of the Great Hunger that they immediately purchased burial plots, as they put it, "just in case."

This grassroots style of politics helped many of the immigrants. In effect, the ward boss could function as a buffer between the newcomer and his alien environment. But, no doubt, it hurt as much as it helped. Large numbers of hardworking innocents were exploited by these ruthless bosses, who made their already difficult lives even worse.

The Irish and the Democratic Party

Since Andrew Jackson's successful presidency in the 1830s, the Democratic Party had become a permanent fixture on the American scene, and it quickly became the affiliation of choice for the Irish immigrants. By the sheer power of their numbers alone, the Irish wielded a great deal of control over the nation's politics, almost from the moment they arrived. Even the lowliest on the economic and

Gift of Gab

The founder of the Democratic Unionist Party, Ian Paisley was both politician and fiery preacher. While delivering a sermon one day, he warned his congregation that sinners are condemned to eternal damnation, where there is much weeping and gnashing of teeth. An old lady exclaimed, "But I don't have no teeth. I wear dentures." Undaunted, Paisley roared, "Teeth will be provided!"

educational scale considered voting and political debate deadly serious duties. Their relationship with the Democratic Party culminated in the election of an Irish Catholic president, Erin's shining son, John Fitzgerald Kennedy.

Gift of Gab

"I want to express my appreciation to the governor for introducing me as potentially the greatest president in the history of this country. I think he is overstating it by a degree or two. George Washington wasn't a bad president, and I want to say a word for Thomas Jefferson, but otherwise I accept the compliment."

—John F. Kennedy in a 1960 speech

JFK, One of Ireland's Finest

John Fitzgerald Kennedy was not only the great-grandson of an Irish Famine emigrant, he was also from the same ancestry as that of Brian Boru, Son of Cennedi, a lineage that sired kings for all countries and all ages. Irishmen seldom agree on anything, but they are unified in their affection for the Kennedy family. They harbored a very special, deep affection for the handsome young man who would become President of the United States. The feeling was mutual.

Returning Home in Triumph

When Kennedy visited Ireland in the summer of 1963, he spoke before the Irish parliament and said, "The Ireland of 1963, one of the youngest of nations and the oldest of civilizations, has discovered that the achievement of nationhood is not an end, but a beginning. Other nations in the world in whom Ireland has long invested her people and her children are now investing their capital as well as their vacations in Ireland. This revolution is not yet over."

Irish commentator Garret Fitzgerald wrote of Kennedy: "He and the crowds understood each other. It was a relationship that no one who is not Irish can ever fully understand. The Irish, contrary to common belief, are not a sentimental people, and they have no time at all for those third or fourth generation Irish Americans who return to Ireland believing it to be full of leprechauns. John Kennedy was unsentimental too. He was tough, loved a laugh, and treated us as we really are. That's why he was different, and that's why we worship the Kennedy family."

The Irish took Kennedy to heart the moment he arrived on Irish soil. The love affair continued long past his assassination, only a year and a half after his visit—an event that was particularly painful for the Irish people. To this day, many homes display his picture in a place of honor, along with a photo of the pope.

A Bard's Tale

One Irish American woman who suffered greatly despite her position in life is Rose Kennedy, a mother who saw two of her sons, John F. Kennedy and Robert Kennedy, assassinated. Her pain and her bravery in the face of heartbreak are well-expressed in these words from an Irish poet that she had framed and placed on her wall:

Lord, I do not grudge
my two sons that I have seen go out to break their
strength and die, they and a few, in bloody protest
for a glorious thing.
They shall be spoken of among their people. The
generations shall remember them and call them
blessed.

But I will speak their names to my heart in
the long nights, the little names that were familiar
once round my dead hearth.
Though I grudge them not, I weary, weary of the
long sorrow.
And yet I have my joy.
They were faithful and they fought.

Workers Unite!

The Irish also found an opportunity to use their talents by organizing and leading labor unions. Already fiercely passionate about the mistreatment of the common man by management or ownership above him, they turned their hatred for English land-lords and Anglo masters toward those who owned businesses and exploited their workers.

Inside many mills and factories, on farms and in stockyards, the Irish immigrants were the unskilled labor. Those chosen for the higher paying jobs, such as supervisors or foremen, didn't come from the existing ranks; Anglos were brought in to fill those positions. As a result, the Irish workers had no way to gain a promotion. The situation looked all too familiar to the Irish immigrant working under an Anglo boss with no opportunity or authority to make his life better.

Irish controlled the unions in the stockyards, along with the Germans, who had immigrated in large numbers between 1865 and 1879. In the 1880s, tens of thousands of workers went on strike across the country. Much of their discontent was the result of agitation from the Irish.

The Molly Maguires: Those Lads Are Sporting Skirts!

The Molly Maguires had been a secret, agrarian society in Ireland from 1835 to 1855 that was formed to oppose landlords and their injustices toward their tenants. An offshoot of the sect, known as the Ancient Order of Hibernians, appeared in the United States and became active in the struggles of the coal miners in Pennsylvania. The members of this clandestine society dressed in disguise as women, hence the name Molly Maguires, when conducting their "business." This "business" consisted of acts of violence, sabotage, and arson. Although their methods may have been questionable, their cause was a worthy one.

Reform was badly needed in the coal industry at that time; the health, even the lives, of the miners was at stake. The miners were subjected to horribly dangerous conditions. They had to work in tunnels that were not always properly secured, and many lives were lost to cave-ins. Often they breathed toxic fumes, and many suffered severe lung ailments. The hours were long, and the pay was ridiculously low. To the Irish workers, these sorts of conditions were all too familiar and not to be tolerated.

The ranks of Molly Maguires expanded considerably after the American Civil War. In 1875, they initiated a strike among the Pennsylvania miners. But their membership was infiltrated by a Pinkerton detective, James McParlan, who turned evidence against them for their illegal acts of terrorism and sabotage. The leaders were executed, and many others were imprisoned. The Molly Maguires in the United States were scattered, and the organization dissolved in 1877.

A Bard's Tale

History had the last word on the matter of the Molly Maguires. In January 1979, Governor Milton J. Shapp of Pennsylvania granted a posthumous pardon for John Kehoe, who had been hanged over 100 years ago for his participation in the Molly Maguires. On that occasion, the governor said, "We can be proud of the men known as the Molly Maguires, because they defiantly faced allegations to make trade unionism a criminal conspiracy. These men gave their lives on behalf of the labor struggle."

Erin's Sons Spill Blood for Their New Country

From the very beginnings of the United States, Irish immigrants have sacrificed their lives for the freedom of their newly adopted nation as they had for the old. Many of the emigrants brought little more with them than the rags on their backs and hearts full of bitterness toward Britain. Once in the United States, many a young man happily added his own energies to whatever revolution or war was going on against England, in America or abroad.

The Troublemaking Irish Spark the Revolution

Irish immigrants supplied much of the energy behind the colonists' revolt against the British in the 18th century. Of those signing the Declaration of Independence, more were of Irish heritage (eight of the signatories) than any other foreign country. Among certain members of the British parliament, Irish Americans were credited with being the major troublemakers who were stoking the fires of rebellion among the colonists. Two witnesses testified before the British House of Commons that half of the Continental Army was Irish. This testimony was so distressing to one member of the House, he exclaimed, "We've lost America to the Irish!" In a sense, they did.

The Civil War, the Irish Blood Price

Although Irish immigrants were ready to go to battle for freedom in their new land, their intentions weren't always received with deserving hospitality. When the Irish crossed the Atlantic, they found the prejudice and bigotry that was present in their home country was rampant in their new one, as well. For all the American rhetoric about being the melting pot of the world and welcoming the huddled masses yearning to breathe freely, the picture wasn't always heartwarming. Sure, many Irish found the United States to be the land of the free and the home of the brave, but only if you were a white, male, Protestant. The earliest European settlers in the United States had been English, and they seemed to have brought their biases with them.

But something happened that gave these Americans cause to reconsider their opinion of the Irish Catholic immigrant: the Civil War or, as it was called at the time it was fought, the War Between the States. So viciously did the war rip the nation apart that Anglos put their grievances (like judging a man on the basis of religion) aside. Always good soldiers, the Irish showed their character and their heroism. They were especially esteemed for their uncommon kindness toward prisoners of war. They showed incredible compassion to their captured enemies, sharing scarce rations with them, caring for their injuries, and getting word to their families about their condition. These deeds caused the Protestant populace to concede the Irishman's worth as a citizen, a soldier, and a human being.

The Irish distinguished themselves on both sides of the Mason-Dixon Line. Ulysses Grant and "Stonewall" Jackson were both of Irish heritage. One distinguished Confederate soldier said he preferred to go to battle with an Irish soldier because of his

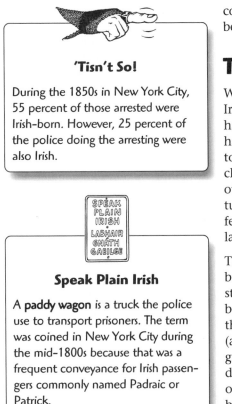

'Tisn't So!

During the 1850s in New York City, 55 percent of those arrested were Irish-born. However, 25 percent of the police doing the arresting were also Irish.

Speak Plain Irish

A **paddy wagon** is a truck the police use to transport prisoners. The term was coined in New York City during the mid-1800s because that was a frequent conveyance for Irish passengers commonly named Padraic or Patrick.

courage, his endurance, cleanliness, cheerfulness, and because he was more amenable to discipline.

The Irish Cop

When the terrible racism of the 1850s began to fade, the Irish began to rise in the ranks of society. Women who had been maids became nurses, and men in low-paying, hard-labor jobs became civil servants. Many Irish men took to walking a policeman's beat, armed with a billy club, that gift of gab that served them so well in all other areas of life, and a "way with people" that could turn a quarrel into a truce. Interestingly, some of the fellows being loaded into the *paddy wagons* as well as the lads loading these vehicles were Irish.

The stereotype of the big, swaggering cop with the Irish brogue twirling his nightstick and dispensing a bit of street justice here and there became a common sight, because many of the peace officers in the large cities of the Eastern Seaboard were Irish. Serving as a cop became (and remains) a family tradition with many. Great-grandfathers who kept the peace now have sons and daughters who proudly wear a badge. If, heaven forbid, one of them falls in the line of duty, sure you'll hear the bagpipes played at their funeral.

Boxing: Those Fighting Irish

The sport of boxing has always been a vehicle by which a poor minority member could rise above his circumstances and make a name for himself, not to mention a hatful of cash. Throughout the history of the sport, a number of groups have been represented by their champions: Italians, Blacks, Jews, Latinos, and, of course, the Irish.

Boxer John L. Sullivan, nicknamed the Boston Strong Boy, boasted upon entering saloons, "I can lick any man in the house." Sullivan was the last heavyweight champion to fight under London Prize Ring rules (bare knuckles, fight-to-the-finish). He later won under Queensberry Rules, with padded gloves, but then lost the championship to James J. Corbert on a 21st round knockout.

Born in Roxbury, Massachusetts on October 15, 1858, of Irish heritage, Sullivan was one of the most colorful, popular boxing champions of all time. Men would proudly claim to have shaken the hand that had shaken the hand that had shaken John L. Sullivan's hand. A heavy drinker, Sullivan gave up alcohol in later years and campaigned on behalf of temperance. He died in 1918 at the age of 59 in Abingdon, Massachusetts. John L. Sullivan held the heavyweight championship title for 10 years and is a member of the Boxing Hall of Fame.

Paddy Makes a Better Name for Himself

Through politics, great sacrifices in war, and athletic competition, the Irish began to be seen as something more than *shanty Irish*. That disparaging slur gave way to the more respectful phrase, *lace curtain Irish*. Though even that was sometimes murmured with contempt in a predominately Anglo-Protestant society, attitudes about the Irish were changing. As they were given the freedom to be themselves and to shape their own destinies, the Irish themselves began to change and evolve into an even more highly refined version of the noble race they had always been.

Speak Plain Irish

Shanty Irish and **lace curtain Irish** were racist terms that made the distinction between respectable and not-so-respectable Irish folk. Shanty Irish could probably be equated with the equally offensive term "white trash" used in the United States. Lace curtain Irish implies a certain level of gentility in those having the good taste to hang gauzy fabric in their windows.

The Least You Need to Know

➤ Possessing an Irishman's share of blarney set the Irish immigrants in good stead for entering the world of American politics, and they did, in droves.

➤ Having negotiated truces between warring factions for centuries, the Irish were skilled mediators, both in politics and in the labor unions. Their contributions to both fields are laudable.

➤ The Democratic Party was the affiliation of choice for the Irish immigrants. By sheer weight of their numbers, they assured the party's success and continuation.

➤ The peak of the Irish Catholic community's political success was the election of John F. Kennedy to the office of U.S. president. They mourned deeply upon his assassination.

➤ Racial bigotry against the Irish began to subdue after the nation saw their courage and great blood sacrifice during the War Between the States.

➤ A traditional occupation for the Irish was that of policeman. To this day, families uphold the tradition, with sons and daughters following in their great-grandparents' steps.

➤ Like many minority groups over the years, the Irish used the sport of boxing to better their difficult circumstances and rise in the world. One of the most famous boxers of all time was the great John L. Sullivan, the Boston Strong Boy, who was heavyweight champion for 10 years.

Chapter 19

The Irish Bards, Keeping the Words Alive

For a country so small, with few notable natural resources other than her emerald fields and spirited people, Ireland has had untold influence on the world's culture. As you know by having read this far (and from your own experience), the talent for stringing words together in attractive patterns is one of the Irish people's greatest gifts, to themselves and the world.

It would be a simplistic explanation to say the gift of gab is in the genetic makeup of a people. It would be fanciful to think it came from pressing your lips to that ever-famous Blarney stone. If the Irish are superb storytellers, it is probably due more to the fact that the storyteller, poet, bard, or *seanchai* has been deeply revered for centuries in Ireland.

Speak Plain Irish

A **seanchai** (pronounced *shawn-a-key*) is a person who is responsible for spreading stories from generation to generation. Usually, one person from each family or small community passes down the family lore.

In many societies, would-be bards hole themselves up in dark attics and bedrooms, pouring their souls out on paper (or on keyboards, as it is at the end of the 20th century), afraid to admit to their family and friends that they fancy themselves a writer. They don't want to be considered a flake in need of a "real" job. In contrast, those who engage in the literary arts in Ireland are highly esteemed; their work is encouraged, nurtured, and applauded. (If it's good, that is; the Irish are discriminating and difficult critics.) Literature is an essential part of Irish culture, and the reading of it is seen as an important pastime. To the Irish, great literature is the tangible expression of a people's soul. It is as much a part of the island as the sweet air, the soft water, and the verdant fields.

It is of little wonder, then, that some of the finest writers of all time have come from Ireland. Unfortunately, we can mention only a few here. It would take many, many thick volumes to do every one of them justice.

William Butler Yeats

Everyone who met William Butler Yeats, whether they were his friend or enemy, supporter or critic, declared him a strangely powerful man. They say his presence was palpable, and you knew he had entered a room even before you laid eyes on him. He was adored by many and hated by some, but no one was indifferent to W. B. Yeats. The man and his words stirred passion in others: sometimes anger, sometimes love, but never apathy.

'Tisn't So!

The story goes that Yeats confided to his close friend, poet F.R. Higgins, "Higgins, do you know that I have never been in a pub in my life, and I'd like to go into one." Higgins complied, but no sooner had they ordered drinks than Yeats declared, "Higgins, I don't like it. Lead me out again."

First published in *The Dublin University Review* in 1885, Yeats went on to pen an enormous and brilliant body of work, consisting of poetry, prose, plays, and political commentaries. Some of his best known pieces include: *Poems and Ballads of Young Ireland,* co-edited with Douglas Hyde, *The Wanderings of Oisin, Crossways,* and the play, *Cathleen ni Houlihan.* One of his last and most ambitious tasks was the editing of the controversial *Oxford Book of Poetry* in 1936. (Yeats' choice of selections for the book were controversial because they were decidedly pro-Irish.)

Yeats was the first Irishman to win a Nobel Prize for literature (in 1923). In 1915, he was offered a knighthood, but in a gracefully rebellious, traditionally Irish manner, he refused the honor, much to the amazement of the literary world and to the chagrin of the British crown.

Speaking to the People from the Stage

Yeats was a founding member of the Irish National Literary Society, and he formed the Irish Literary Theatre with his friend Augusta, also known as Lady Gregory. Both organizations served as vehicles to promote all things Irish: Gaelic culture, folklore, and of course, Irish nationalism. In 1904, the Literary Theatre moved into the Abbey Theatre in Dublin and presented plays that both intrigued and inflamed audiences, who were unaccustomed to Yeats's less than traditional views.

Through the theater, Yeats and Lady Gregory were able to shape public opinion at best and, at least, protect the rights of artists who were controversial, but talented and deserving of being heard. In their fight against censorship, Yeats and Gregory would often vigorously defend the rights of those with whom they disagreed, simply on the principle of artistic freedom.

At that time, both government and the public at large were greatly concerned that the written subject matter not contradict the teachings of the Church or reflect badly on the Irish people as a whole. Sensitive to how they were viewed by the world, the Irish wanted their artists to portray them as pure, virtuous, and moral in every way. But Yeats and the other writers of the Gaelic Revival chose to create characters who were endearing, but flawed. The creators and supporters of this fresh approach paid dearly for their innovation. Some were even pelted with rotten fruit and vegetables, proving that censorship could manifest itself in a number of unpleasant ways.

'Tisn't So!

Fascinated by Celtic mythology, W. B. Yeats was inspired by Standish Hayes O'Grady's translations of the tales of ancient, Irish heroes. Thus, many of his writings centered on the unseen world of the mystic, inhabited by fairy and ghost spirits. He was so fascinated by the spiritual realm that he occasionally sought the services of mediums.

Unrequited Love

The heart of a writer is not consumed by words alone. For W. B. Yeats, his passion for writing spilled over into another passion: the love of a woman he could not have. In one of his plays, *Kathleen ni Houlihan,* Yeats cast in the leading role an exquisitely beautiful, highly spirited actress named Maud Gonne. Maud was quite the activist in her day, supporting the causes of the poor in the slums of Dublin. Yeats fell in love with Maud, but he lost the opportunity to truly court her when in 1903 he conducted a tour across the United States, speaking to 40 enthralled audiences. When he returned, Maud had married another man. Her husband was killed later in the Easter Uprising of 1916, and Yeats proposed marriage to her. She gently refused, and he married Georgie Hyde-Lees, a known psychic medium.

Politics? Maybe Not

Like many Irish writers, Yeats tried his hand at politics, but with minimal success. From 1922 to 1928, he was a member of the Senate of the newly established Irish Free State. But Yeats was more liberal than his counterparts; he even proposed legislation that would allow divorce, making him quite unpopular with the Church and his more conservative opponents. In the end, he decided that literature was the surest road to political reform. He turned his considerable energies in that direction with far more favorable results.

Yeats died on January 28, 1939, in Roquebrune, France. Throughout World War II his body was buried there, but in 1948, it was returned to Ireland and buried in the shadow of that magnificent mountain, Benbulben, in Drumcliff, near Sligo. His gravestone bears the epitaph that he wrote, which says, "Cast a cold eye on life, on death. Horseman, pass by."

A Bard's Tale

The Irish wit is often misunderstood. Quips uttered by the Celtic tongue are often thought a reflection of an insouciant attitude, a character lacking responsibility. This simply isn't so. Sean O'Casey said it best:

"We Irish, when we think, and we often do this, are just as serious and sober as the Englishman; but we never hesitate to give a serious thought the benefit and halo of a laugh. That is why we are so often thought to be irresponsible, whereas, in point of fact, we are critical realists, while Englishmen often mistake sentimental mutterings for everlasting truths."

James Joyce

Born in Dublin in 1882, James Joyce made no secret of the fact that he found his homeland less than ideal. These lines from "Gas from a Burner" express his disenchantment:

> This lovely land that always sent
> Her writers and artists to banishment
> and in a spirit of Irish fun
> Betrayed her own leaders, one by one,
> 'Twas Irish humour, wet and dry,
> Flung quicklime into Parnell's eye...

Considering his sentiments, it is no surprise that Joyce left his homeland when he was 22, but the spirit of Ireland was still with him and was reflected in his work. Supposedly he had rejected his country, his family, and the Church, yet those very subjects dominated his writing, providing the central themes for his poems, short stories, and novels.

Statue of James Joyce.

Life wasn't easy or especially happy for Joyce. He was lonely much of the time and had more than his share of challenges. He was plagued with severe eye problems most of his life and was nearly blind. He endured a number of operations and had to wear a patch over a badly damaged eye. His sight became so compromised that he had to have assistance in researching and assembling *Finnegan's Wake.*

Also, Joyce had serious financial problems, despite his considerable success. Most of his financial support was provided by his brother, his publisher, and an American female benefactor. Some of his money difficulties were the result of poor management, but he also suffered stiff censorship. His works, especially *Ulysses* and *Finnegan's Wake,* were considered obscene and were banned in many English-speaking countries.

'Tisn't So!

When William Butler Yeats met James Joyce, they weren't overly impressed with each other. As Yeats was leaving, Joyce asked him his age. "Thirty-five," Yeats replied. "I've met you too late," Joyce said. "You're too old to be influenced by me." Later Yeats described Joyce thusly: "Never have I encountered so much pretension with so little to show for it."

Joyce's daughter suffered a nervous breakdown soon after the birth of his grandson. In 1940, he was forced to flee the German invasion of France, escaping to Switzerland. The highly innovative writer died in Zurich on January 13, 1941.

Much has been made of all the symbolism and hidden meanings in Joyce's words. Certainly, a richness and depth exists in his work that is rare, even in the highest echelons of literature. But Joyce himself might be amused to see what secret treasures his admirers have "gleaned" from his passages. Radical-fringe Joyceans might be accused of interjecting much of their own symbolism where it never existed before for their own amusement and, perhaps, to appear learned. Joyce once said of himself, "I'm afraid I am more interested in Dublin street names than in the riddle of the universe."

Whether he revered his homeland or despised her, whether his life was happy or miserable, whether his work was as riddled with riddles as some thought or less so, there is no doubt about one thing: James Joyce was a brilliant and important writer. "The Dead," part of his famous collection of stories entitled *Dubliners,* is considered a masterpiece of the short story format. He is also known for his autobiographical novel *The Portrait of the Artist as a Young Man* and *Ulysses,* an enormous novel about a day in the life of a Dublin man.

Joyce's writings were banned in England and burned in New York. Famed psychiatrist Carl Jung proclaimed him schizophrenic. But he was and continues to be held in the highest regard by the Irish and other lovers of literature because he was innovative and imaginative, a true original.

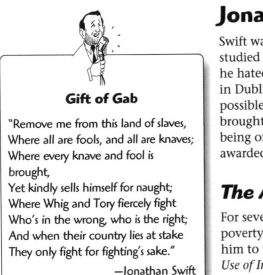

Gift of Gab

"Remove me from this land of slaves,
Where all are fools, and all are knaves;
Where every knave and fool is brought,
Yet kindly sells himself for naught;
Where Whig and Tory fiercely fight
Who's in the wrong, who is the right;
And when their country lies at stake
They only fight for fighting's sake."

—Jonathan Swift

Jonathan Swift

Swift was born in Ireland to Anglo-Irish parents and studied at Trinity College in Dublin for seven years, but he hated Ireland's poverty and hopelessness, especially in Dublin's slums. He escaped to England as soon as possible and began to write political satire, which brought him much acclaim. Swift had high hopes of being offered an English bishopric. Instead, he was awarded a deanery at St. Patrick's in Dublin.

The Anonymous Pen

For seven years he did his job quietly and well, but the poverty of the out-of-work Dublin weavers motivated him to write a pamphlet, *A Proposal for the Universal Use of Irish Manufacture.* In this pamphlet, he encouraged the Irish to "burn everything from England except her coal" and urged them to buy everything Irish. Not surprisingly, he published it anonymously. Because the government didn't know who the author was, it prosecuted the printer. Nine times the jury was sent out and told to reach a guilty verdict. Nine times they refused, and the so-called trial was over.

Three years later, Swift was again moved to protest through his writing. He penned the *Drapier's Letters*, which protested the decision made by Charles II concerning the minting of Irish coins outside of Ireland. The issue wasn't really who was going to mint the ha'penny. It was about Ireland having its own mint. It was about freedom. Once again, the government wanted to prosecute the writer. But although everyone knew that Swift was the infamous drapier, it couldn't be proven because no one would offer evidence against him.

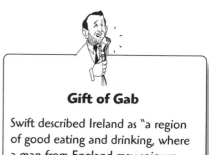

Gift of Gab

Swift described Ireland as "a region of good eating and drinking, where a man from England may sojourn some years with pleasure, make a fortune, and then return home with the spoils he has got by doing us all the mischief he can."

Three years later, between 1727 and 1730, famine hit Ireland, as it has many times over the ages. The bodies of the dead and dying lay openly in the streets, and as many times before, the government did far too little, too late.

Horrified, Swift wrote a shockingly bitter pamphlet under his own name called, "A Modest Proposal for Preventing the Children of Poor People in Ireland from Being a Burden to their Parents or the Country." In this tract he suggested that, "one-fourth part of the infants under two years old be forthwith fattened as dainty bits for land-lords, who, as they have already devoured most of the parents, seem to have best right to eat up the children." His intention was to shock his readers. He succeeded, though it had little effect on policy.

More Than a Kiddie's Tale

Swift's best-known work is *Gulliver's Travels*, written during the turbulent time when he was also composing pamphlets on behalf of Dublin's poor. It is a delightful children's story with complex subtext concerning the conceit of mankind. Many believe that Gulliver was a thinly veiled characterization of Swift himself and his own inner battles: always optimistic, always hoping to win the fight, but suspecting that in the end, his efforts would prove futile.

Padraic Colum: Patriot, Teacher

Padraic Colum was born in Ireland in 1881. His family gave him the names of two of Ireland's most beloved saints, as well as a passion for storytelling and poetry when he was only a lad. As a man he would found the *Irish Review* and fight, with the power of his pen, for Ireland's freedom.

The body and quality of his work is impressive, including lyrical poems, short stories, plays, essays, and children's stories. Lifelong friend of James Joyce, he served as president of the Joyce Society. He was an associate of the Irish Literary Revival and playwright of *The Land,* the Abbey Theatre's first major success.

Colum moved to the United States, living first in Connecticut, then in New York, where he was editor of *Forum,* a literary magazine. He also lectured and taught literature, along with his wife, Mary, at Columbia University. Colum will long be remembered for his incredible versatility. He wrote for rebel rousers, literary theater audiences, and children alike. No matter for whom Colum was writing, his words reflected a deep respect for his audience. He taught the highest ideals through the medium of fine, entertaining literature.

The following is an example of the beauty and sensitivity of Padraic Colum's verse. The passage is taken from his poem, *A Cradle Song:*

> O, men from the fields!
> Come gently within,
> Tread softly, softly,
> O! men coming in.
> Mavourneen is going
> From me and from you,
> Where Mary will fold him
> With mantle of blue.
> From reek of the smoke
> And cold of the floor,
> And the peering of things
> Across the half-door.
> O, men from the fields!
> Softly, softly come through;
> Mary puts round him
> Her mantle of blue.

Maria Edgeworth, the Tiny Lady Who Was All Heart

If physical stature were a measure of a person's value in this world, celebrated writer Maria Edgeworth would certainly not be counted among the 101 reasons for Irish pride. To say she was a wee lass is being generous; as a girl, she was even suspended for periods of time from the neck in hopes of making her taller.

Papa's Slashing Pen

Maria's father, Richard Lovell Edgeworth, married four times and sired 22 children, all of whom were cared for by Maria, who was his eldest daughter. Maria also served as agent for her father's properties and assisted him in the school that he had organized on his estate.

Maria and her father were very close, and he collaborated with her on several of her works, including *Essays on Practical Education* and *Essays on Irish Bulls*. Many thought he took far more credit for Maria's work than he was due. Richard was also a ruthless editor, slashing and rewriting her work to suit his own taste. Once she complained about his editing by referring to his scrawled notes on her manuscript as, "the crooked marks of Papa's critical indignation." One cannot help but wonder how she managed to write as well as she did and speculate how much greater she might have been without his over-the-shoulder censorship.

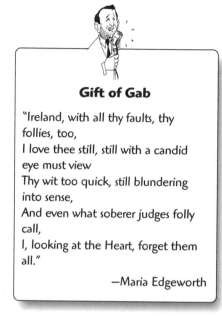

Gift of Gab

"Ireland, with all thy faults, thy follies, too,
I love thee still, still with a candid eye must view
Thy wit too quick, still blundering into sense,
And even what soberer judges folly call,
I, looking at the Heart, forget them all."

—Maria Edgeworth

A Friend in Sir Walter

Her novel *Castle Rackrent* was published in 1800, making Edgeworth internationally famous. Her work brought her to the attention of Sir Walter Scott, the acclaimed Scottish poet and novelist, who acknowledged her in the preface to his novel *Waverly*. She visited Scott in Abbotsford in 1823, and he came to see her in 1825, further cementing their long-standing friendship.

To Miss Edgeworth, for Her Poor

During the Great Hunger, the terrible potato famine from 1845 to 1849, Maria used her own finances, as well as her time and energies, to aid the starving peasantry. As an agent on her father's property, she knew firsthand of their dire circumstances. She pleaded their cause around the world and, as a result, received enormous amounts of donations, which she distributed to the destitute. One of these contributions was a shipment of 150 barrels of flour from Boston. She received the gift in spite of the fact that it was addressed only to "Miss Edgeworth, for her poor."

Maria held strong opinions about the evils of absentee landlordism and the mistreatment of the peasantry by the British. Her novels, set in rural Ireland, mostly followed these themes, enlightening her readers to those problems and sparking efforts toward reform.

Frank McCourt: Bards Still Walk the Green Hills

One of the great gifts of the Irish bard is the ability to wring both tears and laughter out of you in the same moment. Frank McCourt is living evidence that Ireland hasn't given us the last of its bards. They still keep a comin'.

In his phenomenal book *Angela's Ashes,* McCourt displays the same mix of hilarity and tragedy that typifies the Irish spirit. His novel, which details his miserable childhood in Limerick in the 1930s, has sold over 1.8 million copies and has occupied the *New York Times* bestseller list for over a year. It also won him the Pulitzer Prize.

McCourt says of those early years, "It was, of course, a miserable childhood: The happy childhood is hardly worth your while." His alcoholic father spent the meager family income on drink rather than food for his children, three out of seven of whom died of disease and neglect. But the terribly sad novel has its lighter side, as well. The children, innocent, curious, and infinitely forgiving, didn't realize how terrible their lives were and managed to find joy in the most squalid environment.

McCourt immigrated to America in 1949 at the age of 19. In New York, he found jobs on the dock and as a porter in hotels. He attended the New York University, and then became an instructor in a vocational school. Later he taught English for 18 years at the prestigious Stuyvesant High. McCourt's play, *The Irish . . . And How They Got That Way,* has been produced by the Irish Repertory Theatre in New York.

Another mark of a fine Irish writer is the fact that they usually raise the dust clouds of controversy, and McCourt is no different. There are those who feel he has besmirched the name of Ireland, specifically the city of Limerick, and they have let him know about it in no uncertain terms. His reply: "I can do no more than tell the truth. People who think I have insulted Ireland or Limerick or my family have not read the book."

The book shows the dark and the light side of Ireland, Limerick, and on some level, every Irish person. McCourt's novel illuminates the Irish spirit in a way that is fresh and absolutely wonderful.

The Least You Need to Know

➤ William Butler Yeats is considered one of the finest writers of all time. Yeats was fascinated by the mystic world and ancient Celtic mythology and much of his work reflects those interests.

➤ James Joyce was one of the most innovative, experimental writers of all time. Full of metaphors, hidden symbolism, and complex meanings, his works are still diligently dissected and vigorously debated by the academia.

➤ Jonathan Swift made no bones about the fact that he hated Ireland. But her poor, especially those in the Dublin slums, touched his heart. Although he is best known for his children's book, *Gulliver's Travels,* he was an amazing satirist who used his talents to write political pamphlets that exposed the plight of the impoverished.

➤ Padraic Colum displayed both sides of his character, the warrior and the benevolent father, through his writing. On one hand, he was a fierce patriot who used his pen to further the dream of an Irish republic. Yet he wrote beautiful, colorful stories for young people that could be appreciated by children from the ages of 3 to 83.

➤ Maria Edgeworth was a landlord's daughter, but she saw the injustices done in the absentee landlord system, and she exposed those evils in her novel *Castle Rackrent,* a story about such a landlord and his family. When the Great Hunger struck, she used her talents to marshal aid for the victims and saved many lives.

➤ Pulitzer Prize winner Frank McCourt shows the dark and the light side of the Irish people in his wonderful book, *Angela's Ashes.* The novel proves that Ireland is still producing bards, and they are still blessing our spirits with their words.

Chapter 20

Staging a Gaelic Revolution: The Great Irish Theater

In This Chapter

➤ Yeats and Lady Gregory help the Abbey Theatre open to raves and riots

➤ Oscar Wilde: biting, bitter, brilliant

➤ John Synge shocks audiences, and artistic freedom is born

➤ Brendan Behan: the bombastic Borstal Boy

➤ George Bernard Shaw: a noble, Nobel fellow

➤ Sean O'Casey: creating art from painfully humble beginnings

---

If ever a people had a divine calling, it would seem to be the Irish. Their heavenly responsibility is to bring a bit of pathos laced with laughter to every heart that needs to be lifted above and out of its daily toil and trouble. While the good Irish playwrights and actors were boosting the morale of the people, they awoke social consciousness, even though that same society sometimes rioted in the theater as it was waking!

Most cultures value theater on some level. The Irish have raised that level to the stars, rating it a national treasure. Poetic hearts realized long ago that the stage provides the bards with yet another forum and new audiences for their stories and life lessons. In the opinions of most drama aficionados, Ireland has been the fountainhead from which has sprung much of the world's greatest drama. Besides, a night at the theater is grand old fun!

Abbey Theatre, Where the Greats Were Born

In 1904, the National Dramatic Company, owned by the brothers Frank and William Fay, and the Irish Literary Theatre Society (started by William Butler Yeats) merged to form what would become Ireland's National Theatre, the Abbey Theatre in Dublin. The Abbey opened on December 27, 1904, and its first performance was *On Baile's Strand* by Yeats and *Spreading the News* by Lady Gregory.

The Abbey Theatre in Dublin.

Gift of Gab

Apparently, not everyone fully appreciated the Abbey Theatre for its genius and innovation. Playwright Lennox Robinson was so sick of sentimentalists remarking that "The Abbey isn't what it used to be," that he snapped, "It never was!"

After being supported by several philanthropic individuals, the Abbey was given a grant in 1924 by the Free State government, making it the first state-subsidized theater in the English-speaking world. (Did I mention earlier that the Irish love their theater?) In its first 45 years, the theater produced 449 plays. Of those, 384 were written for or inspired by the Abbey itself. Some of the best-known productions were: *The Well of the Saints, Deirdre, The Country Dressmaker, The Workhouse Ward, The Shadow of a Gunman, Juno and the Paycock, The Plough and the Stars,* and, perhaps the most notorious, *The Playboy of the Western World,* which caused riots in the street because of its risqué content.

The Abbey boasted such celebrated directors as Augusta, Lady Gregory, W. B. Yeats, Edward Martyn, J. M. Synge, Ernest Blythe, Brinsley MacNamara, Frank O'Connor, and Walter Macken. The actors and actresses who graced the stage of the Abbey were among the finest of their day and included: F. J. McCormick, Sara Allgood, Barry Fitzgerald, Arthur Sinclair, and Maud Gonne, the object of W. B. Yeats's affection (though it wasn't returned).

Unfortunately, the Abbey Theatre was lost to fire in 1951, a sad demise, indeed. But the tradition continued, and the company was moved to the Queen's Theatre. In 1966, it moved again to its present location in Lower Abbey Street.

Wilde One

Some say that the best components of Irish humor are sarcasm, truthfulness, cynicism, insight, and a drop of ribaldry to spice the mixture. If this is true, then Oscar Wilde was not only one of the greatest Irish playwrights, but also one of her finest humorists. His writings involve all of these components and more.

He was born in Dublin in 1854. His father was Sir William Wilde, a surgeon and writer. His mother was Lady Jane Wilde, a poet and writer of some renown herself. Wilde studied at Trinity College in Dublin and at Magdalen College, Oxford, England, where he won the Newdigate Prize for poetry.

Wilde was a prolific writer, churning out such marvels as *The Happy Prince, Lord Arthur Saville's Crime, The Picture of Dorian Gray, Lady Windermere's Fan, A Woman of No Importance, An Ideal Husband,* and *The Importance of Being Earnest.* He also wrote the play *Salome* in French. It was performed in Paris, and Sarah Bernhardt played the title role.

Gift of Gab

When someone asked Oscar Wilde if he knew fellow playwright, George Moore, Wilde replied, "Know him? Yes, I know him so well I haven't spoken to him in 10 years."

A Bard's Tale

Born Rosine Bernard in 1845, French actress Sarah Bernhardt was the star of the stage in her day. She was famous for her dramatic performances, frequently taking on male or female roles in Shakespearean tragedies. Unfortunately, modern times have not been kind to the memory of Ms. Bernhardt. Her name is often used to demonstrate an overreaction. If you've ever been called a "Sarah Bernhardt," it probably was more of a gentle ribbing than a compliment!

An eccentric, unique character, Wilde became a cult figure in his own time. Known for his biting sarcasm and witty epigrams, he developed quite a following, though some might have considered him more infamous than famous. His views were more than a little irreverent, and he was constantly stirring controversy. Wilde wasn't one to keep his opinions to himself.

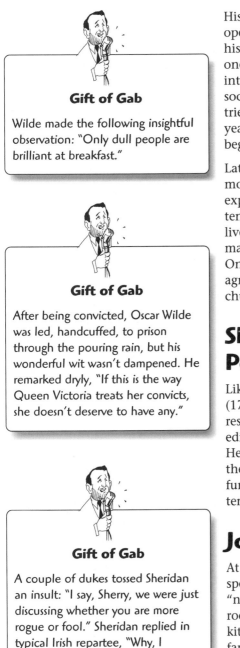

Gift of Gab

Wilde made the following insightful observation: "Only dull people are brilliant at breakfast."

Gift of Gab

After being convicted, Oscar Wilde was led, handcuffed, to prison through the pouring rain, but his wonderful wit wasn't dampened. He remarked dryly, "If this is the way Queen Victoria treats her convicts, she doesn't deserve to have any."

Gift of Gab

A couple of dukes tossed Sheridan an insult: "I say, Sherry, we were just discussing whether you are more rogue or fool." Sheridan replied in typical Irish repartee, "Why, I believe I am between both!"

His tendencies to state his opinions clearly and live an openly homosexual life were not considered virtues in his day. Wilde's enemies were numerous. The father of one of his lovers, Lord Alfred Douglas, pushed Wilde into a lawsuit, which eventually led to his financial and social ruin, as well as eventual incarceration. He was tried and convicted of sodomy and imprisoned for two years, from 1895 to 1897, during which time his health began to fail.

Later his *Ballad of Reading Gaol* was published anonymously and recounted his experiences in prison and explained his side of the story. After serving his sentence, Wilde moved to Italy, and then Paris, where he lived under the alias Sebastian Melmoth. Wilde never made it back to his native Ireland and is buried in Paris. On his deathbed, the man who had lived his life as an agnostic asked to be received into the Roman Catholic church—and was.

Sheridan: From the Drama of Politics to Theater

Like many Irish writers, Richard Brinsley Sheridan (1751–1816) was both artist and politician. He was well-respected in London literary circles for his stage comedies, *The Rivals* (1775) and *The School for Scandal* (1777). He also served as a Westminster MP and was a friend of the Prince of Wales. When Sheridan died in 1816, his funeral was held in Westminster Abbey and was attended by masses of admirers.

John Millington Synge

At the urging of W. B. Yeats, John Millington Synge spent time in the Aran Islands, studying the truly "native" Irish through a hole in his boarding house room floor. By listening to the servants gossip in the kitchen below, the son of an aristocratic, Anglo-Irish family discovered a colorful world filled with animated characters, uttering lively dialogue, which Synge translated into wonderful plays.

To an outsider, those Irish living on the west coast, scraping a life from rock or pulling their food from a stormy sea, had a tough time of it. Certainly, they battled more than their share of challenges. Synge loved these common people of Ireland, admired the nobility of their spirits, and envied the joys of their simple lives. He understood their strengths and weaknesses, relating them to his own and those of his aristocratic friends. It was only natural that the characters of his plays would mirror those traits he had studied in a manner that only a true bard can accomplish.

Not everyone appreciated the complexity of Synge's characters or their honesty. At the time when Synge's play *The Playboy of the Western World* was produced by Abbey Theatre, society's view of what should be presented on stage was narrow. Nationalist propaganda was the fare of the day; the Irish were presented solely as paragons of virtue, flawless, and above all reproach. Yet Synge's two main characters in *Playboy* were a young man on the run, thinking he has killed his father, and an uninhibited, sexual, self-assured woman.

The audience at the Abbey was positively scandalized, and riots broke out. Not only had Synge dared to create a hero and heroine with character foibles, but he had also used the indecent term *shift* (a ladies' undergarment, similar to a slip or chemise) in his dialogue, which was uttered right there in front of God and everybody! Although most of the females in the audience were, no doubt, wearing one, there was a world of difference between wearing a shift and speaking the word aloud in mixed company! Later, W. B. Yeats informed the confused and distressed Synge, "A young doctor (in the audience) has just told me that he can hardly keep himself from jumping onto a seat and pointing out in that howling mob those whom he is treating for venereal disease."

But for all the hoopla, Synge and his ardent supporters, Yeats and the theater director, Lady Gregory, had ushered in a new chapter of theater history. No longer would current political moods dictate the artistic expressions presented on the stage. Society would no longer be able to censor the dramatists of that day. Artistic freedom had been born on the Irish stage and continues to the present day, thanks to courageous playwrights such as Synge, who may have learned a few lessons about courage while his ear was pressed to the floor of his boarding house room.

'Tisn't So!

The playwright Lennox Robinson corrected those who mispronounced John Synge's name by announcing, "You *singe* a cat. You sing Synge."

Augusta, Lady Gregory

Augusta, Lady Gregory was a late bloomer, but what a rose she turned out to be in the end. The first 50 years of her life were spent quietly in relative anonymity. She was born in Roxborough in County Galway in 1852. At the age of 28, she married Sir William Gregory, a distinguished British colonial administrator.

A Bard's Tale

In 1907, the word *shift* (a woman's undergarment) caused an uproar when uttered during a performance of *The Playboy of the Western World* by John Millington Synge. Frantic, Lady Gregory telegraphed W. B. Yeats, who was in London at the time, asking, "What should I do?" He replied, "Leave it on."

Other than editing her father-in-law's papers and her husband's *Autobiography,* she did little writing until after her husband's death. Then, inspired by traditional Irish folklore, she learned the Irish language and traveled from cottage to humble cottage, collecting the colorful tales and sharing a few of her own. Sitting beside the cozy turf fires, the lady found she had much in common with the peasantry. Human tears and trials were the same under every roof, whether it be thatch or slate.

Gift of Gab

When a vicar complained to Lady Gregory that the spire on a new Catholic church was somewhat taller than that of the town's Protestant church, she wisely replied, "Yes, monsignor, but don't they point in the same direction?"

When she met William Butler Yeats in 1896 at the home of a mutual friend, she found a spirit as enthralled with these mystical tales as she was. She invited Yeats to stay often at her home at Coole Park, where they exchanged stories and occasionally collaborated on projects, such as *The Pot of Broth.* But their most important effort was the founding of Abbey Theatre, where she remained one of the directors for the rest of her life. She also wrote a number of works; the two best-known are *Cuchulain of Muirthemne* and *Gods and Fighting Men,* both retellings of ancient Celtic tales.

Brendan Behan, the Boy from Borstal

Brendan Behan led many lives in one, including that of an IRA soldier and subsequently a prisoner, a scholar, and a house painter. But foremost, history will record him as one of Ireland's finest writers.

Born in 1923 to a republican family, Behan was the nephew of Peadar Kearney, author of the Irish national anthem. In 1937, the young teenager joined the IRA and was arrested only two years later at the age of 17 for possessing explosives. He spent three years imprisoned at Borstal, a time when he collected the necessary firsthand "research" he would later use to write his best-selling novel, *Borstal Boy,* published in 1958.

Painful, First-Hand Research

After being released from Borstal, he returned to Dublin, but after only four months was imprisoned again. This time he was accused of attempted murder of a policeman, and his sentence was 14 years. Incarcerated at Mountjoy, he did his "research" once again, gathering material later incorporated into his play, *The Quare Fellow*, produced in the Pike Theatre in 1954.

Before serving his full sentence, Behan was released under general amnesty in late 1946. Once out of prison, he traveled extensively in Kerry and Galway as an ardent student of the Irish language. He spent time in London and Paris, as well, painting houses to earn his keep. Behan never felt hard labor was beneath him, and he harbored no pretensions about his literary work, either. He hated those critics who claimed to have uncovered abstruse meanings in his work. When asked about the messages contained in his plays, he snapped, "What message? I'm a playwright, not a bloody postman!"

Gift of Gab

When Brendan Behan was asked why he hadn't considered a life of sobriety, he gave his reason: "Because the price of a pint of orange juice is twice the price of a pint of stout."

Gift of Gab

An infamous rebel and celebrated writer, Behan once said, "I have a total irreverence for anything connected with society, except that which makes the roads safer, the beer stronger, the old men and women warmer in the winter and happier in the summer."

The Bottle Got Him in the End

Brendan Behan died too soon at the age of 41. A possible explanation of his early demise might be contained in this statement he made on the subject of alcohol usage: "I can only say that in Dublin during the depression when I was growing up, drunkenness was not regarded as a social disgrace. To get enough to eat was regarded as an achievement. To get drunk was a victory." Supposedly, Behan's final words on the planet were these, spoken to the nun who was nursing him: "Thank you, Sister; and may you be the mother of a bishop."

George Bernard Shaw

George Bernard Shaw, one of the great patriarchs of Irish literature, was born in Dublin in 1856 and educated at Wesley College. At the age of 20, he moved to London and took a job with the Edison Telephone Company, but his aspirations were toward writing. He worked hard at his craft, publishing a number of novels, all of which were failures commercially.

Taking a different tack, he became a music critic. He had much better luck at that and soon became one of the most respected members of his field. He wrote in T. P. O'Connor's *Star* and in *The World* using the pen name Corno di Bassetto.

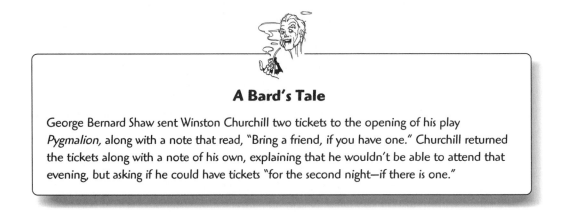

A Bard's Tale

George Bernard Shaw sent Winston Churchill two tickets to the opening of his play *Pygmalion*, along with a note that read, "Bring a friend, if you have one." Churchill returned the tickets along with a note of his own, explaining that he wouldn't be able to attend that evening, but asking if he could have tickets "for the second night—if there is one."

A Political for Politics

Shaw's politics leaned decidedly toward socialism, and in 1882 he joined the Fabian Society and became one of its leaders. The Fabians' intent was to promote socialistic theory through education and peaceful, gradual, political evolution. They did so by presenting lectures internationally, some of which were given by Shaw himself.

Like most of Ireland's fine bards, Shaw's politics landed him in trouble. During World War I, he espoused pacifism, an unpopular stance in a time when political fervor ran hot and patriotism was defined only in militaristic terms. His contrary opinions got him expelled from the Dramatists' Club. Shaw added to the controversy by protesting the execution of the leaders of the Easter Uprising of 1916. Of those killings he said, "An Irishman resorting to arms to achieve the independence of his country is doing only what Englishmen will do if it is their misfortune to be invaded and conquered by the Germans in the course of the present war." He maintained that the executions would only make martyrs of the leaders and leave the country in the hands of Sinn Fein, a group he opposed because of their violent methods.

Finally, Success

Shaw married Charlotte Payne-Townsend in 1882. Because his new wife was wealthy, he was financially able to devote his time fully to writing. Shaw would continue to write for the next 50 years. In 1895, he expanded his career as a critic to include drama and published in the *Saturday Review*. During this time, he continued to hone his own craft. He wrote a play called *Widowers' Houses*, which was staged in 1892, but he didn't receive any real acclaim until he wrote *John Bull's Other Island*. The play was banned by

Lord Chamberlain in England, but it hit the stage in Dublin. The production was a great success, possibly due, in part, to its notoriety as well as its literary genius.

His reputation among the English was restored when he published *St. Joan* in 1924. The next year he was further elevated in their eyes, and those of the world, when he received the Nobel Prize for Literature. Along with William Butler Yeats, he founded the Irish Academy of Letters. He was also offered British honors, the Order of Merit and a peerage, which he refused.

Shaw was a stalwart fellow, both mentally and physically. At the age of 75, he visited Russia, and then took a world tour of four continents. The remainder of Shaw's days were spent in a cottage in Ayot St. Lawrence in Hertfordshire. The site is now a Shaw Museum. At the plucky age of 94, he died from complications resulting from a fall from an apple tree that he had been pruning. His longevity and remarkable vitality may have been due to the fact that he was an avid teetotaler and vegetarian.

Shaw published a number of tracts and pamphlets concerning socialism, including *Fabianism and the Empire* and *The Intelligent Woman's Guide to Socialism and Capitalism.* He contributed many classics to the world of theater, including *Candida, Man and Superman, St. Joan, Caesar and Cleopatra, Heart-break House, Arms and the Man,* and *Doctor's Dilemma.* But he is best known for his wonderful play *Pygmalion,* which was made into the musical *My Fair Lady* that continues to be staged and to delight audiences even today.

Gift of Gab

At a dinner party George Bernard Shaw decided he had enjoyed an arrogant fellow's company as much as he could bear. He told the braggart, "Between the two of us, we know all there is to know...You seem to know everything except that you're a bore, and I know that."

Gift of Gab

"Shaw hasn't an enemy in the world, but none of his friends like him."

—Oscar Wilde

Sean O'Casey

Sean O'Casey was born John Casey in Dublin in 1880 and endured a childhood full of misery. The boy who would become one of the world's most highly esteemed playwrights couldn't even read until he was 13; he suffered horrible vision problems his entire life due to malnutrition and neglect as a child.

O'Casey's poor, Protestant father died when Sean was young, and only 5 of O'Casey's 13 siblings survived to adulthood. Due to his bad eyesight and ill health, his school attendance was sporadic. But once this son of the Dublin slums learned to escape his squalid environment through books, whole new worlds opened for him. He read everything he could get his hands on, and the lad had good taste. His favorites were the Big S's: Shakespeare, Shaw, and Shelley.

A Bard's Tale

Though a great dramatist, Sean O'Casey had received a poor Irish child's education. (He had once disdainfully defined a university as "a place where they polish pebbles and dim diamonds.") When the crowds rioted during one of his controversial plays, and William Butler Yeats took the stage, declaring, "...the fame of O'Casey is born here tonight. This is his apotheosis," O'Casey didn't know whether he had been complimented or insulted. He ran home to the dictionary and, hopefully, felt a lot better. (By the way, *apotheosis* is defined as being exalted to divine rank or stature.)

After taking a part in a local play, O'Casey's appetite for the theater was whetted. He began to write plays, and in 1923, at the age of 43, he had his first play produced. *The Shadow of a Gunman* was performed at the Abbey Theatre to exuberant audiences. O'Casey's work was completely unique. He wrote of what he knew, which was great poverty and sadness. For the first time, theatergoers saw the grim realities of Ireland's slum dwellers presented on the stage.

Shall I Thank You or Punch Your Nose?

O'Casey's third effort, *The Plough and the Stars,* received much harsh criticism, to O'Casey's deep distress. The play was about the ill-fated Easter Uprising of 1916. Thinking the play ridiculed the Irish and their patriotism, audiences rioted as they had 20 years before at the opening of John Synge's *Playboy of the Western World.* The crowd was so abusive that William Butler Yeats himself took the stage and spoke these words in defense of O'Casey, "You have disgraced yourselves again. Is this to be an ever-recurring celebration of the arrival of Irish genius?"

Angry and disillusioned, O'Casey left Ireland and seldom returned except for short visits. When the directors of the Abbey Theatre refused to produce his next play, *The Silver Tassie,* he was devastated. Many critics today consider it his best. His other works include *Within the Gates, Windfalls, The Star Turns Red, Purple Dust, Red Roses for Me, Oakleaves and Lavender, Cock-a-Doodle-Dandy,* and *The Bishop's Bonfire.* He also published the six-volume *Autobiographies,* as well as volumes of essays titled, *The Flying Wasp, The Green Crow, Under a Colored Cap,* and *Blasts and Benedictions.*

The rest of his life was plagued with sadness. He and his wife lost one of their three children to leukemia, and O'Casey himself was almost completely blind when he died at the age of 84.

A Bard's Tale

The portrayal of a prostitute in Sean O'Casey's *The Plough and the Stars* caused riots inside the theater. The cast was actually stoned! One fiercely patriotic, though somewhat naïve, critic insisted there were no prostitutes in Dublin. Apparently, he was the only fellow in town who was unaware of the city's notorious red-light district that was liberally sprinkled with blatant streetwalkers.

Make 'Em Laugh; Make 'Em Weep

O'Casey was once asked if he thought the Irish people were sincere. He replied, "Sincere? Man, I should say so. In fact, there's no more sincere people in the world than the Irish. Why, an Irishman would murder his own father or brother over a difference in creed or politics. If you want more evidence of sincerity than that, I don't know where you can find it."

Indeed, O'Casey's sincerity in his own work made him one of the great writers of the twentieth century. In spite of his bitterness and misfortune, he will be remembered as a great Irish playwright, whose true talent lay in his ability to make us laugh uproariously, suddenly strike us with sadness, and then raise us up again with more laughter. O'Casey's balance between comedy and tragedy is the hallmark of true Irish wit and talent at its best.

Gift of Gab

Sean O'Casey wrote in *Drums Under the Window:* "Though I should mingle with the dust, or fall to ashes in flame, the plough will always remain to furrow the earth, the stars will always be there to unveil the beauty of the night, and a newer people, living a newer life, will sing like the sons of the morning."

Trinity's Sons

Trinity College in Dublin has produced a number of notable playwrights, and one of the best was George Farquhar. Born in Londonderry in 1678, Farquhar was a former army soldier turned actor. Though he lived modestly and died in relative poverty, he paved the way for Ireland's future playwrights and enriched the stage with his comedies, such as *The Recruiting Officer* and *The Beaux' Stratagem,* which was an enormous success in its time and continues to play even today.

Another Trinity man was Oliver Goldsmith, who was born in Elphin in County Roscommon in 1728. He was the fifth of eight children of a poor Anglican clergyman.

'Tisn't So!

Although many believe that truly good writers come from truly good schools, others have reservations about the effect of universities upon their students. When asked whether she believed that college stifles writers, the American, Southern writer of Irish descent Flannery O'Connor, replied, "It doesn't stifle half enough of them!"

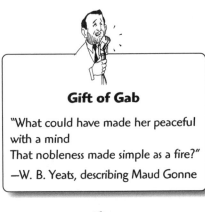

Gift of Gab

"What could have made her peaceful with a mind
That nobleness made simple as a fire?"
—W. B. Yeats, describing Maud Gonne

Gift of Gab

When Maude Gonne rejected the affections of W. B. Yeats, she gave him the following reason:

"You make beautiful poetry out of what you call your unhappiness, and you are happy in that. Marriage would be such a dull affair. Poets should never marry. The world should thank me for not marrying you."

Oliver was a slight, awkward child, disfigured by small-pox. But he was also known for his wit and cleverness and was well-liked by other children.

Goldsmith became a star in the literary circles of London with such works as the play *She Stoops to Conquer* (1773), his poems *The Traveller* and *The Deserted Village,* and the novel *The Vicar of Wakefield* (1766). He lived only 46 years before dying on April 4, 1774 of a fever, which he had determined to cure himself. He is buried in London.

Maude Gonne

Many Irishmen considered Maud Gonne the most beautiful woman in Ireland in her day. Judging from the powerful and famous men who fell in love with her, they may have been right. Maud was an actress who received much fame and acclaim from her roles at the Abbey Theatre. But Maud Gonne was so much more than a pretty face. She was a spitfire who used her beauty and her passionate nature to further the cause of freedom for the Irish.

Considering her privileged upbringing—her father was an Irish officer in the British army—one might have assumed Maud would be spoiled. But at an early age, she expressed her own opinions, which were in direct variance to her parents, and pledged her life to the cause of Irish freedom.

Already a stunning beauty at the age of 17, she was presented to Albert Edward, Prince of Wales, at the Viceregal Court in Dublin Castle. During a ball there, the prince was so taken by her beauty that he escorted her to the platform. The feisty young lady took full advantage of the situation. She entertained the royal court by singing, "The Wearing of the Green." Whether the prince was still taken by her after that, we can only surmise.

William Butler Yeats was another man who was completely smitten with the lovely Maud. He fell madly in love with her, making her the star of his renowned play, *Kathleen ni Houlihan.* He was bitterly disappointed when she married a fellow named MacBride. When MacBride was killed during the Easter Uprising, Yeats proposed marriage to her, but she refused. Her husband's death made her all the more emphatic about her mission.

Maud fought not only for political reform, but she also battled poverty and sickness in the slums of Dublin. In 1900, she founded the Daughters of Erin, a group of equally radical women bent on accomplishing the same goals. For the remainder of her days, Maud worked on behalf of the republicans, fighting for an independent Ireland. In January 1923, during the Irish Civil War, she was imprisoned. She went on a hunger strike and was released after 20 days. The great actress and patriot died in 1953. In the end, Maud Gonne was loved, not for her beauty, but for the way she spent her time, her energy, and her talents in the pursuit of the Irish dream.

The Least You Need to Know

➤ The Abbey Theatre, the National Theater of Ireland, was the first state-subsidized theater in the English-speaking world. Founded by such greats as William Butler Yeats and his friend Lady Gregory, the theater produced the first plays of many wonderful dramatists.

➤ Oscar Wilde possessed a biting, sharp wit seldom matched in the art of wordsmithing. His quips and his biting retorts were his charm as well as his downfall.

➤ John Millington Synge (pronounced *sing*) wrote *The Playboy of the Western World,* which caused riots in the audience at the Abbey Theatre. He helped to set the stage for even more artistic freedom to come.

➤ Time spent imprisoned gave Brendan Behan material for his play *The Quare Fellow.* He died early of hard living and heavy drinking, but he will always be remembered for his boisterous personality and irreverent, but insightful, view of life.

➤ George Bernard Shaw was awarded the Nobel Prize for Literature as well as a place of honor among the literary greats of all time. His play, *Pygmalion,* continues to be staged today.

➤ Sean O'Casey survived a dreadful childhood in the slums of Dublin and wrote plays about the horrors of that life. This subject matter had never been presented on stage before. He was known for his remarkable gift for bringing his audience to tears with both laughter and pathos, as in his remarkable play, *The Plough and the Stars.*

➤ Maud Gonne was a beautiful actress who starred in W. B. Yeats's renowned play, *Kathleen ni Houlihan,* during which she captured Yeats's heart, though she never returned his love. But more important than being Yeats's muse, she campaigned endlessly for Ireland's freedom.

Part 5

Ireland and All It Has to Offer: A Story Still Tellin'

From enchanting lore to exquisite crystal to the fine knit of an Aran sweater, the beauty of modern Ireland is as much a reflection of its past as it is a view into the future. The Irish of today are a fiercely proud people for more reasons than any society has the right to boast. In Part 5, you'll see what it means to be Irish in the 20th century. 'Tis grand, indeed! If by now you're itching to trace your own Irish family tree, I'll help you do that, too.

Chapter 21

Mythical Ireland: Its Lovely Lore

> **In This Chapter**
>
> ➤ Amergin, the poet druid and the battle of the enchantments
>
> ➤ Is that a fairy flitting about?
>
> ➤ Those little green men: leprechauns

Every society has its mythology. Every culture has heroes dimly viewed through the mists of time and legend. But the Irish cherish their ancient tales on a level that most others consider overly sentimental and whimsical to the point of folly. Why is that?

Maybe it's because such an extreme effort was made to deny the Irish their sagas by those who didn't want the Irish to think of themselves as descended from mighty warriors of yore. Maybe it's because the stories reminded the Irish that they *were* warriors, no matter how servile their existence at any given moment, and helped them maintain the belief that their suppression as a people was temporary. Or maybe it's just because their legends are so much better than others. (The arrogance reflected in that last statement is also quintessentially Irish. Our wonderful sagas, our rapier wit, and our smashing good looks are surpassed only by our humility.)

Colorful Mythology

When the Irish paint a story, they do so with a full palette. Their lore is filled with tales of golden-haired maidens, black seas, and, of course, lush, green terrain. The following Ossianic poem vividly describes how the Fenian warriors bounded away on a deer hunt in the company of 3,000 hounds with golden chains:

Thus we were arrayed and armed
When we went to pursue the deer.
No Fenian warrior went forth
Without a shirt of satin and two hounds,
A garment of smooth silk,
A coat of mail, a sharp blue glittering dart,
A helmet set in stones of gold,
And two spears in the hand of each hero,
A green shield that oft was upreared in victory,
And well-tempered sword that scattered heads.
Thou might wander o'er the white-foaming bays of ocean
Without beholding a man like Finn.
We came to a green mount above a valley,
Where the trees were leafy and pleasant,
Where the joyful birds made music,
And the sound of the cuckoo resounded
From the top of the cliff.

A Bard's Tale

Michael Quirke, a modern-day bard and butcher in Sligo who would much prefer to share an ancient story than trim a pork chop, once told me, "The reason I love the Celtic stories is because they're so very colorful." I thought he meant figuratively, only to realize that he was being literal. He went on to explain by telling me the story of Princess Niav of the Golden Hair, rising up out of the black waters of Killarney on a white stallion and beckoning to Ossian to follow her to The Land of the Ever Young. "You see," he said, "the stories are full of color."

Amergin, the Poet Druid

The old legend about a powerful druid named Amergin has been handed down for literally thousands of years, though it goes too far back into the mists of time to set an accurate date. Amergin's chant, the song of creation, or some close version of it has appeared in the literature and mythology of other peoples. It closely resembles the song of Sri Krishna in the *Bhagavad-Gita*.

Amergin was one of the nine sons of Mil and chief poet-druid of his people. When the Milesians arrived in 30 ships in Kenmare Bay on the southwest coast of Ireland, they demanded that the current residents, the Tuatha De Danann, surrender to them. In a typical display of Celtic equity, Amergin told the Tuatha De Danann that his warriors' ships would pull back "nine waves from shore" to give the Tuatha De Danann time to make ready.

Rather than prepare for surrender, the Tuatha De Danann used their considerable mystic powers to conjure a druidic wind. The wind blew no higher than the masts of the Milesian ships, but that was enough to destroy the fleet. In the magical hurricane, five of Amergin's brothers were killed.

Amergin and his remaining brothers managed to make it to shore, and when they stepped upon the beach, Amergin chanted an ancient song, summoned from the distant haze of time:

> I am wind on Sea,
> I am Ocean-wave,
> I am Roar of Sea,
> I am Bull of Seven Fights,
> I am Vulture of Cliff,
> I am Dewdrop,
> I am Fairest of Flowers,
> I am Boar for Boldness,
> I am Salmon in Pool
> I am Lake on Plain
> I am Word of Skill,
> I am the Point of a Weapon
> I am God who fashioneth Fire for a Head.
> Who smootheth the ruggedness of a mountain?
> Who is He who announceth the ages of the Moon?
> And who, the place where falleth the sunset?
> Who calleth the cattle from the House of Tethra?
> On whom do the cattle of Tethra smile?
> Who is the troop, who the god who fashioneth edges?
> Enchantments about a spear?
> Enchantments of Wind?

Amergin and his warriors fought the Tuatha De Danann in two mighty battles, the first in the mountains of the Slieve Mish in Kerry and the second at Taillten in Meath. Finally the Milesians triumphed. The poet druid divided Ireland, awarding the upper earth to his brothers and the territory beneath the earth and under the sea to the Tuatha De Danann. Legend says the Tuatha De Danann still live in fairy forms below the earth and the sea in golden palaces. Occasionally, they emerge to influence the affairs of men.

217

Amergin's words of invocation echo through time. St. Patrick's most famous poem, *Faedh Fiada, Cry of the Deer,* in which the saint petitions the forces of the sun, moon, fire, wind, rocks, lightning, and the ocean to defeat evil, sounds strangely reminiscent of Amergin's pagan song, chanted that day on the seashore of Kenmare.

The World of Fairy

In the 1700s, a fellow by the name of Crofton Croker studied the subject of fairies thoroughly and described them as being only a few inches high. He claimed that their bodies are airy and have a transparent quality. They are so delicate that they could dance on a dewdrop without shattering its surface. Their clothing is white as snow and shines like silver, and their caps are made from red foxglove blossoms. He claimed they love to eat. Though Croker's vision of the Gentle People is quite whimsical, there are those who believe they are far more than dainty creatures, flitting from flower to leaf like ethereal bees.

Just in case you want to call the Gentle People by their proper Irish names (and 'tis an intelligent lad or lass you are if you do so), here are their names and the pronunciations, too:

English	Irish	Pronunciation
fairy (one)	shidheog	shee-hogue
fairy people	daoine sidhe	deenee shee
mermaids	moruadh	merrow
leprechauns	leith bhrogan	leith phrogan
banshee	bean sidhe	ban she
pooka	puca	poo ka
water horse	each-uisge	augh-ishka
ghosts	taidhbhse	thevshi

Long ago, some of the earliest inhabitants of the Island of Eire were the above-mentioned Tuatha De Danann. A mystical race of beings, they were defeated by the militarily superior Milesians. Because everything beneath the earth's surface and below the sea belongs to the Tuatha De Danann, some believe that these beings still exist, living in the fairy forts in the ocean, loughs (lakes), and rivers. Few Irishmen can be found who would disturb a fairy fort or even spend much time in one. A common good-bye warning is, "Safe home and around the fairy forts!"

At times the Tuatha De Danann emerge from their subterranean dwellings to influence the affairs of men. They are credited with assisting in the defeat of Bloody Cromwell at

Cluan-mealla in Tipperary, where over 2,000 of his men were killed in battle. It would seem that, at times, Ireland could have used even more help from these spiritual beings. But who knows how much worse things might have been without them?

Leprechauns: Surely, I Believe; Don't You?

If you want to make an Irishman crazy and display your ignorance and bad manners, ask him if he truly believes in leprechauns. The Irish are all too aware that many of their Anglo neighbors consider them rather daft for harboring these foolish, childish superstitions. They're a bit sensitive about the subject and feel they are being set up to play the fool when some tourist asks them the leprechaun question. Of course they don't believe in this folklore that, nowadays, is little more than a collection of children's stories that promotes the sale of *Wee People* souvenirs. Or do they?

The fellow who has been questioned about the matter may not be a true believer, but he isn't about to say so aloud. 'Twould be foolish, indeed. After all, "they" are everywhere, and you can be sure they will hear. There's no point in inviting disaster upon your own head. Everyone knows how vindictive the little devils can be.

Leprechauns need to hire a new public relations firm, because their present one has done them a gross injustice. To those outside Ireland, leprechauns are thought of as cutesy, Disney-type dwarves who wear pointed caps, pointed shoes, and have pointed ears. They are known for their cobbling skills, their pots of gold, and their ability to locate that elusive end of the rainbow.

True leprechauns deserve far more respect. Not only are they a dignified lot, but cunning, as well. One of the most popular leprechaun stories is that of Owen-a-Kieran, a fellow who was fortunate enough to nab one of the diminutive fellows. Tradition says that you can prevent a leprechaun from escaping just by keeping an eye on him, but not losing sight of one of these wily lads is a difficult task. Owen managed to accomplish this and forced the fellow to tell him where his gold was hidden. This particular leprechaun didn't store his at the end of a rainbow, but beneath a

Gift of Gab

"I am not making a plea for the existence of ghosts and extra-human influences. I would be more inclined to argue that in the context of Ireland the traveler would be well advised to suspend both belief and disbelief in this connection."

—Owen Dudley Edwards

Speak Plain Irish

The term **Wee People** is more American than Irish. On the island, they more commonly refer to their spirited neighbors as the **Good People** or the **Gentle People**.

bouchaillin-buidhe, also known as Benweed. Having this valuable information, Owen released the leprechaun and, because there were bouchaillin-buidhe covering the field, he tied a red kerchief on the particular one to distinguish it. Then he hurried away to get a shovel. But when he returned, he found he had been outwitted by the leprechaun. Every bouchaillin-buidhe in the field was sporting a red kerchief.

So even though we all know that such creatures don't exist, don't say so; don't even think it too loudly. If you're ever lucky enough to see one of these fellows, keep your eye on him until his treasure is safely in your hands. Because if you don't show up with the pot of gold, your neighbors will never believe your story. They'll think you more than a little daft. If they're Irish, don't worry; they won't say so—not out loud.

Folklore to Help Us Believe Again

Irish lore is filled with quaint tales of those "other" beings who live among us, of whom we only catch fleeting glances from the corners of our eyes. When walking a wooded path, we can feel them watching us, as curious about us as we are about them. Because of the stories that have been handed down to us, we know them well.

We also know about these other creatures because the child's spirit within us bears witness to their existence. We know fairies are there, perched in sun-spangled trees, crouching behind moss-covered rocks, or sleeping in a half-opened matchbox in the back of the cupboard. Then there is the odd mischievous one that hides beneath our bed, waiting to grab our toes should we run around in the middle of the night. Don't believe in fairies, you say? You used to. We all did. And wouldn't it be nice if, even for a moment, we could believe again?

The Least You Need to Know

➤ The Irish treasure their mythology and folklore more than most societies, possibly because it was outlawed during times of oppression or because it reminds them of what a great people they were and are again or just because it's such good stuff!

➤ Amergin, the poet druid, is the story of a powerful druid from Mil who battled the Tuatha De Danann with an ancient chant summoned from the misty beginnings of time.

➤ Usually, the Irish refer to the Wee People as the Good People to stay in their favor, because fairy folk are known to have a vindictive nature.

➤ Some believe that the fairies of Ireland are far more than cute little creatures or whimsical folklore. Those of a more mystical mindset believe they were once the spiritual beings, the Tuatha De Danann, who lived in Ireland even before the Celts arrived. They think the Tuatha De Danann still live below the earth, where they were banished long ago, and occasionally surface to come to the aid of men.

Chapter 22

Tourism: Erin's Children Return in Droves!

In This Chapter

➤ They're coming home to visit, to live, and work!

➤ Shop, golf, and take in some castles

➤ Driving backwards (well, it just seems that way)

➤ Ride public transport and make some friends

➤ Hang your hat in a castle, B&B, or a thatched cottage and call it home

➤ Is that English you're speakin'?

By the thousands, Erin's sons and daughters come home every year. Some of them have never even set foot on Irish soil. Someone, maybe an elderly aunt or great-grandfather, said something one Thanksgiving years ago about the family being from County Kerry or from the Sligo area. So the eager American family saves their pennies and takes off for the "auld" country in search of long-lost relatives. Do they find them? Indeed, they often do. As they sit down to share a pint in some dark, cozy pub with a fellow who has the same name and maybe the same shade of copper hair, they find a part of themselves, as well.

Those pilgrimages, undertaken by Irish Americans and Irish from all parts of the world (along with visits from curious non-Irish guests), provide an enormous amount of revenue for Ireland. Tourism is big business on the Emerald Isle.

Speak Plain Irish

When venturing on a trip to Innisfail (the Isle of Destiny), you're sure to get the following greeting (in English or Irish): **Cead Mile Failte,** or One Hundred Thousand Welcomes.

'Tisn't So!

Beware of smart-aleck Irish tour bus drivers who entertain themselves at their American patrons' expense. When asked the common question, "Why do some of those sheep on the roadside have a big blue spot painted on their backsides?" a driver may reply, "Tis to tell the lads from the lasses; the girls wear pink, they do." Of course, 'tisn't so. The colored markings designate ownership.

'Tisn't So!

When you stop into a pub and order yourself a nice pint of Guinness to whet your whistle, *do not* tip the bartender. It's just not done in Ireland. If you do leave a punt or two on the bar, the barkeep will call you back to tell you that you forgot your money on the bar.

Exploring the Homeland

One of the easiest ways to view the homeland is looking through the window of a tour bus while someone with a charming brogue fills you in on all the fanciful details about the countryside. These types of tours are readily available through tourist agencies. For the most part, they are well-organized, and they provide a quick look at the island with minimal effort on the part of the sight-seer. The downside is the rigid schedule and the lack of opportunity to wander where you will. Also, you may find yourself spending more time with the other tourists on the bus than with the natives, and that's a shame. No matter how entertaining that lovely lady from Cleveland may be who's sitting in the bus seat beside you, she won't be as much fun as almost any Irish man, woman, or child who would be sitting on public transportation.

Theme Tours: Golfing, Shopping, Visiting Castles

Another structured, but satisfying, type of tour is a theme tour, which is designed to appeal to those with a certain hobby or favorite pastime. For example, golfing tours take you from one sumptuous green to the next in the marvelous golf courses that are spread across the island. If you love to shop 'til you drop, the tour operators will drop you off at the best spots in the country. There you'll find wonderful products unique to Ireland at mostly affordable prices (if you're a savvy buyer). The crystal, woolens, linens, porcelain, books, recordings, hand crafts, jewelry, art, and antiques will tempt you far beyond what you're able to resist. The workmanship on most of these products will assure you a lifetime of use and pleasure.

Writers or avid, adoring readers can take literary tours and view the birthplaces, burial sites, childhood homes, and creative environs (pubs and, in some cases, the jail cells) of some of your favorite writers. Dublin and Sligo are especially ripe with such landmarks.

Those of you who like castles will be in heaven, because there seems to be some sort of castle ruin in every backyard in Ireland. Castle tours will take you from one medieval (or older) fortress to the next, and guides will fill you in on all the deliciously gory details of the happenings on those spots.

Driving Yourself: Stay on the Wrong Side!

To see the country on your schedule, rent a car and motor about yourself. This method of travel has a couple of drawbacks though. The Irish drive on the left side of the street, and their steering wheels are on the right. Adjusting to this style of driving if you're unfamiliar with it can be difficult, but it isn't something you can take or leave at your leisure. Until you have it straight, you're a traffic hazard.

Also, some of the roads (especially in rural areas) are notoriously narrow. In places, the car you're driving may seem wider than the road itself. The Irish blithely cruise down the center of such country lanes, and then whip to the left when they see someone coming. This style of driving can make that wonderful breakfast you ate at your B&B do flip-flops in your tummy, but it certainly adds a thrill to an otherwise peaceful country ride.

You'll often hear the natives complain bitterly, "Aarah...but petrol is dear." Translation: "Gasoline is expensive." And it is, though maybe not enough to warrant so many complaints. To hear the Irish tell it, everything is "dear."

Public Transport: Ye'll Never Be Lonely

If you truly want to get to know the Irish, and believe me, you do, the best way to go is public transportation. You can purchase a pass for 8 days, 15, 21, or even a month. The pass will get you on either bus and/or train, depending on your destination.

Speak Plain Irish

A favorite pastime in Ireland is **slagging** or playing a harmless game of fooling the tourist, so don't believe everything you hear from your new Irish mates. If you think you're being had, look for the mischievous sparkle in an Irishman's eyes. If the twinkle's there, chances are good that you've just been handed a line of blarney.

Gift of Gab

When an Irish train stopped abruptly in the middle of the countryside, an impatient American passenger yelled to the engineer, "Why did we stop?" "'Tis an auld cow on the line," was the calm answer. A few minutes later, the train was underway, but not for long. When the train stopped for a second time, the American shouted, "What's wrong? Another cow on the tracks, I suppose." The Irish engineer replied dryly, "No, 'tis the same one."

But be warned. If you ride a public conveyance, you must be prepared to converse. The foreign custom of sitting there with headphones on your ears and your nose in a book won't do on a trip from Waterford to Dublin. If you want peace and quiet and a solitary train ride alone with your thoughts and your best-seller, save it for your commute to work when you get back home 'cause sure you won't find it in Ireland.

Speak Plain Irish

DART (Dublin Area Rapid Transport) is the primary system of transportation in Dublin. This above-ground transit system runs only along the water in Dublin, but there has been recent talk of laying track to give the DART a few new, inland stops. Here's a silly inside-Dublin joke: "Isn't it a fine thing, now, that Dublin wasn't named Florence?"

Someone will plop themselves down on the seat across from you or beside you and give you a mournful, gently aggrieved look until you close your book or remove the headphones and begin a conversation. It's worth putting the Walkman away just for the bright smile you receive when you capitulate.

Bicycling: They Say You Never Forget How

Many of the larger towns have places that will rent you a bicycle for an afternoon, a day, week, or longer. Riding a bicycle is a lovely way to see the countryside, smell the delicious air, and feel the wind in your face. Of course, depending on the time of year, that wind can be full of rain, so you have to be a hardy soul who isn't afraid of melting. One of those "soft rains" might come misting down and bloody well drown you.

Accommodations: Where to Lay Your Weary Head

Whether your inclination is a royal palace or a thatch-roofed cottage, Ireland has a place for you to call home, at least for a night or two. With tourism being a major source of revenue for the country, there are more hotels and bed-and-breakfast establishments than you can shake a shillelagh at. The Irish Tourist Board has kindly rated and listed most of them in publications, which they will be delighted to send to you (along with an envelope full of other grand stuff). You can access information from the Irish Tourist Board at this web site: **http://www.ireland.travel.ie/home/index.asp**. Or call or write them at:

The Irish Tourist Board
345 Park Avenue
New York, NY 10145
1-800-223-6470

A Man's Castle Is His Home

Many of Ireland's castles have been converted into hotels; some are fairly rustic, and some are wonderfully deluxe. Of the castles that remain in private hands, many have rooms set aside for overnight guests. The prices can be reasonable, or they can be "dear," but how often do you get to spend the night in a real castle? For that matter, until you left the United States, had you ever even *seen* a real castle? (No, the one in the Magic Kingdom doesn't count!)

Bed and More Breakfast Than You Can Eat

It seems as though everyone in Ireland with an extra bedroom and the need for some extra punts puts a sign out on the lawn and announces that they are a bed-and-breakfast. Most are the real thing and are run by charming people, but review the listings in the Irish Tourist Board publications and check their rating before you agree to stay there.

Staying at a bed-and-breakfast is one of the nicest ways to get to know the Irish people. Often, you can pass the evening sitting by a fragrant turf fire while the family watches television, reads, or plays games around you. The conversation you overhear alone is worth the price of the bed (which is generally very economical).

Later, you sleep in the bedroom at the end of the hallway, lined with rooms for the family's dozen children, who are surprisingly quiet, courteous, and altogether delightful. If the night is chilly, and most are, your thoughtful hostess may slip a hot water bottle between the sheets for you, just before you retire. Don't expect the heat to be on during the night or any time soon when you arise. The cost of heating a house in Ireland is also apparently considered "dear."

The next morning you have breakfast in the dining room, and you'd better make sure your appetite awakens with you, because this is no coffee and piece of toast affair. You rise to a bowl full of cereal and a glass of juice waiting for you. This is followed by the largest meal of the day: eggs, their version of sausages and bacon (far more substantial than American fare), and soda bread or brown bread toast. Sometimes fried potatoes or tomatoes are added, and if you ask the night before, a bowl of "mush" will also be provided, which you will be relieved to know is oatmeal, cooked to perfection.

If you don't devour every morsel of this cardiac nightmare, you will see a mournful, worried look on your hostess's face. As she tries to force more food down you, she'll say something like, "Eat, eat, eat. I'll not be havin' you faint dead away in the street today. If you do, by nightfall, 'twill be said all over town, 'Mary O'Flagherty doesn't feed her guests properly!'"

'Tisn't So!

A bed-and-breakfast is exactly what it says: a bed and a breakfast. By seven o'clock in the evening, when your appetite is asking for dinner, your host will be sitting by the fireplace with her feet up, and she'll have no patience at all with you when you ask about the possibilities of dinner. Make sure you make your dinner plans elsewhere.

Gift of Gab

"Food is golden in the morning, silver at noon, and lead at night."

An old Irish proverb, which probably accounts for why it's such a challenge to wrap your teeth around a good dinner in Ireland (outside of a fine hotel).

Rent a Not-So-Humble Cottage

For those of you who really want to get into the spirit of the place, consider renting one of those charming, quaint cottages, some of which even have thatched roofs. You can pretend to be an oppressed, but gloriously jolly, Irish peasant for a night or a fortnight. I say, "pretend" because you will enjoy such luxuries as central heating and indoor plumbing, such as your ancestors never saw. Of course, you'll have to do without the chickens roosting in the rafters and the cow tied at the end of the main room, but you can still live the fantasy.

Speaking the Language

Even if an American isn't speaking the Gaelic language, he or she can misunderstand and be misunderstood in Ireland to the point where the people trying to communicate wonder if they are communicating in the same language. For example, I had scoured County Kerry for a certain elderly historian who was an expert on the historical event I was researching. When I finally had him on the telephone, I begged him for an interview, and he graciously accepted.

'Tisn't So!

Irish lads and lasses rarely worry about punctuality. It's not that they don't care about their engagements—they do. They just have a much more laid-back way of dealing with time. You might find yourself annoyed when you agreed to meet Irish friends at two in a pub, and they don't show until three, but take a deep breath, relax, and remember: You're on Irish time now.

I asked, "Could I drop by your home for a few minutes tomorrow?" He replied, "Call at three." I assumed he was a busy fellow, unsure of tomorrow's schedule, so I happily agreed, hoping he would have time to squeeze me in. At three o'clock the next day, I dialed his number, and the instant I identified myself, he snapped, "Where are ye?"

"Here at my B&B," I said, "phoning because you asked me to call and..."

"Aye, where are ye?"

It took several of these exchanges before I realized his *call* meant *visit*. He had been expecting me to arrive at three and was irritated that I had stood him up.

A few other terms might give you a problem:

➤ The term *craic* (pronounced *crack*) means fun and lots of it. So if some sweet-faced young Irish lady is telling you what great craic she had at a party last evening, don't be scandalized and recommend that she head for the nearest drug rehabilitation clinic.

➤ When referring to time, the Irish use the term *half* to refer to the half-hour mark. For instance, if you plan to go to a show at the Abbey Theatre at 7:30 p.m., you'd say "half-seven." You'll also notice that instead of saying *after* (quarter after seven), the Irish use the word *past* (quarter past seven).

➤ As mentioned before, *call* means visit, but *ring* means call. Got that? If not, ring me, and I'll pick up the phone and explain it to you, but don't call, because I won't answer the door.

➤ Irish people don't have all that many more holidays than anyone else, but they do call their vacations holidays. So if they ask you if you're on holiday, don't look at your calendar to see if it's Thanksgiving or Halloween.

➤ Ladies, if a handsome Irish lad suggests that you allow him to "knock you up at half-ten," don't slap his face. He's not being *cheeky* (fresh), he's only asking if he can knock on your door or call on you if you please.

The Least You Need to Know

➤ Tourism is big business in Ireland, as thousands return to the homes of their ancestors to get in touch with their family roots.

➤ Between the shopping, sightseeing, golfing, fishing, and chatting up the residents of a local pub, you'll never be bored or lonely while in Ireland.

➤ Whether you stay in a bed-and-breakfast, a remodeled castle, or a winsome thatched cottage, the Irish make you feel at home.

➤ Although the Irish speak English, you may be confused by some of the terminology. Take a crash course in Irishisms before you go, or you might find yourself "knocked up at half-eight!"

The Irish: Musical, Athletic, and Crafty!

In This Chapter

➤ Reviving the old tunes

➤ Tweed and sweaters, lace and linen

➤ Fire and sand become crystal magic

➤ The Claddagh: symbol of love and loyalty

➤ Gaelic football, hurling, rugby, and horse racing: the Irish are still fighting amongst themselves

The newest generation of Irish are a robust, well-grounded people as demonstrated by the music they play, the crafts they create, the sports in which they compete, the new industry they promote and the politics they embrace. They retain a love of their heritage while looking to a bright future, showing all the strength and optimism of their ancestors. It's never been a brighter day to be Irish.

Erin's Song

Since the days of the druids, musicians have been greatly revered, even feared, in Ireland. In ancient times, a harpist/minstrel could destroy your standing in the community by composing a scathing satire of you. It was in a person's best interest, then, to stay in the good graces of these folks with singing harps and searing tongues. This tradition of music with a message has continued into the present day. Whether it be a fiery tune with politics at its core or a melodic love song that would break even the stoniest of hearts, the music of the Irish is one of great passion.

Traditionally, musicians served a greater calling than merely the production of pretty melodies. Their primary duties were to write glowing reviews of kings, chieftains, and other prominent individuals, recording their virtues and victories, even if that meant embellishing the truth a bit. Equally important, they were expected to ridicule a nobleman's enemies. Far more than mere entertainers, these musicians could, with one composition, promote or demote an individual within his social structure. Thus, the interweaving of music and poetry with political and social commentary has its roots deep in ancient Celtic tradition.

A Bard's Tale

For periods of time in Ireland's troubled history, Irish music (and literature) was banned. Understanding the power that composers and musicians have over their people, the British government, under Elizabeth I, outlawed all traditional music. The Queen proclaimed, "Hang all the harpers where found, and burn the instruments."

The Old Tunes Are Heard Again

The Irish have always enjoyed a poignant ballad or a rollicking jig or reel. In a country where the weather isn't always conducive to outdoor activities, indoor music making has long been a popular pastime for royal and peasant alike. A combination of traditional instruments, including the harp, the tin whistle, the accordion, the flute, the bodhran (a round, hand-held drum), and the Uilleann (an elbow bagpipe), are employed to create that distinctive sound that causes any Irishman's pulse to leap a beat or two.

Recently, a modern revival of Irish folk music has been fired by the talents of such wonderful groups as: Makem and Clancy, The Chieftains, the Clancy Brothers, Horslips, the Wolfe Tones, and The Dubliners. Some Irish songs have become old standbys around the world. How could St. Patrick's Day be properly celebrated without the crooning of at least one verse of "The Londonderry Air" and "The Rose of Tralee"?

New Lads and Lasses on the Block

A particularly exciting occurrence has been the effect of Irish music on the pop charts. Never a group to shrink from challenge, Irish musicians have managed to combine traditional aspects of Celtic tunes with that of the modern music beat.

Popular music pioneers such as Van Morrison (who has been on the scene for over 30 years now) have paved the way for many a band to bring their brand of Irish rock to American stages and radio waves. Probably the most well-known of Ireland's rock 'n roll success stories is the enormously popular U2, a band whose lyrics contain many political and spiritual references, which delineate them as quintessentially Irish. U2 has maintained a strong American following since they burst onto the American music scene in the early 80s, with songs that go from politics to love to just plain fun.

Also popular, in spite of her controversial views, is Sinead O'Connor. Best known for her striking appearance (up until recently, this beautiful Irish lass spent many years shaving her head bald as a cue ball) and her appearance on *Saturday Night Live* when she tore up a picture of Pope John Paul III, O'Connor's intensely beautiful voice has outlasted the repercussions of her in-your-face style of political debate.

In addition, listeners the world over have become enthralled by the ethereal, lilting quality of Enya, the strong chords and unpredictable notes of the Cranberries, as well as bands such as the ever-raucous Pogues and ex-Pogues singer Shane McGowen and the Popes, the Scotch/Irish Waterboys, the Hothouse Flowers, Therapy, Ash, the Corrs, the Proclaimers, and Mary Coughlan, to name just a few.

Those Nimble-Footed Dancers

Traditional Irish dance is an art form packed with energy and passion. Wearing hard shoes called horn pipe shoes, Irish dancers can pound out a number to rival that of the spiciest Mediterranean variety. Theater goers worldwide have been flocking to see the magnificent productions of *Riverdance,* and its more recent offshoot, *Lord of the Dance,* which celebrate the Irish dance tradition. As a result, dance classes are overflowing with youngsters and adults alike learning the traditional Irish dances. Irish musicians with agile fingers and dancers with magic in their feet are introducing a whole new generation to the wonders of Celtic music.

A Bard's Tale

Riverdance began as a half-time show on the Eurovision Song Contest, an annual event in which European countries compete against each other for the best musical act. Whichever country wins the contest hosts it the following year and gets to feature one of its home acts in the interval during the competition. Ireland won several years in a row and presented a group of Irish dancers during the half-time show. The dancers were so popular that they began to tour as a dance troupe, and *Riverdance* was born.

A Crafty Lot, the Irish Are

The word *craft* may bring fond memories of sitting in your schoolroom with a pile of wooden Popsicle sticks and a bottle of white glue, but to the Irish, crafts are part of a long, Celtic tradition. Their textiles are magnificent creations that no automated machine loom can even simulate. Until you slip into an Irish sweater, run your hand across a piece of fine Irish linen, or study the intricate work on a bit of their lace, you don't know the quality you've been missing.

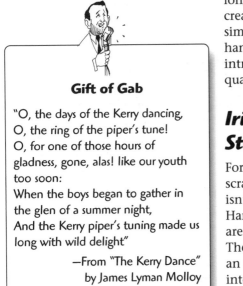

Gift of Gab

"O, the days of the Kerry dancing,
O, the ring of the piper's tune!
O, for one of those hours of gladness, gone, alas! like our youth too soon:
When the boys began to gather in the glen of a summer night,
And the Kerry piper's tuning made us long with wild delight"

—From "The Kerry Dance"
by James Lyman Molloy

Irish Tweed, Not That Auld Stiff Stuff

For many, the word *tweed* may bring to mind a stiff, scratchy, brown fabric dotted with bits of beige. But that isn't the sort of tweed that the Irish are so proud of. Hardworking folks in many different parts of the island are master craftsmen at the art of hand-weaving tweed. They produce a soft, lightweight material that comes in an assortment of delicious colors. The fabric is fashioned into everything from a man's hunting jacket to stunning dresses and striking scarves.

Although Donegal is most famous for its marvelous tweeds, the craft is widespread throughout the country. Masters weave their magic in Dublin, around County Wicklow, and also in Kerry and Connemara. Some of the best Irish stores specialize in tweeds. Kevin and Howlin in Dublin carries a variety of sports jackets and suits, as do McGee's of Donegal and Martin Standun in Spiddal, County Galway.

The selections at these stores include traditional styles as well as cutting-edge fashions and even the unusual, bordering on the absurd. The old tweed cap has been back for more than a decade, and some fellows find that tweed neckties are lightweight and comfortable and lend a certain aristocratic flair to a gentleman's wardrobe. Women's skirts come in a wide range of sizes, colors, and styles, providing fashion as well as long-wearing value.

The fine, undyed tweed material called *bainin* has been used traditionally for the Aran Island fishermen's jackets, but now it is made with a finer weave and is used for a multitude of purposes in the crafting of garments. Home furnishings also include a touch of tweed here and there. Bedspreads, curtains, pillows, cushions, placemats, and throw rugs are popular in distinguished tweed.

So the next time you want to take a stroll across the lush green countryside with a faithful hound at your heels, a pipe in your hand, and an aristocratic lift to your chin, slip into a jacket made of fine Irish tweed, put on a tweed cap, tilted slightly to one side, and, if the weather's particularly nippy, wind a nice tweed wrapper around your throat. You'll look and feel quite the country gentleman or lady, as the case may be. (Yes, some women still smoke pipes in Ireland.)

Linen and Lace, Quintessential Femininity

Ladies of discriminating taste have always treasured a gift of Irish linen and lace. For generations, hope chests have been filled with tablecloths, napkins, sheets, pillow slips, doilies, and tablemats (not to mention the gentlewoman's lingerie) made of durable and elegant Irish linen and trimmed with delicate, intricate Irish lace. Many a bride has glided down the aisle, her face hidden demurely behind an Irish lace veil.

Traditional Irish crochet dates back to the 1840s when it began in the cottages of Limerick, Kenmare, and Carrickmacross. Originally, the lacemakers used cotton thread exclusively, but now they also use wool. Irish lace decorates a variety of goods, including scarves and shawls, collar and cuff sets, blouses and dresses, pillow slips and sheet edges, and tablecloths and tablemats.

The heart of the linen industry is located south of Belfast in Antrim, Down, and Armagh. At Lisburn in Country Antrim, the Irish Linen Centre shows visitors how flax is transformed into linen through audio-visual presentations and live demonstrations by local weavers and artisans. The art of *sprigging,* hand-embroidering domestic linen and handkerchiefs, began in County Donegal as a cottage craft, but it is far more widespread now as an industry.

Whether a lady is giving a gift, decorating her own home, or building her trousseau, fine Irish linen and lace are some of the best in the world and will remain serviceable and beautiful for a lifetime.

Aran Sweaters

There's nothing like an Aran sweater to keep you warmer than a freshly baked loaf of soda bread. These gorgeous sweaters have become very popular with the tourists lately, and that popularity has caused the prices to become "dear," indeed. They vary in quality and weight, though almost all are fine garments. Some are hand-knit; some are knit by machine. The machine-knit sweaters will cost you less, but they aren't as traditional. It all depends upon your taste.

Shimmering Crystal

Of all its many hand-crafted imports, Ireland must surely be best-known for its crystal. (It's debatable whether Guinness is hand-crafted.) The name Waterford crystal is synonymous with perfection and high level craftsmanship.

In Waterford, County Cork, where Waterford crystal is created, visitors may tour the factory, assisted by friendly guides. Visitors are lead through the process, step by meticulous step, as the simple ingredients of silica sand, litharge, potash, and the heat from mighty furnaces are used to create a miracle of light. At the factory there in Waterford, crystal is transformed into everything from Superbowl trophies to chandeliers to hang in the palaces of the world's kings.

George and William Penrose opened a small factory there in 1783, and since that time master glassblowers and their apprentices have used the traditional tools to work their alchemy: hollow iron rods, wooden molds, and countless years of experience. Special attention is paid to the thickness of the glass, because it will later be carved with multifacets, the trademark of Waterford crystal.

'Tisn't So!

Some folks scour the Irish countryside trying to save a few coins by buying a *second* or slightly defective piece of Waterford crystal, but they are searching in vain. Inspections are performed at the factory every step of the way. If a piece is anything other than absolutely perfect, it is immediately destroyed. There are no Waterford crystal seconds.

After the crystal shape has been blown, it is *annealed*. This specialized process of slowly cooling the glass prevents tiny cracks or stresses from developing in the piece that might later cause it to break. The cooling is done gradually in annealing ovens, which control the rate at which the glass cools. A sports trophy might require as much as 16 hours to anneal properly.

The true mastery of the craftsmen is revealed as they grind the crystal. With diamond-tipped cutting wheels, they create the exquisite, deeply cut patterns that Waterford has been known for since George and William began so long ago.

Waterford crystal can be purchased in many locations across the island, as well as in the factory gift shop. The prices don't vary much, but you can find good buys at the Shannon and Dublin airport where you can purchase items duty-free. But whether you carry home a wine glass, purchase a paperweight, or ship a chandelier to your palace in Beverly Hills, your Waterford crystal will be a source of pride and delight to you and your heirs for generations to come. (By the way, although Waterford is the best-known name in crystal, the glass coming out of Tipperary is also exquisite. For sheer beauty and craftsmanship, they are a worthy competitor to Waterford and are less expensive.)

The Claddagh

Ireland has many choices for jewelry lovers, from the reproductions of the beautiful Tara Brooch, to rosaries made of beads of Connemara marble, to the most popular item of all, the Claddagh. This lovely design has captured the hearts of Irish folk and tourists alike. This symbol adorns everything from necklaces to door knockers, but the most popular rendition is the Claddagh ring.

The pattern is a heart with a crown at the top and a pair of hands on either side. The heart represents love, the crown loyalty, and the hands friendship. It is little wonder that the Claddagh is a favorite wedding ring; Claddagh rings are crafted in gold or silver and are sometimes adorned with emeralds and diamonds.

Claddaghs are sold throughout Ireland in every gift shop and jewelry store. Bringing one home to a sweetheart or a dear friend is to give that person a part of old Ireland.

From Harvesting Spuds to Power-Lunch Duds

For all the Irish complaining about the state of affairs, the Irish economy is doing far better than it has in the past. Throughout the ages, the island's income was primarily agricultural. But the government realized that this was not the best for the people, and they have invested a great deal in industry. With subsidies and other forms of support, they have encouraged international companies, especially in the field of computer technology, to build factories and plants in Ireland. This growing industry has lead to more jobs, which in turn has resulted in fewer young people leaving home to find work.

Industry in Ireland can now be considered successful by any standard and has become the center of the economy. Currently Irish industry accounts for 37 percent of the domestic product, over 75 percent of exports, and 29 percent of the work force. Most of the Irish still work in the area of service (57 percent). Although unemployment rates remain high (between 15 and 18 percent), things are definitely looking up. For instance, emigration levels are low, and more of the teenagers are staying home rather than trotting off to the United States or Great Britain in search of jobs.

All this work at the dawn of the millennium seems to be having an interesting effect on things at home, as well. For one thing, the marriage rate is down. The next generation doesn't seem to feel the need to rush into matrimony at a young age. For those who are married, the birth rate is much lower than that of their parents and grandparents. At 2.1 births per childbearing woman, the rate isn't even high enough to replace the current generation. Not to worry, the Irish are hardly an endangered species. Left to their own devices, they will continue to triumph. Optimism is still a rare commodity on the world market, but a valuable one, and Ireland has more than her share of that.

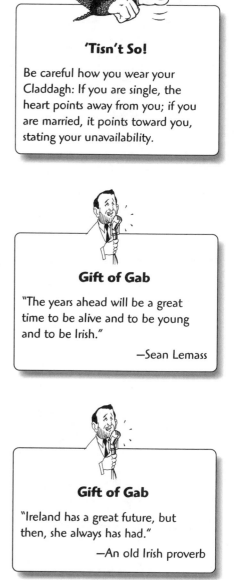

'Tisn't So!

Be careful how you wear your Claddagh: If you are single, the heart points away from you; if you are married, it points toward you, stating your unavailability.

Gift of Gab

"The years ahead will be a great time to be alive and to be young and to be Irish."

—Sean Lemass

Gift of Gab

"Ireland has a great future, but then, she always has had."

—An old Irish proverb

Sports: The "Clans" Still Wage War

From the days when the ancient Celts drove their chariots from miles away to gather in assemblies and participate in athletic competition until now, the Irish have been crazy for their sports. The Irish are passionately competitive with each other and outsiders. If there's anything an Irishman loves more than his Guinness, it's his Gaelic football. Of course, he would see no reason to have to choose between the two.

Gift of Gab

"The condition of Irish sport is frequently desperate but never serious."

—Tony O'Reilly

Gaelic Football: The Manly Man's Sport

Imagine a cross between rugby and soccer, played with an exuberance unmatched in American football or European soccer and executed at breakneck speed. That's Gaelic football. More accurate than saying it is a mixture of these games would be to say it was the progenitor of these games.

Gaelic football is certainly not a sport for the meek, and its heroes are widely touted. Many a young Irish boy grows up with dreams of leading his team to victory and claiming the All-Ireland title, the equivalent of winning the American Superbowl. A career in Gaelic football can lead you far. A lad named Jack Lynch captained a team that won six All-Ireland titles, and he was rewarded by being elected prime minister—twice!

Hurling: Older Than the Irish

None of the Irish people's sports are complacent; hurling is another example of how vigorous these Celtic athletes can be. The game has been around as long as recorded history, probably dating back to the days of the ancient Celts. The name comes from the *hurley*, a stick approximately three-feet long and curved on the end that is used to hurl a ball down field and through your opponent's goal posts.

'Tisn't So!

If you aren't an ardent sports devotee, you might want to keep silent about it. Former Prime Minster Garret Fitzgerald once made the mistake of admitting that he would prefer to study a train timetable than watch a football game. The confession cost him several points in the popularity polls.

The scoring may be confusing to novice onlookers, but the enthusiasm with which the sport is played and observed by fans is contagious. It is played all summer long, and the All-Ireland finals are in September in Dublin.

Rugby, Where North Meets South

To the untrained eye, rugby looks like football, only without all the boring starts and stops. Hearty lads attempt to run a ball through their opponents' defenses, inflicting damage along the way and sustaining plenty of their own.

Rugby began as a Protestant game, but it was taken up by the Catholics and is now enjoyed by all. The international teams are made up of players from both sides of the border, and in a rare display of unity, political differences are swept aside as they represent old Erin's isle abroad.

Horse Racing: An Ongoing Love Between Man and Beast

No one loves horses more than the Irish people. They worship them. For centuries, the aristocrats of Europe have traveled to Ireland to buy some of the best horses bred in the world. The elite also congregate in Ireland for the wildly exciting races held there annually.

Racing is more than a national pastime; it's an obsession. Even on workdays the tracks are humming in places such as the Curragh, Leopardstown, Phoenix Park, Fairyhouse, Tralee, and Galway. The crowd alone is worth watching; it's comprised of kings and paupers, young and old, winning and losing fortunes and enjoying every moment no matter what their luck.

Whether the Irish turn their hands to knitting, jewelry making, lace tatting, or linen embroidery, they create pure magic. Whether they are spinning sand into priceless crystal or racing a thoroughbred toward the finish line, they are champions. On athletic fields, competing before screaming throngs, or in quiet, dark pub corners, strumming guitars, they transport their spectators to another world. In this world of Erin, ancient tradition is translated by the creativity of the modern Irish, who preserve the old and yet strive for innovation. They are an industrious, crafty, and quietly (and sometimes not so quietly) ambitious lot. In other words, after all these centuries, the Celts haven't really changed at all, just improved. And we're all the better for it.

The Least You Need to Know

➤ The Irish have revived their traditional music, and the latest generation of Erin's sons and daughters are, once again, singing the songs that were once outlawed.

➤ The old traditions of lace making, weaving, knitting, and making glorious crystal are alive and thriving in Ireland.

➤ After a long, difficult recession, Ireland is doing well with new industries opening and thriving, providing much-needed jobs and stability.

➤ The sports of Gaelic football, hurling, rugby, and horse racing are just as much a part of the nation's spirit as ever. The Irish never need an excuse to compete with one another on an athletic field.

Chapter 24

Tracing Those Irish Grandfa'rs

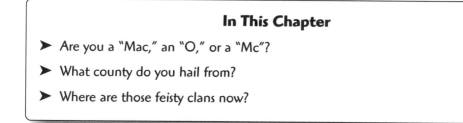

In This Chapter

➤ Are you a "Mac," an "O," or a "Mc"?

➤ What county do you hail from?

➤ Where are those feisty clans now?

Some of you may already know the names of your Irish ancestors, what counties they hailed from, and maybe even whether there was a king or a horse thief among them. (Sometimes the kings and the horse thieves were one and the same.) But for those of you who haven't a clue where your Irish ancestry began, you may want to search these counties and the names of some of their more prominent families.

If you can't find your name, look for it without the O, Mac, or Mc. When coming to the United States, many families shed their O's and Mc's to appear more American. *O* merely means *of*, and *Mac* means "son or grandson of." *Mc* is short for *Mac*. There you have it—easy got as a wet foot!

You may find your name listed under more than one county. Although some families tended to stay in one area generation after generation, others traveled about, making it more difficult for their American children's children to find them. If they got around that quickly, they probably had a horse, which brings us back to that king/horse thief theory.

Keep in mind that this list is limited, and you may not find your surname. A more detailed book of Irish names at your local library would probably point you in the right direction. I've also included a list of books on genealogy at the end of the chapter as well as addresses and phone numbers of places to buy Irish genealogy books.

Families of County Antrim

Diamond	McElvenny	O'Hamill
Earle	McNally	O'Hara
McAllister	McQuillan	O'Keevan
McClean	Mulholland	O'Shiel
McDonald	O'Donnellan	Stewart
McDougall	O'Flynn	

Families of County Armagh

Callan	McAlinden	McSherry
Keiran	McCann	McVeagh
Larkin	McEvoy	O'Garvey
MacGee	McGivern	O'Hanratty
Marron	McPartlan	O'Neill

Families of County Carlow

Bolger	Gahan	O'Cavanagh
Cahill	Hayden	O'Doyle
Carew	Kinsella	Ryan
Fortune	Nolan	

Families of County Cavan

Brady	Dolan	Fleming
Brogan	Drum	Gaffney
Carolan	Fitzsimon	Kiernan

McCabe	McTiernan	O'Farrelly
McGovern	Mulligan	O'Lynch
McGowan	O'Clery	O'Reilly
McHugh	O'Curry	Smith
McNulty	O'Daly	Tully
McSharry	O'Donohoe	

Families of County Clare

Boland	McMahon	O'Griffey
Brody	McNamara	O'Halloran
Carmody	Melody	O'Loughlin
Considine	Minogue	O'Moloney
Culligan	Mullins	O'Morony
Deegan	Neilan	O'Hehir
Durack	O'Brien	Shannon
Gallery	O'Cullenan	Sheedy
Hanrahan	O'Daly	Slattery
Liddy	O'Flattery	
McInerney	O'Grady	

Families of County Cork

Ahern	Cagney	Corry
Barrett	Canty	Cotter
Barry	Coakley	Coughlan
Begley	Coleman	Cowley
Bohane	Collins	Cremin
Bradley	Cooney	Crowley
Buckley	Coppinger	Cullinane

continues

DeCourcy	MacAuliffe	O'Driscoll
Dinneen	McCarthy	O'Fineily
Donnegan	McDonough	O'Harlihy
Fitzgerald	McSheehy	O'Hoolaghan
Goggin	McSherry	O'Hurley
Gould	McSweeny	O'Leary
Harnett	Mullan	O'Looney
Harrington	Murphy	O'Riordan
Hartigan	Nagle	O'Scannell
Healy	Noonan	O'Tuomey
Hennigan	O'Callaghan	Regan
Horgan	O'Curry	Roche
Kearney	O'Daly	Rynne
Lucy	O'Doheny	
Lyons	O'Donavan	

Families of County Derry

Bradley	McGilligan	O'Carolan
Cassidy	McGinn	O'Connell
Deary	Mullen	O'Conor
McCracken	Mulligan	O'Friel
McCrilly	Mulvenna	O'Kane
McDonnell	Murray	O'Quigley

Families of County Donegal

Cannon	Gallagher	McClean
Coyle	Gillespie	McCloskey
Donelly	Kenny	McCool
Farren	McBride	McCrossan

McFadden	McWard	O'Gormley
McGinty	O'Boyle	O'Quinn
McHugh	O'Clery	O'Sheeran
McLeach	O'Curran	O'Shiel
McLinchy	O'Doherty	Pattan
McLoughlin	O'Donnell	Roddy
McRoarty	O'Dornin	Toner
McSweeney	O'Dorrian	

Families of County Down

Campbell	Lowry	O'Garvey
Colter	Macken	O'Loughnan
Copeland	Mandeville	O'Moore
Devaney	Martell	O'Moran
Donlevy	McGuinness	O'Rogan
Jordan	McRory	Rooney
Lawlor	Murray	Savage

Families of County Dublin

Baggot	Harold	Segrave
Casey	Hennessy	St. Lawrence
Cruise	Plunkett	Talbot
Fagan	Preston	Taylor
Fitzwilliam	Ronan	Tyrell

Families of County Fermanagh

Breslin	Maguire	McManus
Connolly	McCaffrey	McTiernan
Corcoran	McEntaggart	Muldoon
Corrigan	McGarrahan	O'Casey
Corry	McGillinen	O'Glanagan
Devine	McGrath	O'Gorman
Keenan	McGuigan	
MacAuley	McGuire	

Families of County Galway

Birmingham	Flaherty	Mulkerin
Blake	French	Mullally
Brehan	Gilduff	Mullarky
Broder	Gilkelly	Naughton
Browne	Hannon	O'Callanan
Burke	Haverty	O'Conealy
Cahill	Hynes	O'Daly
Cawley	Jennings	O'Donnellan
Cook	Joyce	O'Flaherty
Day	Kenny	O'Kelly
Deane	Kirwan	O'Moran
Devaney	Larkin	O'Sheehan
Divilly	Lennon	Page
Doorly	Lynch	Ruane
Doyle	Manning	Tormey
Duane	Martin	Tracy
Fahy	McEgan	Tuohy
Feeney	McNevin	Ward

Families of County Kerry

Brennan	Hallissey	O'Daly
Brosnan	Healy	O'Donoghoe
Cahill	Joy	O'Gallivan
Clancy	Kelleher	O'Grady
Clifford	Kissane	O'Hagarty
Creagh	Leahy	O'Mahony
Cronin	Long	O'Moore
Delany	Magrath	O'Moran
Doolin	McCarthy	O'Mullane
Downey	McElligott	O'Quill
Egan	McGillicuddy	O'Quinlan
Falvey	McKenna	O'Rahilly
Fenton	Moriarty	O'Shea
Ferriter	Moynihan	O'Sullivan
Fitzmaurice	O'Carroll	Stack
Foley	O'Casey	Trant
Griffin	O'Connell	
Guiney	O'Conor	

Families of County Kildare

Bermingham	Colgan	Morrin
Bracken	Cullen	O'Conor
Burke	Dunn	O'Kelly
Carey	Fitzhenry	Woulfe

Families of County Kilkenny

Birch	Cody	O'Donoghue
Bookie	Comerford	O'Loughnan
Brennan	Dunphy	Purcell
Broder	Forrestal	Roth
Butler	Gaul	Ryan
Callan	Grace	Shortall
Cantwell	Marnell	Sweetman
Cleere	Mullins	Walsh

Families of County Leitrim

Clancy	McDorcy	McTeigue
Finn	McFergus	Meehan
Gallon	McGoldrick	Muvey
Ganly	McGowan	O'Carroll
Gilmartin	McKeon	O'Cuirneen
Goggan	McMorrow	O'Rourke
Kenny	McRannall	Reynolds
MacElroy	McShanley	Roddy

Families of County Leix

Breen	Delaney	Lalor
Brophy	Doran	McCashin
Butler	Dowling	McEvoy
Campion	FitzPatrick	Mooney
Costigan	Gilpatrick	Mulhall
Deegan	Hely	O'Moore

Families of County Limerick

Condon	Kinealy	O'Donovan
Crawford	Kirby	O'Scanlan
Culhane	McArthur	O'Sheehan
Cummins	McCurtin	Quinn
Fitzgibbon	McEnery	Roche
Fitzharris	Mulcahy	Russell
Harold	Nestor	Sheehy
Hely	O'Conlan	Troy
Kiely	O'Connell	

Families of County Longford

Conway	McGilligan	O'Quinn
Fleming	McHugh	Ronan
Flood	McMaster	Sheridan
Gaynor	Mulroy	Slevin
McCormac	O'Farrell	Tuite

Families of County Louth

Bellew	Geehan	O'Scanlon
Branigan	Heaney	Rice
Carragher	Kenny	Verdon
Coleman	McMahon	
Devereaux	O'Genry	

Families of County Mayo

Bannon	Kearns	Murray
Barrett	Killeen	O'Beirne
Brady	Lawless	O'Gormley
Canny	Lynott	O'Hara
Connegan	McAndrew	O'Malley
Costello	McGarry	Petit
Coyne	McNally	Philbin
Dorcey	McPhillips	Prendergast
Dugan	Milford	Ronan
Finnegan	Morris	Tierney
Jordan	Mulroy	

Families of County Meath

Barnwall	Hand	O'Carolan
Bates	Hayes	O'Connolly
Conlon	Hussey	O'Gogary
Cusack	Langan	O'Halligan
Darcy	Loughnane	O'Kelly
Devane	Mortimer	O'Regan
Drake	Murtagh	O'Rory
Dunn	Nangle	Peppard
Fagan	Netherville	Traynor
Gibney	Nugent	

Families of County Monaghan

Boylan	Kelaghan	McQuade
Cosgrave	McArdell	O'Coigley
Gernon	McKenna	O'Duffy
Gilroy	McNally	Tully
Hughes	McNeany	

Families of County Offaly

Bannan	Collier	Molloy
Beary	Cunneen	Mooney
Behan	Delahunt	Mulvany
Bergin	Dempsey	O'Carroll
Carey	Gill	O'Flanagan
Coghlan	Holohan	O'Hart
Colgan	Kearney	Warren

Families of County Roscommon

Brennan	Lavan	Monahan
Concannon	McDermott	Morehan
Conroy	McEoin	Mulready
Cooney	McGeraghty	Norton
Cox	McGlynn	O'Duffy
Dillan	McGreevey	O'Flynn
Duignan	McWeeney	O'Gormley
Fallon	Molloy	O'Hanley

Families of County Sligo

Coleman	McGorley	O'Gavaghan
Conway	Mongan	O'Harte
Devlin	Morrison	O'Keeran
Durkin	Morrissey	O'Mullany
Kernanghan	O'Creane	O'Mulvany
McDermott	O'Dowd	O'Rafferty
McDonagh	O'Flannelly	Spelman
McFirbis	O'Gara	

Families of County Tipperary

Corcoran	Looby	O'Meara
Dermody	Lynch	O'Slattery
Donegan	Mathew	O'Sullivan
Duggan	McGrath	Quinlan
Fanning	Meagher	Quirke
Fennessy	Morrissey	Reidy
Fogarty	Mulcahy	Ryan
Gleason	O'Brien	Scully
Halley	O'Callaghan	Sexton
Hickey	O'Donnell	Spillane
Hogan	O'Dwyer	Tobin
Lannigan	O'Harigan	White
Lee	O'Hurley	

Families of County Tyrone

Cooney	Hughes	McConmee
Donnegan	Laverty	McCourt
Green	McCarvill	McCrossan

McEtigan	O'Connelan	O'Neill
McGoldrick	O'Corry	O'Quinn
McIntyre	O'Duvany	O'Rafferty
McRory	O'Henry	Tighe
McShane	O'Hussey	Tomalty
McTaggart	O'Kelly	
Mellah	O'Lunney	

Families of County Waterford

Brick	Henebry	Phelan
Crotty	Merry	Power
Dennehy	O'Flannagan	Sherlock
Foley	O'Keane	Wadding
Geary	O'Mullany	Wall
Harper	Ormonde	Wyse

Families of County Westmeath

Barberry	Delamere	Mulcady
Carey	Dooley	O'Daly
Coffey	Fay	O'Kearney
Coleman	Fenlon	O'Scully
Corrigan	Fox	Toler
Dalton	Malone	

Families of County Wexford

Browne	Corish	Esmond
Codd	Deveraux	Fitzharris
Colclough	Doran	Fitzhenry

continues

Fitzstephen	Larkin	Redmond
Garvey	Lynam	Rossiter
Hartley	Masterson	Sinnott
Hayes	McMurrough	Stafford
Keating	Morgan	Sutton
Keogh	Murphy	Walsh

Families of County Wicklow

Bollard	Doyle	O'Toole
Butler	Fitzwilliam	Tallon
Cheevers	Furlong	Tighe
Cooke	Lombard	Walsh
Cosgrove	O'Byrne	

Whatcha Say?

By the way, if you do trace your family roots all the way back to the old country and meet some long-lost relatives, you will want to be able to properly pronounce their names and not make a donkey's hind leg of yourself when you're introduced. These are some of the more commonly mispronounced given names and the way to speak them in plain Irish:

Name	Pronunciation
Aine	OWN ya
Aoife	EE fa
Caitriona	Ka trina
Ciaran	KEER un
Colm	CALL um
Donough	DUN uh
Eamon	Ay mon
Eoin	Owen
Kathleen	KAT leen

Name	Pronunciation
Liam	LEE um
Maeve	Mayve
Malachi	MAL akey
Moire	MOY ra
Niall	Neel
Niamh	Neev
Sean	Shawn
Seamus	SHAY mus
Sinead	Shi NAY ud
Siobahn	SHI vawn

Tools to Help You Uncover Your Heritage

Tracing your ancestors can be a time-consuming and fairly complicated matter. I can't go into all the ins and outs of such a search in this book, but these wonderful books may help you:

The Ancestor Trail in Ireland: Companion Guide by Donal F. Begley

Directory of Irish Archives, edited by Seamus Helferty and Raymond Refausse

Irish Families by Edward MacLysaght

Irish Family History by Marilyn Yurdan, Bastford, 1990

Irish Genealogy by Donal Begley, published by Heraldic Artists Ltd.

The Irish Roots Guild by Tony McCarthy, Lilliput, 1991

Surnames of Ireland by Edward MacLysaght

Tracing the Past by Dr. William Nolan

Tracing Your Irish Roots by Christine Kinealy, Blackstaff Press, 1990

You can purchase these books at leading bookstores or by ordering from the following bookstores:

The Genealogy Bookshop
(Heraldic Artists Ltd.)
3 Nassau Street, Dublin 2
Telephone: (01) 679 7020

Historic Families
8 Fleet Street, Dublin 2
Telephone: (01) 677 7034

Mullins of Dublin
Heraldic House
36 Upper O'Connell Street, Dublin 1
Telephone: (01) 674 1133

Bernard Sheehan
3 Sir Harry's Mall, Limerick
Telephone: (061) 52794

The Irish Tourist Board will also send you information sheets concerning your genealogical search upon request (see Chapter 22).

The Least You Need to Know

➤ Everyone should find out, at least, what county their Irish ancestors were from and then pay that area a visit. There's nothing like coming home to Mother Erin!

➤ The families of Ireland have moved about a bit, but there are concentrations of certain names in many regions. With a bit of research, you can ferret out your family's information.

➤ A number of publications can help you with your genealogical search. A few are listed in this chapter, and the research librarian at your local public library can probably point you in the right direction.

Speak Plain
Irish Glossary

agitation   Irish term for a movement to sway public opinion toward a particular political agenda.

agrarian sects   Underground terrorist groups organized by the Catholic peasantry in retaliation against oppression by the British. They inflicted covert punishments on Protestant landlords, such as mutilating livestock, burning houses, and beating and even killing the aristocrats themselves.

Ard Ri   The Irish word for high king or emperor.

barbarian   A term coined by the Greeks for anyone who couldn't master the Greek language.

bard   One of an ancient Celtic order of poets who recited verses about the exploits of their tribes.

Black and Tans   British soldiers/police known for their mixed uniforms (black and tan) and their brutality when dealing with the Irish public.

black rent   A colorful name for extorted "protection" money.

blarney   The truth as only an Irishman can tell it.

Blarney stone   Stone found at Blarney Castle. It is said that if you kiss this stone, you will be rewarded with the gift of gab.

bodhran   A traditional Irish drum.

brehon   A judge or arbitrator of old Celtic law.

cairn   Stones heaped over the grave immediately following a burial to keep animals from digging up those who were trying to rest in peace. It also provided a monument for the dead. Sometimes cairns were used to show the spot were someone lost his or her life, especially if that death was violent or untimely.

Cead Mile Failte   Irish greeting meaning "one hundred thousand welcomes."

Celts   Ancient people from western Russia who conquered much of Europe from 500 to 300 B.C.

changeling   In Irish folklore, a fairy baby left in place of a stolen human baby.

claddagh   A heart with a crown at the top and a pair of hands on either side. The heart represents love, the crown loyalty, and the hands friendship. The symbol adorns everything from necklaces to door knockers, but the most popular rendition is the Claddagh ring.

DART   Dublin Area Rapid Transport.

dragoon   A heavily armed, mounted soldier.

druid   A member of a Celtic religious order of priests, judges, fortune tellers, and poets.

Eire, Erin, or **Eirrinn**   The Gaelic (or Irish) equivalent of the word Ireland.

Fenians   A rebel group formed in 1858 for the purpose of severing all Irish ties with England. Later divided into the Irish Republican Brotherhood and the Fenians.

Gael   A Celt of Ireland, Scotland, or the Isle of Man.

gallowglasses   Foreign warriors, usually from the Western Isles, who fought as mercenaries for Ireland.

gaol   Jail.

Good People   Also known as the Gentle People, these fairies sometimes protect and sometimes play tricks on their human neighbors.

The Great Hunger   Period between 1845 and 1847 in which thousands of Irish people died of hunger and disease. This blight was due to a fungus that arrived on ships from America, which infested potatoes, a staple crop in Ireland, and turned them into foul-smelling, black, inedible mush.

Home Rule   The idea that Ireland should have an Irish parliament based on the British House of Commons and House of Lords.

hurling   A game probably dating back to the days of the ancient Celts. The name comes from the *hurley,* a stick approximately three-feet long and curved on the end that is used to hurl a ball down field and through an opponent's goal posts.

Irish Republican Army (IRA)   A revolutionary group which is expert in guerrilla warfare. It was the right arm of Michael Collins during the War of Independence and is still active today.

Irish Republican Brotherhood (IRB)   A revolutionary group founded in 1858 and considered the most effective of all Ireland's revolutionary national movements. It launched the Easter Uprising of 1916.

keen   To wail for the dead.

lace-curtain Irish   Racist term that made the distinction between respectable and not-so-respectable Irish folk. Lace-curtain Irish implies a certain level of gentility in those having the good taste to hang gauzy fabric in their windows. (See also *shanty Irish*.)

leprechauns   Fairy creatures known for their cobbling skills, their pots of gold, and their ability to locate that elusive end of the rainbow.

Mass rocks   Stones where Catholic priests held secret masses during Cromwell's wrath.

Orangemen   Protestant terrorists whose main objective was to drive Catholics from their homes. They were called the Orangemen after English ruler William of Orange and carried orange banners symbolizing William's victory over the Catholic James II. The tradition of wearing orange sashes and marching through Catholic areas continues even today, as does much of the animosity spawned during those harsh times.

paddy   American slang for an Irish male (after the common Irish name of Patrick). Usually considered derogatory.

paddy wagon   A truck the police use to transport prisoners. The term was coined in New York City during the mid-1800s because it was a frequent conveyance for Irish passengers commonly named Padraic or Patrick.

Pale   The area around Dublin that was ruled by the Anglo-Irish. The phrase "beyond the Pale" means "outside of acceptable limits."

Penal Laws   Enacted by the Protestant English ruler William of Orange, these laws forbade Catholics from holding office, marrying Protestants, carrying arms, taking a land dispute to court, or even owning a horse valued at more than £5.

pooka   A fairy spirit who often appears in the form of an animal.

Protestant Ascendancy   The period of time from 1690 to 1800 that marked an era of Protestant rule in Ireland.

publican   A saloon- or innkeeper.

punt   Another word for the Irish unit of currency, the pound.

Royal Irish Constabulary (RIC)   The British military-style police who enforced law on behalf of the British Crown in Ireland.

shanty Irish   Racist term that made the distinction between respectable and not-so-respectable Irish folk. Shanty Irish could probably be equated with the equally offensive term "white trash" used in the United States. (See also *lace-curtain Irish*.)

seanchai   (Pronounced *shawn*-a-key) A person who is responsible for spreading stories from generation to generation. Usually, one person from a family or small community passes down the family lore.

Sinn Fein   A revolutionary group formed in 1905 that supported cultural reforms as well as political, advocating a revival of the Gaelic language, Gaelic literature, and music. Restructured around 1917 to include the IRB, it's still called Sinn Fein.

slagging   Irish slang for teasing or verbally pulling a tourist's leg.

souperism   The betrayal by a Catholic of his or her religion by converting to Protestantism in order to receive food from the English soup kitchens during the Great Famine.

Tory   The Conservative party of England's two major political parties. A Tory is a member of Britain's Conservative Party. Ironically, before the late 17th century in Ireland, a Tory was an Irish outlaw who favored the killing of English soldiers and settlers and who survived by means of plunder.

Tuatha De Danann   Members of a mystical super-race who, according to mythology, were the first inhabitants of Ireland.

tuaths   Divisions or sects of Celtic tribes belonging to a particular family branch. Specifically, a tuath consisted of the five generations of descendants from one patriarch. The leader of the tuath was elected by the majority.

wake   An Irish funeral, traditionally lively with plenty of food, drink, dancing, and games.

Wee People   See *Good People*.

Whig   The other major political party in 18th and 19th century England. Now known as the Liberal Party, Whigs championed reform and parliamentary rights.

Young Ireland   A group of intellectuals, which was founded in the 1840s for the purpose of establishing Irish independence through forceful means.

Index

V

Valera, Eamon de, 158, 165-166
Van Morrison, 231
verbal contracts, 40
Victoria, Queen, 133
Vikings, 55-67
  contributions to Irish
    civilization, 66
  invasions
    causes of, 56
    first invasion, 57-58
    second invasion, 60-61
  longphorts, 58
  monasteries, pillaging
    of, 57
  retaliation against, 58-59
  river raids, 57-58
  Sitric Silkbeard, 63-65
    Dublin, battle of, 63
  *The War of the Gaedhil with
    the Gaill*, 58
  words absorbed into Gaelic,
    60
Villiers, George, 102

W-X

wakes, 19
War of Independence, 158-159
*The War of the Gaedhil with the
  Gaill*, 58
War of the Roses, 88-90
ward bosses, 178-179
warfare
  Celtic, 39
  dragoons, 104

warriors, 41
Waterford crystal, 233-234
weapons, shillelaghs, 19
Web sites, Irish Tourist
  Board, 224
weddings, 19
Wee People, 219
Whigs, 129
Whiteboys (agrarian sect), 112
Wilde, Oscar, 201-202
William of Orange, 107-108
wit, 190
women
  Celtic law, 6, 42
  English versus Irish, 96
  immigrants, 139
World War II, 166
writers, 187-197
  Augusta, Lady Gregory,
    203-204
  Behan, Brendan, 204-205
  censorship
    Joyce, James, 191-192
    Yeats, William Butler,
      189
  Colum, Padraic, 193-194
    "A Cradle Song", 194
  Edgeworth, Maria, 194-196
  Fahrquhar, George,
    209-210
  Goldsmith, Oliver, 209-210
  Joyce, James, 190-192
    death of, 192
    symbolism, 192
  McCourt, Frank, 196
  O'Casey, Sean, 207-209
    The Plough and the Stars,
      208-209

Shaw, George Bernard,
  205-207
  political involvement,
    206
Sheridan, Richard
  Brinsley, 202
Swift, Jonathan, 192-193
  *A Proposal for the
    Universal Use of Irish
    Manufacture*, 192
  anonymous works,
    192-193
  Drapier's Letters, 193
  Gulliver's Travels, 193
Synge, John Millington,
  202-203
  *The Playboy of the
    Western World*, 203
Wilde, Oscar, 201-202
Yeats, William Butler,
  188-190
  Gonne, Maud, 189
  political involvement,
    190
see also literature;
  storytelling

Y-Z

Yeats, William Butler, 188-190
  censorship, 189
  Gonne, Maud, 189
  Irish National Literary
    Society, 189
  political involvement, 190
Yellow Ford, battle of, 96
Young Ireland, 119, 156